Robert Cassels, Charles H. Masters

The Practice of the Supreme Court of Canada

Robert Cassels, Charles H. Masters
The Practice of the Supreme Court of Canada
ISBN/EAN: 9783337189471

Printed in Europe, USA, Canada, Australia, Japan

Cover: Foto ©Suzi / pixelio.de

More available books at **www.hansebooks.com**

THE PRACTICE

OF THE

SUPREME COURT

OF

CANADA.

BY

ROBERT CASSELS,
ONE OF HER MAJESTY'S COUNSEL,
AND
REGISTRAR OF THE COURT.

SECOND EDITION
BY
C. H. MASTERS,
REPORTER OF THE COURT.

TORONTO:
THE CARSWELL COMPANY LIMITED.
1899.

Entered according to Act of the Parliament of Canada, in the year one thousand eight hundred and ninety-nine, by C. H. MASTERS, in the Department of Agriculture.

TORONTO
PRINTED BY THE CARSWELL CO., LIMITED
22, 30 Adelaide St. East

CONTENTS.

	PAGE
LIST OF CHIEF JUSTICES, JUDGES AND OFFICERS OF THE SUPREME COURT OF CANADA	v
LIST OF MINISTERS OF JUSTICE AND ATTORNEYS-GENERAL AND OF SOLICITORS-GENERAL OF THE DOMINION SINCE THE ORGANIZATION OF THE COURT	vi
INTRODUCTION TO FIRST EDITION	vii
PREFACE TO SECOND EDITION	ix
TABLE OF ABBREVIATIONS	xi
TABLE OF CASES CITED	xiii

PART I.

OUTLINE OF STATUTES RESPECTING THE SUPREME COURT	1
SUMMARY OF PROCEEDINGS ON APPEAL TO SUPREME COURT	4

PART II.

SUPREME AND EXCHEQUER COURTS ACT	11

PART III.

APPEALS UNDER SPECIAL ACTS:

Criminal Appeals	101
Exchequer Appeals	106
Election Appeals	112
Appeals under the Winding-up Act	121

PART IV.

RULES OF THE SUPREME COURT OF CANADA	127

PART V.

APPENDIX:

County Court jurisdiction in the Provinces of Nova Scotia, New Brunswick, British Columbia and Prince Edward Island	190
50-51 Victoria, c. 16, amending the Supreme and Exchequer Courts Act	196
Supreme Court Act, 1888	197
Supreme Court Act, 1889	198

CONTENTS.

APPENDIX—*Continued.*   PAGE

    Exchequer Court Act, 1890 200
    Supreme Court Act, 1891 200
    Exchequer Court Act, 1891 203
    Supreme Court Act, 1893 204
    Supreme Court Act, 1896 205
    Revised Statutes of Ontario, c. 42, respecting the Supreme Court of Canada and the Exchequer Court of Canada 205
    Extracts from Imperial Statutes and Orders in Council relating to the practice in appeals to the Judicial Committee of the Privy Council 207
    Forms 219

ADDENDA:
    ADDITIONAL CASES ON THE JURISDICTION OF THE COURT. 231
    REFERENCES UNDER THE RAILWAY ACT 231

INDEX 233

Chief Justices and Judges

—OF THE—

Supreme Court of Canada.

CHIEF JUSTICES.

HON. SIR WILLIAM BUELL RICHARDS, Knight.
    Appointed 8th October, 1875.
    Resigned 10th January, 1879.

HON. SIR WILLIAM JOHNSTONE RITCHIE, Knight.
    Appointed 11th January, 1879.
    Died 12th September, 1892.

RIGHT HON. SIR SAMUEL HENRY STRONG, Knight.
    Appointed 13th December, 1892.

JUDGES.

HON. SIR WILLIAM JOHNSTONE RITCHIE, Knight.
    Appointed 8th October, 1875.

HON. SAMUEL HENRY STRONG.
    Appointed 8th October, 1875.

HON. JEAN THOMAS TASCHEREAU.
    Appointed 8th October, 1875.
    Resigned 6th October, 1878.

HON. TELESPHORE FOURNIER.
    Appointed 8th October, 1875.
    Resigned 12th September, 1895.

HON. WILLIAM ALEXANDER HENRY.
    Appointed 8th October, 1875.
    Died 5th May, 1888.

HON. HENRI ELZEAR TASCHEREAU.
    Appointed 7th October, 1878.

HON. JOHN WELLINGTON GWYNNE.
    Appointed 14th January, 1879.

HON. CHRISTOPHER SALMON PATTERSON.
    Appointed 27th October, 1888.
    Died 24th May, 1893.

HON. ROBERT SEDGEWICK.
    Appointed 18th February, 1893.

HON. GEORGE EDWIN KING.
    Appointed 21st September, 1893.

HON. DESIRE GIROUARD.
    Appointed 28th September, 1895.

OFFICERS OF THE COURT.

ROBERT CASSELS, Q.C.
    Appointed Registrar 8th October, 1875.
    Died 17th June, 1898.

EDWARD ROBERT CAMERON, Barrister-at-Law.
    Appointed Registrar 2nd July, 1898.

GEORGE DUVAL, Q.C.
    Appointed Reporter 20th January, 1876.
    Died 6th June, 1895.

ARCHIBALD SANDWITH CAMPBELL, Solicitor.
    Appointed Assistant Reporter 3rd March, 1886.
    Died 3rd September, 1886.

CHARLES H. MASTERS, Barrister-at-Law.
    Appointed Assistant Reporter 1st October, 1886.
    Appointed Reporter 2nd October, 1895.

LOUIS WILLIAM COUTLEE, Barrister-at-Law.
    Appointed Assistant Reporter 2nd December, 1895.

MINISTERS OF JUSTICE AND ATTORNEYS-GENERAL OF THE DOMINION OF CANADA SINCE THE ORGANIZATION OF THE COURT.

HON. EDWARD BLAKE, Q.C.
    Appointed 19th May, 1875.

HON. RUDOLPHE LAFLAMME, Q.C.
    Appointed 8th June, 1877.

HON. JAMES McDONALD, Q.C.
    Appointed 17th October, 1878.

HON. SIR ALEXANDER CAMPBELL, K.C.M.G., Q.C.
    Appointed 20th May, 1881.

RIGHT HON. SIR JOHN SPARROW DAVID THOMPSON, K.C.M.G., Q.C.
    Appointed 25th September, 1885.

HON. SIR CHARLES HIBBERT TUPPER, K.C.M.G., Q.C.
    Appointed 21st December, 1894.

HON. ARTHUR RUPERT DICKIE, Q.C.
    Appointed 15th January, 1896.

HON. SIR OLIVER MOWAT, G.C.M.G., Q.C.
    Appointed 13th July, 1896.

HON. DAVID MILLS, Q.C.
    Appointed 18th November, 1897.

SOLICITORS-GENERAL.

HON. JOHN JOSEPH CURRAN, Q.C., L.L.D.
    Appointed 5th December, 1892.

HON. SIR CHARLES HIBBERT TUPPER, K.C.M.G., Q.C.
    Appointed 1st May, 1896.

HON. CHARLES FITZPATRICK, Q.C.
    Appointed 13th July, 1896.

INTRODUCTION TO FIRST EDITION.

By section 101 of the British North America Act, 1867, the Parliament of Canada was authorized to provide for the constitution, maintenance and organization of a general Court of Appeal for Canada, and for the establishment of any additional courts for the better administration of the laws of Canada. Under the power given by this section of the constitution, the Parliament of Canada, on the 8th April, 1875, passed an Act, 38 Vic. c. 11, establishing the Supreme Court of Canada and the Exchequer Court of Canada, the former to have an appellate, civil and criminal jurisdiction within and throughout the Dominion of Canada, and the latter court to exercise concurrent original jurisdiction with the courts of the Provinces in the Dominion of Canada in all cases in which it should be sought to enforce any law of the Dominion relating to the revenue, and in all other suits of a civil nature at common law or equity in which the Crown in the interest of the Dominion should be plaintiff or petitioner, and exclusive or original jurisdiction in all cases in which demand should be made or relief sought in respect of any matter which might in England be the subject of a suit or action in the Court of Exchequer on its revenue side against the Crown, or any officer of the Crown. As the scope of this work is confined entirely to the jurisdiction and practice of the Supreme Court of Canada, no further reference need be made to the Exchequer Court beyond mention of the fact that until the passing of 50-51 Victoria c. 16, the Judges of the Supreme Court were also Judges of the Exchequer Court, each Judge, sitting alone, constituting the latter court, and all the Judges, or at least five, constituting the appellate tribunal.

On the 17th September, 1875, by proclamation, the Act passed on the 8th April preceding, was brought into force as respected the appointment of judges, registrar, clerks and servants of the court, the organization thereof, and the making of general rules and orders. On the 8th of October following the judges and registrar were appointed; and the Chief Justice, the Hon. William Buell Richards, afterwards Sir William Buell Richards, took the oath of office before His Excellency Lieutenant-General Sir William O'Grady Haly, the Administrator of the Government, in Council. On the 8th of November following, the Chief Justice administered the oath of office to the puisne judges of the Court. On the 10th January, 1876, by proclamation, the 11th day of January, 1876, was appointed as the day and time at and after which the judicial functions of the Court should take effect and be exercised. And on the 7th February, 1876, general rules relating to the practice of the Supreme Court were promulgated by the judges. The first sitting of the Supreme Court for the hearing of appeals was on the 17th of January, 1876, but no appeals were ready to be heard. The first session of the Court at which appeals were heard was on the 5th day of June, 1876, when three appeals were argued. Since the organization of the Court over 800 appeals have been filed, representing directly in themselves a considerable amount of valuable results, and indirectly, no doubt, a far reaching beneficial influence on the jurisprudence and administration of justice throughout the country. The business of the Court has been steadily increasing, until for the present sittings, the third of the year, there stand inscribed for hearing about 60 appeals, sent from all parts of the Dominion.

Since 1875, ten or eleven statutes have been passed affecting the jurisdiction or practice, or both, of the Supreme Court, and numerous amendments and additions to the rules have been made. Under these circumstances a work consolidating the statutes and rules and noting the many decisions given by the Court relating to the practice and jurisdiction of the Court, may be found convenient.

PREFACE TO SECOND EDITION.

Since the first edition of this work was issued, in 1888, the Parliament of Canada has passed a number of Acts affecting the Supreme Court, by some of which the jurisdiction of the Court has been extended, and by others the procedure has been altered. The rules of the Court, also, have been to some extent amended, and many decisions have been given on questions relating to its practice and procedure. A second edition will, therefore, be a convenience to those practising before the Court.

The late Mr. Cassels realized the necessity for a second edition some time before he died, but was never able to undertake it. When he requested me to do so in his stead it was his intention to go over the whole of the original work with me and arrange the scope of the alterations and additions to be made, but after carrying out this intention in respect to the first fifty sections of the Supreme Court Act he was obliged to abandon it, and I had to complete it without further assistance.

The form of the original edition has been closely followed, except in one respect. The instructions to practitioners, which in this volume appears in Part I., was, in the former work, a part of the introduction.

Every decision of the Court relating to the construction of the Act, or to points of practice and procedure under it and the Rules of Court down to the October session of 1898, has been noted, and an endeavour has been made to have the index exhaustive as well as accurate.

In 1888 about 800 appeals had been filed in the Court since its organization. At the present time the number is over 1,800. It cannot be claimed that the annual business of the Court has increased during the last few years, but that is to be attributed to the like state of affairs in the Provincial Courts.

C. H. MASTERS.

Ottawa, November 25, 1898.

ABBREVIATIONS

A. & E. . . . . Adolphus and Ellis.
App. Cas. . . . . Law Reports, Appeal Cases.
Art. . . . . Article.
C. . . . . Chapter.
Can. S. C. R. . . . . Reports of the Supreme Court of Canada.
C. C. P. . . . . Code of Civil Procedure of the Province of Quebec
Ch. D. . . . . Law Reports, Chancery Division.
C. J. . . . . Chief Justice.
C. L. J. . . . . Canada Law Journal.
C. L. T. . . . . Canadian Law Times.
C. P. D. . . . . Law Reports, Common Pleas Division.
C. S. N. B. . . . . Consolidated Statutes of New Brunswick.
Dig. . . . . } Cassels' Digest of Supreme Court Decisions, edi-
Dig. S. C. D. . . } tion 1893.
H. M. . . . . Her Majesty.
Ibid. . . . . At the same place.
J. . . . . Judge.
JJ. . . . . Judges.
L. R. . . . . Law Reports.
L. T. . . . . Law Times Reports, New Series.
M. L. R. Q. B. . . . Montreal Law Reports, Queen's Bench.
M. R. . . . . Master of the Rolls.
N. B. . . . . New Brunswick.
O. R. . . . . Ontario Reports.
Ont. App. R. . . . . . Ontario Appeal Reports.
Ont. P. R. . . . . Ontario Practice Reports.
P. . . . . Page.
P. D. . . . . Law Reports, Probate Division.
Prac. P. C. . . . . Practice of the Privy Council.
P. Q. . . . . Province of Quebec.
Q. B. . . . . Queen's Bench.

ABBREVIATIONS.

Q. B. D..........Law Reports, Queen's Bench Division.
R. S. C..........Revised Statutes of Canada.
R. S. O.........Revised Statutes of Ontario.
S................Section.
SS...............Sections.
S-S..............Sub-section.
S. C.............Same case.
Sch..............Schedule.
S. & E. C. A.....Supreme and Exchequer Courts Act.
Times L. R.......Times Law Reports.
V................Victoria.
W. R............Weekly Reporter.
West. L. T......Western Law Times.

TABLE OF CASES CITED

[The blank spaces in this list indicate that part or the whole of the case preceding a blank is repeated.]

A.

Abbott, Fraser v., Dig. 695 No. 125; 63, 68.
    Macdonald v., 3 Can. S. C. R. 278; 23, 28, 66.
Accident Ins. Co. v. McLachlan, 18 Can. S. C. R. 627; 22, 32.
Ætna Insurance Co. v. Brodie, Dig. 673 No. 18; 66, 86, 131.
Agricultural Ins. Co. of Watertown v. Sargent, 16 Ont. P. R. 297; 74.
Allan v. Pratt, 13 App. Cas. 780; 49.
Amer v. The Queen, 2 Can. S. C. R. 592; 103.
Ames, Fuller v. Dig. 140 No. 10; 144.
Anderson, Bain v.; 51.
Anglo-Continental Guano Works, Emerald Phosphate Co. v., 21 Can. S. C. R. 422; 45.
Angus v. Calgary School Trustees, 16 Can. S. C. R. 716; 26, 27.
Arabin, *in re*; 55.
Archbald v. deLisle, 25 Can. S. C. R. 1; 31.
Archer v. Severn, 12 Ont. P. R. 472; 70.
Arpin v. Merchants Bank, 24 Can. S. C. R. 142; 31.
    v. The Queen, 14 Can. S. C. R. 736; 31.
Arscott v. Lilley, 14 Ont. App. R. 283; 164.
Attorney-General v. Flint, 16 Can. S. C. R. 707; 23.
    v. Vaughan Road Co.; 37.
Auer Incandescent Light Mfg. Co., Dreschel v., 28 Can. S. C. R. 268; 40.
Ayotte v. Boucher, 9 Can. S. C. R. 460; 40.

B.

Bain v. Anderson; 51.
Baird, Ellis v., 16 Can. S. C. R. 147; 31.
Bank British North America v. Walker, Dig. 425 No. 30; 30.
                                  Dig. 671 No. 8; 35.
                                  Dig. 673 No. 17; 65, 83.
Bank of Hamilton v. Halstead; 69.
Bank of Montreal, Demers v., 27 Can. S. C. R. 197; 33.
Bank of Toronto v. Le Cure et les Marguilliers, etc., de la Paroisse de la Nativite, 12 Can. S. C. R. 25; 41, 43.
                        Dig. 432 No. 40; 81.
Baptist v. Baptist, 21 Can. S. C. R. 425; 33.
Barbeau, Labelle v., 16 Can. S. C. R. 390; 41.
Barnard, Molson v., 18 Can. S. C. R. 622; 32.

TABLE OF CASES CITED.

Barrington v. City of Montreal 25 Can. S. C. R. 202; 23, 48.
    v. Scottish Union & National Ins. Co., 18 Can. S. C. R. 615; 21, 32.
Bartram v. London West, 24 Can. S. C. R. 705; 37.
Bazinet v. Godomy; 69.
Beamish v. Kaulbach, 3 Can. S. C. R. 704; 26, 27.
    Dig. 677 No. 44; 81.
Beatty, O'Donohoe v., 19 Can. S. C. R. 356; 31.
Beaubien v. Bernatchez, Dig. 433 No. 41; 43.
Beaudoin, Lefeunteum v., 28 Can. S. C. R. 89; 31.
Beeswing, The, 10 P. D. 18; 163.
Beland, Laine v.; 69.
Bell Telephone Co. v. City of Quebec, 20 Can. S. C. R. 230; 24.
Bellechasse Election Case, 5 Can. S. C. R. 91; 112, 115.
Bender, Carrier v., Dig. 674 No. 22; 65, 66, 134.
Bernatchez, Beaubien v., Dig. 433 No. 41; 43.
Berthier Election Case, 9 Can. S. C. R. 102; 112.
Bessey v. Eddy; 148.
Bickford v. Hawkins, 19 Can. S. C. R. 362; 31.
Blachford v. McBain, 19 Can. S. C. R. 42; 27, 35.
Black, Wheeler v., M. L. R. 2 Q. B. 159; 43, 70.
Blanchard, Bourget v., Dig. 423 No. 27; 40.
Boak v. Merchants' Marine Insurance Co., Dig. 677 No. 45; 83, 160.
Bossom, Wallace v., 2 Can. S. C. R. 488; 20.
Bouchard Conture v., 21 Can. S. C. R. 281; 47, 48.
Boucher, Ayotte v., 9 Can. S. C. R. 460; 30.
    In re, Dig. 325 No. 2; 54.
Bourget v. Blanchard, Dig. 423 No. 27; 40.
Bourne, O'Donohue v., 27 Can. S. C. R. 654; 38.
Brampton, Haggart v.; 82.
Brassard v. Langevin, 1 Can. S. C. R. 201; 157.
Breakey v. Carter, Dig. 463; 144.
British Columbia Towing Co., Sewell v., Dig. 670 No. 7; 36.
    v., Dig. 675 No. 31; 55.
Brodie, Ætna Insurance Co. v., Dig. 673 No. 18; 66, 86, 131.
Brown, Dominion Salvage & Wrecking Co. v., 20 Can. S. C. R. 203; 45.
Brunet, Pilon v., 5 Can. S. C. R. 319; 164.
Bull, Gilmour v., 1 Kerr (N. B.), 94; 141.

C.

Cahan, In re, 21 Can. S. C. R. 100; 33, 68.
Cairns, Dominion Cartridge Co. v.; 68, 157.
Caldwell v. Stadacona Fire & Life Insurance Co., 11 Can. S. C. R. 212; 78.
Calgary School Trustees, Angus v., 16 Can. S. C. R. 716; 26, 27.

TABLE OF CASES CITED.

Cameron, Domville v., Dig. 421 No. 23; 81.
    McDougall v., 21 Can. S. C. R. 379; 83.
Canada Atlantic Railway Co., Stanton v., Dig. 430 No. 37; 31.
Canada Co. v. Kyle, 15 Can. S. C. R. 188; 86.
Canadian Pacific Railway Co. v. Cobban Mfg. Co., 22 Can. S. C. R. 132; 22, 32.
    v. Fleming, 22 Can. S. C. R. 33; 21.
    v. Robinson, 14 Can. S. C. R. 105; 164.
    Shaw, v., 16 Can. S. C. R. 703; 30.
    v. Ste. Therese, 16 Can. S. C. R. 606; 27.
Canada Southern Railway Co. v. Norvell, Dig. 34 No. 5; 83.
    Rowlands v., 13 Ont. P. R. 93; 62, 63.
Carrier v. Bender, Dig. 674 No. 22; 65, 66, 134.
Carson, Martley v., 13 Can. S. C. R. 439; 60.
Carter, Breakey v., Dig. 463; 144.
    Holmes v., 16 Can. S. C. R. 473; 40.
    Milson v., 69 L. T. 735; 69.
    Muir v., 16 Can. S. C. R. 473; 40.
Casey v. Gabourie, 12 Ont. P. R. 252; 63, 168.
Cattley, Mason v., Law Notes, 1885, p. 15; 163.
Cavender's Trusts, in re, 16 Ch. D. 270; 163.
Central Bank of Canada, in re, 17 Ont. P. R. 395; 37, 63.
Chagnon v. Normand, 16 Can. S. C. R. 661; 43.
Chamberland v. Fortier, 23 Can. S. C. R. 371; 44, 46.
Champoux v. Lapierre, Dig. 426, No. 31; 40, 81.
Chaussée, Stephens v., 15 Can. S. C. R. 379; 164.
Charlevoix Election Case, Dig. 695 No. 124; 677 No. 43; 133, 140.
Chevallier v. Cuvillier, 4 Can. S. C. R. 605; 30.
Chicoutimi & Saguenay Election Case, Dig. 682 No. 72; 75.
Chisholm v. Kenny, Dig. 539; 23.
Christie, Toronto Junction v., 25 Can. S. C. R. 551; 165.
Citizens' Light and Power Co. v. Parent, 27 Can. S. C. R. 316; 48, 49.
Clark v. Scottish Imperial Insurance Co., Dig. 688 No. 100; 87.
Clarke, in re, Virtue v. Hayes, 16 Can. S. C. R. 721; 32, 38.
Clarkson v. Ryan, 17 Can. S. C. R. 251; 50.
Cleveland, Lamb v., 19 Can. S. C. R. 78; 26.
Cobban Mfg. Co., Canadian Pacific Railway Co, v.. 22 Can. S. C. R. 132; 22, 32.
Colchester South v. Valade, 24 Can. S. C. R. 622; 31.
Coleman v. Miller, Dig. 683 No. 78; 144.
Colville, Migotti v., 4 C. P. D. 233; 169.
    Titus v., 18 Can. S. C. R. 709; 31.
    v.; 149.
Commissaires d'Ecoles de St. Marc., Langevin v., 18 Can. S. C. R. 599; 23, 32, 52.
Common, McCasgill v.; 123.

TABLE OF CASES CITED.

Cornwall Minerals Railway Co., Harrison v., 18 Ch. D. 346; 164.
Cosgrave Brewing and Malting Co., Starrs v., Dig. 697 No. 130; 63, 69.
Cossette v. Dun, 18 Can. S. C. R. 222; 49.
Cote v. Stadacona Assurance Co., Dig. 682 No. 68; 133.
         Dig. 683 No. 77; 143.
Couture v. Bouchard, 21 Can. S. C. R. 281; 47, 48.
Cowen v. Evans, 22 Can. S. C. R. 328; 41.
    22 Can. S. C. R. 331; 48.
Criminal Code, *in re*, Bigamy sections, 27 Can. S. C. R. 461; 59.
Crowley, Dorion v., Dig. 694 No. 120; 78.
   v. Dig. 709 No. 12; 83 144.
Cummings, Gladwin v., Dig. 426 No. 32; 31.
Cusson, Delorme v., 28 Can. S. C. R. 66; 46.
Cuvillier, Chevallier v., 4 Can. S. C. R. 605; 30.
Curé, le, et les Marguilliers, etc., de la Paroisse de la Nativité, Bank of Toronto v., 12 Can. S. C. R. 25; 41, 43.
       Dig. 432 No. 40; 81.

D.

Danjou v. Marquis, 3 Can. S. C. R. 251; 23, 28, 81, 82, 107.
Dansereau, Letourneux v., Dig. 677 No. 46; 84.
   Turcotte v., 26 Can. S. C. R. 578; 40, 42.
Darling v. Ryan, Dig. 435 No. 44; 43.
Dartmouth, Town of, The Queen v., 9 Can. S. C. R. 509; 23.
Davidson, Lord v., Dig. 683 No. 80; 143.
Dawson v. Dumont, 20 Can. S. C. R. 709; 49.
   v. Union Bank, Dig. 428 No. 35; 31, 85.
deLisle, Archbald v., 25 Can. S. C. R. 1; 31.
Delorme v. Cusson, 28 Can. S. C. R. 66; 46.
Demers v. Bank of Montreal, 27 Can. S. C. R. 197; 33.
   v. Montreal Steam Laundry Co., 27 Can. S. C. R. 537; 31.
Denyssen, Hiddingh v., 12 App. Cas. 107; 163.
Desmarteau, Hurtubise v., 19 Can. S. C. R. 562; 47.
Dinck, Guest v.; 150.
Dickson, Kearney v., Dig. 431 No. 38; 31.
Dominion Cartridge Co. v. Cairns; 68, 157.
Dominion Salvage & Wrecking Co. v. Brown, 20 Can. S. C. R. 203; 45.
Domville v. Cameron, Dig. 421 No. 23; 81.
Donovan, Herbert v., Dig. 706 No. 149; 170.
   Roberts v.; 37.
Dorion v. Crowley, Dig. 694 No. 120; 78.
     Dig. 709 No. 12; 83, 144.
Drakes, Robinson v., 23 Ch. D. 98; 164.
Draper v. Radenhurst, 14 Ont. P. R. 376; 62.

Dreschel v. Auer Incandescent Light Mfg. Co., 28 Can. S. C. R. 268; 40.
Dubois v. Village of Ste. Rose, 21 Can. S. C. R. 65; 24, 45.
Dufresne v. Guevremont, 26 Can. S. C. R. 216; 48, 49.
Dumont, Dawson v., 20 Can. S. C. R. 709; 40.
Dumoulin, Langtry v., 13 Can. S. C. R. 258; 36, 78.
Dun, Cossette v., 18 Can. S. C. R. 222; 49.
Dupuis, King v., 28 Can. S. C. R. 388; 40.

E.

Earl of Strathmore, *Ex parte. In re* Riddell, 20 Q. B. D. 512; 33.
Ecclesiastiques du Seminaire, etc., de Montreal v. La Cite de Montreal, 16 Can. S. C. R. 399; 44.
Eddy, Bessey v.; 148.
Ellis v. Baird, 16 Can. S. C. R. 147; 31.
    v. The Queen, 22 Can. S. C. R. 7; 31, 104.
Emerald Phosphate Co. v. Anglo-Continental Guano Works, 21 Can. S. C. R. 422; 45.
Equitable Life Assurance Soc., Laberge v., 24 Can. S. C. R. 59; 49.
Eureka Woolen Mills v. Moss, 11 Can. S. C. R. 91; 82.
Evans, Cowen v., 22 Can. S. C. R. 328; 41.
    v. 22 Can. S. C. R. 331; 48.
Exchange Bank v. Gilman, 17 Can. S. C. R. 108; 65.
    v. Springer; 141.

F.

Fauteux, Montreal Loan & Mortgage Co. v. Dig. 20 No. 11; 65.
Ferland, Flatt v., 21 Can. S. C. R. 32; 41.
Ferrier v. Trepannier, 24 Can. S. C. R. 86; 31.
Fisher v. Fisher, 28 Can. S. C. R. 494; 51.
Flatt v. Ferland, 21 Can. S. C. R. 32; 41.
Fleming, Canadian Pacific Railway Co. v., 22 Can. S. C. R. 33; 21.
Flint, Attorney-General v., 16 Can. S. C. R. 707; 23.
Foran v. Handley; 76, 149.
Forristal v. Macdonald, Dig. 422 No. 25; 50.
Fortier, Chamberland v., 23 Can. S. C. R. 371; 44, 46.
Fraser v. Abbott, Dig. 695 No. 125; 63, 68.
    v. Tupper, Dig. 421 No. 24; 53, 54, 83.
Freeman v. Read, 11 W. R. 802; 169.
Fuller v. Ames, Dig. 140 No. 10; 144.

G.

Gabourie, Casey v., 12 Ont. P. R. 252; 63, 168.
Galarneau v. Guilbault, 16 Can. S. C. R. 579; 45.
Galivan, Macdonald v., 28 Can. S. C. R. 258; 42.
Geddes, Wilkins v., 3 Can. S. C. R. 203; 29.

C.S.E.C.—b

Gendron v. McDougall. Dig. 429 No. 36; 40. 81.
Gerriken, Reeves v., Dig. 689 No. 106; 86.
Gerow, Providence Washington Insurance Co. v., 14 Can. S. C. R. 731: 86.
Gibbs, Wheeler v.: 84, 120.
Guilbault, Galarneau v., 16 Can. S. C. R. 579; 45.
Gilbert v. Gilman, 16 Can. S. C. R. 189; 44.
Gilman, Exchange Bank v., 17 Can. S. C. R. 108; 65.
  Gilbert v., 16 Can. S. C. R. 189; 44.
Gilmour v. Bull, 1 Kerr. (N. B.) 94; 141.
Gladwin v. Cummings, Dig. 426 No. 32; 31.
Glengarry Election Case (Kennedy v. Purcell). 14 Can. S. C. R. 453; 113.
  59 L. T. 279; 116.
Gloucester Election Case, 8 Can. S .C. R. 205; 113.
Godomy, Bazinet v.; 69.
Godson v. City of Toronto, 18 Can. S. C. R. 36; 23.
Goldie, Smith v., Dig. 689 No. 109; 86.
Gougeon, Ste. Cunegonde v., 25 Can. S. C. R. 78; 24, 29, 35.
Grand Trunk Railway Co., Platt v., 12 Ont. P. R. 380; 63. 168.
Grant v. Maclaren; 18.
  23 Can. S. C. R. 310; 38.
Gregory, Halifax & Cape Breton Coal & Ry. Co. v., Dig. S. C. D. 727; 11 App. Cas. 229; 20.
  O'Dell v., 24 Can. S. C. R. 661; 46.
Griffith, Walmsley v., 13 Can. S. C. R. 434; 60, 63.
  v., Dig. 670 No. 6; 69.
  v., Dig. 697 No. 129; 63.
  v., Dig. 699 No. 134; 63.
Guest v. Dinck; 150.
Guevremont, Dufresne v., 26 Can. S. C. R. 216; 48, 49.

H.

Haggart v. Brampton; 82.
Halifax, City of. v. Reeves. 23 Can. S. C. R. 340: 27.
Halifax and Cape Breton Coal & R. Co., Gregory v., Dig. 727: 11 App. Cas. 229; 20.
Halifax Street Railway Co. v. Joyce. 17 Can. S. C. R. 709; 21.
Hall Mines Co. v. Moore; 149.
Halstead. Bank of Hamilton v.; 69.
Halton Election Case, 19 Can. S. C. R. 557; 75, 116, 133.
Hamel v. Hamel. 26 Can. S. C. R. 17; 33.
Hampson, Wineberg v., 19 Can. S. C. R. 369; 44, 45.
Hancock, Long, v.; 78.
Handley, Foran v.; 76, 149.
Harris, Robertson v., 14 Ont. P. R. 373; 68, 71.
Harrison v. Cornwall Minerals Ry. Co., 18 Ch. D. 346; 164.

Hart, Joyce v., 1 Can. S. C. R. 321; 48.
Harty, O'Sullivan, v., 13 Can. S. C. R. 431; 60.
Harwich, Township of, v. Raleigh; 22.
Hawkins, Bickford v., 19 Can. S. C. R. 362; 31.
Hayes, Virtue v. In re Clarke, 16 Can. S. C. R. 721; 32, 38.
Heffernan, Walsh v., 14 Can. S. C. R. 738; 231.
Helsby, in re, 42 W. R. 218; 61.
Henderson, The Queen v., 28 Can. S. C. R. 425; 87.
Herbert v. Donovan, Dig. 706 No. 149; 170.
Hiddingh v. Denyssen, 12 App. Cas. 107; 183.
Hinchinbrooke, Township of, McKay v., 24 Can. S. C. R. 55; 24, 31.
Hinds, Pilcher v., 11 Ch. D. 905; 167.
Hogaboom v. Receiver-General; 78.
Holmes v. Carter, 16 Can. S. C. R. 473; 40.
Hood v. Sangster, 16 Can. S. C. R. 723; 41.
Hovey, Whiting v., 14 Can. S. C. R. 515; 30.
Howe, Lewin v., 14 Can. S. C. R. 722; 36.
Hunt v. Taplin, 24 Can. S. C. R. 36; 42.
Huntingdon, Village of, Moir v., 19 Can. S. C. R. 363; 24, 31.
Huron, Wright v., Dig. 673 No. 20; 65, 86.
Hurtubise v. Desmarteau, 19 Can. S. C. R. 562; 47.
Hyde v. Lindsay; 231.

I.

Irvine, Williams v., 22 Can. S. C. R. 108; 47.

J.

James, Scammell v., 16 Can. S. C. R. 593; 38, 68.
Jermyn v. Tew, 28 Can. S. C. R. 497; 51.
Johnson, in re, Dig. 677 No. 41; 329 No. 5; 53, 83.
Joyce v. Hart, 1 Can. S. C. R. 321; 48.
    Halifax Street Railway Co. v., 17 Can. S. C. R. 709; 21.

K.

Kandick v. Morrison, 2 Can. S. C. R. 12; 30.
Kaulbach, Beamish v., 3 Can. S. C. R. 704; 26, 27.
    v., Dig. 677 No. 44; 81.
Kean, Kearney v., Dig. 672 No. 14; 64, 85.
Kearney v. Dickson, Dig. 431 No. 38; 31.
    v. Kean, Dig. 672 No. 14; 64, 85.
Keefer, Merchant's Bank v., Dig. 688 No. 103; 78.
Kelly v. Sulivan, 1 Can. S. C. R. 1; 28.
Kenny, Chisholm v., Dig. 539; 23.
Kennedy, Purcell v. (Glengarry Election Case), 14 Can. S. C. R. 453; 113.
    v. (Glengarry Election Case); 59 L. T. 279; 116.

Keronck, Mackinnon v., 15 Can. S. C. R. 111; 30.
King v. Dupuis, 28 Can. S. C. R. 388; 40.
King's County (N.S.) Election Case, 8 Can. S. C. R. 192; 113.
Kinghorn v. Larue, 22 Can. S. C. R. 347; 42.
Knight, McCorkill v., Dig. 694 No. 116; 40.
    Penrose v., Dig. 689 No. 108; 86.
Kyle, Canada Co. v., 15 Can. S. C. R. 188; 36.

L.

Labelle v. Barbeau, 16 Can. S. C. R. 390; 41.
    City of Montreal v., 14 Can. S. C. R. 741; 164.
Laberge v. Equitable Life Assurance Soc., 24 Can. S. C. R. 59; 49.
Lachance v. Societé de Prêts et de Placements de Quebec, 16 Can. S. C. R. 200; 42.
Lainé v. Beland; 69.
Lakin v. Nuttall, 3 Can. S. C. R. 691; 63, 69.
Laliberté v. The Queen, 1 Can. S. C. R. 117; 21.
Lamb, *Ex parte*, 19 Ch. D. 169; 67, 168.
    v. Cleveland, 19 Can. S. C. R. 78; 26.
Lambe, Molson v., 15 Can. S. C. R. 253; 23.
Landry, Theberge v., 2 App. Cas. 102; 117.
Langdon v. Robertson, 12 Ont. P. R. 139; 63, 168.
Langevin, Brassard v., 1 Can. S. C. R. 201; 157.
    v. Les Commissaires d'ecoles de St. Marc., 18 Can. S. C. R. 599; 23, 32, 52.
Langlois, Valin v., 5 App. Cas. 115; 117.
Langtry v. Dumoulin, 13 Can. S. C. R. 258; 36, 78.
Lapierre, Champoux v., Dig. 426 No. 31; 40, 81.
    Rodier v., 21 Can. S. C. R. 69; 45.
Lariviere v. School Commissioners of Three Rivers, 23 Can. S. C. R. 723; 43, 46.
Larue, Kinghorn v., 22 Can. S. C. R. 347; 42.
L'Assomption Election Case, 14 Can. S. C. R. 429; 113.
Lauretta, The, 4 P. D. 25; 164.
Leamy, McGoey v., 27 Can S. C. R. 193; 46.
Lees, Webster v., 3 C. L. T. 504; 168 .
Lefebvre, Monette v., 16 Can. S. C. R. 387; 49.
Lefeunteum v. Beaudoin, 28 Can. S. C. R. 89; 31.
    v. Veronneau, 22 Can. S. C. R. 203; 45.
Lenior v. Ritchie, 3 Can. S. C. R. 575; 29.
Leonard, Williams v., 26 Can. S. C. R. 406; 31, 38.
Letourneux v. Dansereau, Dig. 677 No. 46; 84.
Levi v. Reed, 6 Can. S. C. R. 482; 48.
Lewin v. Howe, 14 Can. S. C. R. 722; 36.
    v. Wilson, 14 Can. S. C. R. 722; 80.
Lewis v. City of London; 37.

TABLE OF CASES CITED. xxi

Leys, Wright v., 10 Ont. P. R. 354; 109.
    Sievewright v., 9 Ont. P. R. 200; 63.
Lilley, Arscott v., 14 Ont. App. R. 283; 164.
Limoges, Mills v., 22 Can. S. C. R. 331; 48.
Lindsay, Hyde v., 231.
Lionais v. Molsons Bank, 10 Can. S. C. R. 526; 65.
London, City of, Lewis v.; 37.
    West, Village of, Bartram v., 24 Can. S. C. R. 705; 37.
London & Canadian Loan & Agency Co. v. Morris, 19 Can. S. C. R. 434; 32, 38.
London & Canadian Loan & Agency Co. v. Morris, 1 West. L. T. 215; 69.
Long v. Hancock; 78.
Lord v. Davidson, Dig. 683 No. 80; 143.
Lynch v. Seymour, 15 Can. S. C. R. 341; 30.

M.

Macrae, News Printing Co. v., 26 Can. S. C. R. 696; 60, 61, 63, 170.
Maire, &c., de Terrebonne v. Les Sœurs de l'Asile de la Providence, Dig. 434 No. 43; 27, 81.
Major v. Corporation of the City of Three Rivers, Dig. 422 No. 26; 27, 81.
Manchester Economic Building Society, *in re*, 24 Ch. D. 488; 64.
Manitoba Statutes relating to Education, *in re*, 22 Can. S. C. R. 577; 58, 59.
Marcheterre, Ontario & Quebec Railway Co. v., 17 Can. S. C. R. 141; 32, 49, 70.
Maritime Bank of Canada v. Stewart, 20 Can. S. C. R. 105; 32, 38.
Marquette Election Case, 27 Can. S. C. R. 219; 113.
Marquis, Danjou v., 3 Can. S. C. R. 251; 23, 28, 81, 82, 107.
Martin v. Moore, 18 Can. S. C. R. 634; 32.
    v. Roy, Dig. 682 No. 69; 75, 132.
    v. Sampson, 26 Can. S. C. R. 707; 60.
Martley v. Carson, 13 Can. S. C. R. 439; 60.
Marx, Rumohr v., 18 C. L. J. 444; 19 C. L. J. 10; 3 C. L. T. 31; 168.
Mason v. Cattley, Law Notes, 1885, p. 15; 163.
Mathien, Quebec, &c., Railway Co. v., 19 Can. S. C. R. 426; 41.
May v. McArthur, Dig. 674 No. 23; 135.
Mayhew v. Stone, 26 Can. S. C. R. 58; 65.
Maxwell v. Scarfe, 18 O. R. 529; 67.
Merchants Bank, Arpin v., 24 Can. S. C. R. 142; 31.
    v. Keefer, Dig. 688 No. 103; 78.
    Moffat v., 11 Can. S. C. R. 46; 36.
    v. Smith, Dig. 688 No. 102; 78.
    Whitfield v., Dig. 681 No. 66; 75, 133, 144.
Merchants' Marine Ins. Co., Boak v., Dig. 677 No. 45; 83, 160.
Migotti v. Colvill, 4 C. P. D. 233; 169.

TABLE OF CASES CITED.

Miller, Coleman v., Dig. 683 No. 78; 144.
Mills v. Limoges, 22 Can. S. C. R. 331; 48.
Milson v. Carter, 69 L. T. 735; 69.
Mitchell v. Trenholme, 22 Can. S. C. R. 331; 48.
Mockler, McGowan v., Dig. 421 No. 22; 81. 82.
Moffat v. The Merchants' Bank, 11 Can. S. C. R. 46; 36.
Moir v. Village of Huntingdon, 19 Can. S. C. R. 363; 24, 31.
Molson v. Barnard, 18 Can. S. C. R. 622; 32.
    v. Lambe, 15 Can. S. C. R. 253; 23.
Molsons Bank, Lionais v., 10 Can. S. C. R. 526; 65.
Montcalm Election Case, 9 Can. S. C. R. 93; 112.
Monette v. Lefebvre, 16 Can. S. C. R. 387; 49.
Montreal, City of, Barrington v., 25 Can. S. C. R. 202; 23, 48.
    Ecclesiastiques du Seminaire de St. Sulpice de Montreal v., 16 Can. S. C. R. 399; 44.
    v. Labelle, 14 Can. S. C. R. 741; 164.
    Stevenson v., 27 Can. S. C. R. 187; 44.
    City Passenger Railway Co., Parker v., Dig. 674 No. 24; 86, 132.
    Loan & Mortgage Co. v. Fauteux, Dig. 20 No. 11; 65.
    Park & Island Railway Co. v. Shannon, 28 Can. S. C. R. 374; 23.
    Steam Laundry Co., Demers v., 27 Can. S. C. R. 537; 31.
Moore, Hall Mines Co. v.; 149.
    Martin v., 18 Can. S. C. R. 634; 32.
Morris, Rural Municipality of, v. London & Canadian Loan & Agency Co., 19 Can. S. C. R. 434; 32, 38.
Morris, Rural Municipality of, London & Canadian Loan & Agency Co. v., 1 West. L. T. 215; 69.
Morrison, Kandick v., 2 Can. S. C. R. 12; 30.
Moss, Eureka Woolen Mills v., 11 Can. S. C. R. 91; 82.
Muir v. Carter, 16 Can. S. C. R. 473; 40.
Muirhead v. Shireff, 14 Can. S. C R. 735; 78.
Murray, Warner v., 17 Can. S. C. R. 720; 31.
    v. Westmount, 27 Can. S. C. R. 579; 24, 46.

Mc.

Macdonald, Ex parte, 27 Can. S. C. R. 683; 55.
    v. Abbott, 3 Can. S. C. R. 278; 23, 28, 66.
    Forristal v., Dig. 422 No. 25; 50.
    v. Galivan, 28 Can. S. C. R. 258; 42.
Macdougall, Gendron v., Dig. 420 No. 36; 40, 81.
Mackinnon v. Keronack, 15 Can. S. C. R. 111; 30.
Maclaren, Grant v.; 18.
    v., 23 Can. S. C. R. 310; 38.
    Raphael v., 27 Can. S. C. R. 319; 46.
McArthur, May v., Dig. 674 No. 23; 135.

xxiii

McBain, Blachford v., 19 Can. S. C. R. 42; 27, 35.
McCall v. Wolff, Dig. 673 No. 19; 86, 131.
McCasgill v. Common; 123.
McCorkill v. Knight, Dig. 694 No. 116; 40.
McDougall v. Cameron, 21 Can. S. C. R. 379; 33.
    McGreevy v.; 148.
McGauley, Reg. v., 12 Ont. P. R. 259; 62.
McGhee, Phœnix Ins. Co. v., 18 Can. S. C. R. 61; 31.
McGoey v. Leamy, 27 Can. S. C. R. 193; 46.
McGowan v. Mockler, Dig. 421 No. 22; 81, 82.
McGreevy v. McDougall, 148.
McGugan v. McGugan, 21 Can. S. C. R. 267; 27, 33, 38.
McIntosh v. The Queen, 23 Can. S. C. R. 180; 104.
McKay v. Township of Hinchinbrooke, 24 Can. S. C. R. 55; 24, 31.
McLachlan, Accident Ins. Co. v., 18 Can. S. C. R. 627; 22, 32.
McLean, The Queen v., Dig. 399 No. 6; 87.
McManamy, City of Sherbrooke v., 18 Can. S. C. R. 594; 24, 42, 45.
    v., 13 Legal News, 290; 70.
McNab v. Wagler, Dig. 690 No. 133; 70.
McQueen v. The Phœnix Mutual Fire Ins. Co., Dig. 688 No. 99; 87.
McQueen v. The Queen; 108.

N.

Neill v. Travellers' Ins. Co., 9 Ont. App. R. 54; 63.
Nevins, The Queen v., Dig. 427 No. 33; 27, 81.
News Printing Co. v. Macrae, 26 Can. S. C. R. 695; 60, 61, 63, 170.
Normand v. Chagnon v., 16 Can. S. C. R. 661; 43.
North British & Mercantile Ins. Co. v. Tourville, 25 Can. S. C. R. 177; 31.
North Ontario Election Case, 3 Can. S. C. R. 374; 84, 115, 120.
North Shore Ry. Co., Pion v.; 88.
Norvell, Canada Southern Ry. Co. v., Dig. 34 No. 5; 83.
North York Eection Case, Dig. 682 No. 71; 75, 120, 133.
Nuttall, Lakin v., 3 Can. S. C. R. 691; 63, 69.

O.

O'Brien, in re, 16 Can. S. C. R. 197; 12, 31, 38.
O'Dell v. Gregory, 24 Can. S. C. R. 661; 46.
O'Donohoe v. Beatty, 19 Can. S. C. R. 356; 31.
    v. Bourne, 27 Can. S. C. R. 654; 38.
Oliver, Vernon v., 11 Can. S. C. R. 156; 144.
Ontario & Quebec Railway Co. v. Marcheterre, 17 Can. S. C. R. 141; 32, 49, 70.
Ontario & Quebec Railway Co. v. Philbrick, Dig. 688 No. 104; 78.
Ostrom v. Sills; 150.
O'Sullivan v. Harty, 13 Can. S. C. R. 431; 60.

TABLE OF CASES CITED.

O'Toole, Wallace v., Dig. 713; 23.
Ouimet v. La Société de Construction Permanente des Artisans; 44.

P.

Palliser, Simpson v.; 48.
Parent, Citizens Light & Power Co. v., 27 Can. S. C. R. 316; 48, 49.
Parker v. Montreal City Passenger Railway Co., Dig. 674 No. 24, 86, 132.
    White v., 16 Can. S. C. R. 699; 79.
Peak, Shields v., 8 Can. S. C. R. 579; 30.
Penrose v. Knight, Dig. 689 No. 108; 86.
Philbrick, Ontario & Quebec Railway Co. v., Dig. 688 No. 104; 78.
Phœnix Ins. Co. v. McGhee, 18 Can. S. C. R. 61; 31.
    McQueen v., Dig. 688 No. 99; 87.
Piché v. City of Quebec, Dig. 497 No. 6; 85.
Pilcher v. Hinds, 11 Ch. D. 905; 107.
Pilon v. Brunet, 5 Can. S. C. R. 319; 164.
Pion v. North Shore Railway Co.; 88.
Platt v. Grand Trunk Railway Co., 12 Ont. P. R. 380; 63, 168.
Poitvin, *in re*, Dig. 327 No. 3; 54.
Pontiac Election Case, 20 Can. S. C. R. 626; 113.
Poulin v. Corporation of Quebec, 9 Can. S. C. R. 185; 23.
Pratt, Allan v., 13 App. Cas. 780; 49.
Prohibitory Liquor Laws, *in re*, 24 Can. S. C. R. 170; 59.
Providence Washington Ins. Co. v. Gerow, 14 Can. S. C. R. 731; 86.
Provincial Fisheries, *in re*, 26 Can. S. C. R. 444; 58, 59.
Purcell v. Kennedy (Glengarry Election Case), 14 Can. S. C. R. 453; 113.
    (Glengarry Election Case), 59 L. T. 279; 116.

Q.

Quebec, City of, Bell Telephone Co. v. 20 Can. S. C. R. 230; 24.
    Piché v., Dig. 497 No. 6; 85.
    Poulin v., 9 Can. S. C. R. 185; 23.
    Quebec Gas Co. v., 20 Can. S. C. R. 230; 24.
  Gas Co. v. City of Quebec, 20 Can. S. C. R. 230; 24.
    &c., Railway Co. v. Mathieu, 19 Can. S. C. R. 426; 41.
Queen, The, Amer v., 2 Can. S. C. R. 592; 103.
    Arpin v., 14 Can. S. C. R. 736; 31.
    v. Dartmouth, 9 Can. S. C. R. 509; 23.
    Ellis v., 22 Can. S. C. R. 7; 31, 104.
    v. Henderson, 28 Can. S. C. R. 425; 87.
    Laliberté v., 1 Can. S. C. R. 117; 21.
    McIntosh v., 23 Can. S. C. R. 180; 104.
    v. McLean, Dig. 399 No. 6; 87.

TABLE OF CASES CITED.   XXV

The Queen, McQueen v., 108.
   v. Nevins, Dig. 427 No. 33; 27, 81.
   St. Louis v., 25 Can. S. C. R. 665; 87.
   v. Taylor, 1 Can. S. C. R. 65; 48, 61, 63.
   Toronto Railway Co. v.; 87.
   Viau v.; 103.

R.

Radenhurst, Draper v., 14 Ont. P. R. 376; 62.
Raleigh, Township of, Harwich v.; 22.
Ramsay, Reid v., Dig. 420 No. 21; 30, 64, 81.
Rankin, Roblee v., 11 Can. S. C. R. 137; 30.
Raphael v. Maclaren, 27 Can. S. C. R. 319; 46.
Rattray v. Young, Dig. 692 No. 110; 86, 149.
Read, Freeman v., 11 W. R. 802; 169.
Reburn v. La Corporation de la Paroisse de Ste. Anne du Bout de L'Isle, 15 Can. S. C. R. 92; 44.
Receiver-General, Hogaboom v.; 78.
Reed, Levi v., 6 Can. S. C. R. 482; 48.
Reeves v. Gerriken, Dig. 689 No. 106; 86.
   Halifax, City of, v., 23 Can. S. C. R. 340; 27.
Reg. v. McGauley, 12 Ont. P. R. 259; 62.
   v. Shropshire Justices, 8 A. & E. 173; 168.
Reid v. Ramsay, Dig. 420, No. 21; 30, 64, 81.
Richardson, Vaughan v., 17 Can. S. C. R. 703; 21, 62, 63.
Riddell, *in re*, *Ex parte* Earl of Strathmore, 20 Q. B. D. 512; 33.
Ritchie, Lenoir v., 3 Can. S. C. R. 575; 29.
Roberts v. Donovan; 37.
Robertson v. Harris, 14 Ont. P. R. 373; 68, 71.
   Langdon v., 12 Ont. P. R. 139; 63, 168.
Robinson, Canadian Pacific Railway Co. v., 14 Can S. C. R. 105; 164.
   v. Drakes, 23 Ch. D. 98; 164.
Roblee v. Rankin, 11 Can. S. C. R. 137; 30.
Rodier v. Lapierre, 21 Can. S. C. R. 69; 45.
Rooney, Schroeder v., Dig. 403 No. 6; 29.
Rowlands v. Canada Southern Railway Co., 13 Ont. P. R. 93; 62, 63.
Roy, Martin v., Dig. 682 No. 69; 75, 132.
Rumohr v. Marx, 18 C. L. J. 444; 19 C. L. J. 10; 3 C. L. T. 31; 168.
Ryan, Clarkson v., 17 Can. S. C. R. 251; 50.
   Darling, v., Dig. 435 No. 44; 43.

S.

Saffrey, *Ex parte*, 5 Ch. D. 365; 62.
Sampson, Martin v., 26 Can. S. C. R. 707; 60.
Sangster, Hood v., 16 Can. S. C. R. 723; 41.

TABLE OF CASES CITED.

Sargeut, Agricultural Ins. Co. of Waterdown v., 16 Ont. P. R. 297; 74.
Scammell v. James, 16 Can. S. C. R. 593; 38, 68.
Scarfe, Maxwell v., 18 O. R. 529; 67.
School Commissioners of Three Rivers, Lariviere v., 23 Can. S. C. R. 723; 43, 46.
Schroeder v. Rooney, Dig. 403 No. 6; 29.
Schwersenski v. Vineberg, 19 Can. S. C. R. 243; 31.
Schultz v. Wood, 6 Can. S. C. R. 585; 35.
Scottish Imperial Insurance Co., Clark v., D'g. 688 No. 100; 87.
Scottish Union & National Ins. Co., Barrington v., 18 Can. S. C. R. 615; 21, 32.
Severn, Archer v., 12 Ont. P. R. 472; 70.
Sewell v. British Columbia Towing Co., Dig. 670 No. 7; 675, No. 31; 36, 55.
Seymour, Lynch v., 15 Can. S. C. R. 341; 30.
Shannon, Montreal Park & Island Railway Co. v., 28 Can. S. C. R. 374; 23.
Shaw v. Canadian Pacific Railway Co., 16 Can. S. C. R. 703; 30.
— v. St. Louis, 8 Can. S. C. R. 385; 30.
Sherbrooke, City of, v. McManamy, 18 Can. S. C. R. 594; 24, 42, 45, 13 Legal News, 290; 70.
— Webster v., 24 Can. S. C. R. 52; 24.
Shields v. Peak, 8 Can. S. C. R. 579; 30.
Shireff, Muirhead v., 14 Can. S. C. R. 735; 78.
— Swim v., Dig. 142 No. 14; 85.
Shoolbred, Union Fire Ins. Co. v.; 71.
Shropshire Justices, Reg. v., 8 A. & E. 173; 168.
Sievewright v. Leys, 9 Ont. P. R. 200; 63.
Sills, Ostrom v.; 150.
Simpson v. Palliser; 48.
Skulthorpe, Stewart v.; 37.
Smart, *in re*, 16 Can. S. C. R. 396; 53, 61.
Smith v. Goldie, Dig. 689 No. 109; 86.
— Merchants' Bank v., Dig. 688 No. 102; 78.
— v. Smith, 11 Ont. P. R. 6; 62.
Société de Construction Permanente des Artisans, Ouimet v.; 44.
Société de Prêts et de Placements de Quebec, Lachance v., 26 Can. S. C. R. 200; 42.
Sœurs de L'Asile de la Providence, Le Marie, etc., de Terrebonne v., Dig. 434 No. 43; 27.
Soulanges Election Case, Dig. 682 No. 70; 120.
Souther, Wallace v., Dig. 672 No. 15; 682 No. 73; 64, 85, 144.
Springer, Exchange Bank v.; 141.
Sproule, *in re*, 12 Can. S. C. R. 140; 54.
Stadacona Fire & Life Assurance Co., Caldwell v., 11 Can. S. C. R. 212; 78.

Stadacona Fire & Life Assurance Co., Coté v., Dig. 682 No. 68; 133.
          v., Dig. 683 No. 77; 143.
Stanton v. Canada Atlantic Railway Co., Dig. 430 No. 37; 31.
Starrs v. Cosgrave Brewing and Malting Co., Dig. 697 No. 130; 63. 69.
Steam Propeller St. Magnus, *In re*,; 133.
Ste. Anne du Bout de l'Isle, Corporation de la Paroisse de, Reburn v., 15 Can. S. C. R. 92; 44.
Ste. Cunegonde de Montreal v. Gougeon, 25 Can. S. C. R. 78; 24, 29, 35.
Stephens v. Chaussé, 15 Can. S. C. R. 379; 164.
Ste. Rose, Village of, Dubois v., 21 Can. S. C. R. 65; 24, 45
Ste. Thérése. Canadian Pacific Railway Co. v., 16 Can. S. C. R. 606; 27.
Stevenson, *Ex parte* [1892], 1 Q. B. 394; 37.
          3 Times, L. R. 486; 63.
          v. City of Montreal, 27 Can. S. C. R. 187; 44.
Stewart, Maritime Bank of Canada v., 20 Can. S. C. R. 105; 32, 38.
          v. Skulthorpe; 37.
St. Louis v. The Queen, 25 Can. S. C. R. 665; 87.
          Shaw v., 8 Can. S. C. R. 385; 30.
Stone, Mayhew v., 26 Can. S. C. R. 58; 65.
Strathmore (Earl of), *Ex parte, In re* Riddell, 20 Q. B. D. 512; 33.
Sulivan. Kelly v., 1 Can. S. C. R. 1; 28.
Swim v. Sheriff, Dig. 142 No. 14; 85.

T.

Taplin. Hunt v., 24 Can. S. C. R. 36; 42.
Taylor v. The Queen, 1 Can. S. C. R. 65; 48, 61, 63.
Tew, Jermyn v., 28 Can. S. C. R. 497; 51.
Theberge v. Landry, 2 App. Cas. 102; 117.
Thrasher Case, Dig. 480 No. 12; 59.
Three Rivers, City of, Major v., Dig. 422, No. 26; 27.
Titus v. Colville, 18 Can. S. C. R. 700; 31.
Titus v. Colville; 149.
Toronto, City of, Godson v., 18 Can. S. C. R. 36; 23.
          v. Toronto Railway Co., 27 Can. S. C. R. 640; 26.
          Junction v. Christie, 25 Can. S. C. R. 551; 165.
          Railway Co. v. The Queen; 87.
          Toronto, City of, v., 27 Can. S. C. R. 640; 26.
Tourville. North British & Mercantile Ins. Co. v., 25 Can. S. C. R. 177; 31.
Travellers' Ins. Co., Neill v., 9 Ont. App. R. 54; 63.
Trenholme. Mitchell v., 22 Can. S. C. R. 331; 48.
Trepannier, *In re*, 12 Can. S. C. R. 111; 54, 55.
          Ferrier v., 24 Can. S. C. R. 86; 31.

Tupper, Fraser v., Dig. 421 No. 24; 53, 54, 83.
Turcotte v. Dansereau, 26 Can. S. C. R. 578; 40, 42.

U.

Union Bank, Dawson v., Dig. 428 No. 35; 31, 85.
    v. Whitman, 16 Can. S. C. R. 410; 69.
Union Fire Ins. Co. v. Shoolbred; 71.

V.

Valade, South Colchester v., 24 Can. S. C. R. 622; 31.
Valin v. Langlois, 5 App. Cas.; 115; 117.
Varennes, Village of, County of Vercheres, v.. 19 Can. S. C. R. 365; 24, 45.
Vaudreuil Election Case, 22 Can. S. C. R. 1; 113.
Vaughan v. Richardson, 17 Can. S. C. R. 703; 21, 62, 63.
Vaughan Road Co., Attorney-General v.; 37.
Vercheres, County of, v. Village of Varennes, 19 Can. S. C. R. 365; 24, 45.
Vernon v. Oliver, 11 Can. S. C. R. 156; 144.
Veronneau, Lefeuntum v., 22 Can. S. C. R. 203; 45.
Vian v. The Queen; 103.
Vineberg, Schwersenski v.. 19 Can. S. C. R. 243; 31.
Virtue v. Hayes, *In re* Clarke, 16 Can. S. C. R. 721; 32, 38.

W.

Wagler, McNab v., Dig. 699 No. 133; 70.
Walker, Bank B. N. A. v., Dig. 425 No. 30; 30.
    v. Dig. 671 No. 8; 35.
    v. Dig. 673 No. 17; 65, 85.
Wallace v. Bossom, 2 Can. S. C. R. 488; 29.
    v. O'Toole, Dig. 713; 23.
    v. Souther. Dig. 672 No. 15; 682 No. 73; 64, 85, 144.
Walmsley v. Griffith, 13 Can. S. C. R. 434; 60, 63.
    Dig. 670 No. 6; 69.
    Dig. 697 No. 129; 63.
    Dig. 699 No. 134; 63.
Walsh v. Heffernan, 14 Can. S. C. R. 738; 231.
Warner v. Murray, 19 Can. S. C. R. 720; 31.
Webster v. Lees, 3 C. L. T. 504; 168.
    v. Sherbrooke, City of, 24 Can. S. C. R. 52; 24.
Welland Election Case, 20 Can. S. C. R. 376; 31.
West Assiniboia Election Case, 27 Can. S. C. R. 215; 113.
Western Counties Ry. Co. v. Windsor & Annapolis Ry. Co., Dig. 683 No. 75; 144.

Westmount, Town of, Murray v., 27 Can. S. C. R. 579; 24, 46.
Wheeler v. Black, M. L. R. 2 Q. B. 159; 43, 70.
    v. Gibbs; 84, 120.
White v. Parker, 16 Can. S. C. R. 699; 79.
Whitfield v. The Merchants' Bank, Dig. 681 No. 66; 75, 133, 144.
Whiting v. Hovey, 14 Can. S. C. R. 515; 39.
Whitman, Union Bank v., 16 Can. S. C. R. 410; 69.
Wilkins v. Geddes, 3 Can. S. C. R. 203; 29.
Williams v. Irvine, 22 Can. S. C. R. 108; 47
    v. Leonard, 26 Can. S. C. R. 406; 31, 38.
Wilson, Lewin v., 14 Can. S. C. R. 722; 89.
Windsor & Annapolis Railway Co., Western Counties Railway Co. v., Dig. 683, No. 75; 144.
Wineberg v. Hampson, 19 Can. S. C. R. 369; 44, 45.
Winnipeg v. Wright, 13 Can. S. C. R. 441; 75, 133.
Wood, Schultz v., 6 Can. S. C. R. 585; 35.
Wolff, McCall v., Dig. 673 No. 19; 86, 131.
Wright v. Huron, Dig. 673 No. 20; 65, 86.
Wright v. Leys, 10 Ont. P. R. 354; 169.
Wright, Winnipeg v., 13 Can. S. C. R. 441; 75, 133.

Y.

Young, Rattray v., Dig. 692 No. 110; 86, 149.

PART I.

OUTLINE OF STATUTES AND SUMMARY OF PROCEEDINGS ON APPEAL

PART I.

OUTLINE OF STATUTES AND SUMMARY OF PROCEEDINGS ON APPEAL.

I. OUTLINE OF STATUTES AFFECTING THE SUPREME COURT.

The Revised Statutes of Canada came into force on the 1st day of March, 1887, by proclamation issued on the 24th January, 1887 (see R. S. C. p. xv.), under the authority of section 4 of chapter 4 of 49 Victoria. Thereupon among other Acts which were repealed were:

(*a*) The Supreme and Exchequer Courts Act, 38 V. c. 11, by which the Supreme and Exchequer Courts of Canada were originally established.

(*b*) The Supreme Court Amendment Act, 1876, 39 V. c. 26.

(*c*) The Supreme Court Amendment Act, 1877, 40 V. c. 22.

(*d*) The Supreme Court Amendment Act, 1879, 42 V. c. 39.

(*e*) The Supreme Court Amendment Act, 1880, 43 V. c. 34.

These repealed Acts were consolidated by R. S. C. c. 135, which by s. 1 "may be cited as 'The Supreme and Exchequer Courts Act.'"

49 V. c. 4, s. 8, provides:

"**8.** The said Revised Statutes shall not be held to operate as new laws, but shall be construed and have effect as a consolidation, and as declaratory of the law as contained in the said Acts and parts of Acts so repealed, and for which the said Revised Statutes are substituted:

" 2. But if upon any point the provisions of the said Revised Statutes are not in effect the same as those of the repealed Acts and parts of Acts for which they are substituted, then, as respects all transactions, matters and things subsequent to the time when the said Revised Statutes take effect, the provisions contained in them shall prevail, but as respects all transactions, matters and things anterior to the said time, the provisions of the said repealed Acts and parts of Acts shall prevail."

By 50-51 V. c. 16, " An Act to amend 'The Supreme and Exchequer Courts Act' and to make better provision for the trial of claims against the Crown," numerous amendments were made in the jurisdiction and practice of the Supreme Court. The most important change made by this Act was the taking away of all original Exchequer Court jurisdiction from the Supreme Court Judges, and the establishing of a separate Court of Exchequer.

By 50-51 V. c. 50, "An Act to amend the law respecting Procedure in Criminal Cases," the sections in the Supreme and Exchequer Courts Act relating to criminal appeals were repealed and substantially re-enacted as part of the Criminal Procedure Act. It contained also a provision making the judgment of the Supreme Court final in any such case, and taking away any appeal to England. By 51 V. c. 43, the sub-section dealing with this question of appeal was repealed and re-enacted, in terms intended to make it still clearer that no appeal to the Privy Council should lie in criminal matters. These provisions will now be found in the Criminal Code, 1892, Part LII.

By 51 V. c. 37, the nineteenth section of the Supreme and Exchequer Courts Act, relating to the quorum of the court, as amended by 50-51 V. c. 16, sch. A, was repealed and another section substituted to enable a majority to give judgments in certain circumstances; and the jurisdiction of the court was further extended to certain cases not arising in a superior court.

By 52 V. c. 37, a further amendment was made to s. 19 by the addition of a sub-section disqualifying a judge from hearing an appeal in a case in which he had been concerned in the court appealed from, and making four judges a quorum to hear any such appeal; by an addition to s. 24, the jurisdiction of the court was extended to cases respecting provincial or municipal assessments, and to probate cases, though not originating in a Superior Court; further provision was made for the procedure in case of the death of parties to an appeal, and the court was authorized to direct the order in which the cases from the different provinces should be entered on the lists numbered one and three mentioned in s. 58.

By 53 V. c. 35, section 51 of The Exchequer Court Act (50-51 V. c. 16) was repealed and another section substituted therefor, making further provisions for appeals from judgments of the Exchequer Court in which the actual amount in controversy exceeds five hundred dollars.

By 54-55 V. c. 25, several important amendments to the Act were made; section 20 was amended by changing the time for the October session from the fourth to the first Tuesday; s. 24 (*d*), by striking out the words "upon the ground that the judge has not ruled according to law," which followed the section as it now stands, and so allowing an appeal from any judgment on motion for a new trial; and s. 24 (*g*), by extending the jurisdiction to cases of *certiorari* and prohibition; sub-sec. 2 of s. 29 was repealed and other sub-sections substituted, the effect of which is that certain cases from the Province of Quebec may be appealed though not originating in the Superior Court; provision was also made for an appeal direct from judgments of the Court of Review in the cases specified, and a mode of determining the amount in controversy was adopted; s. 37 was repealed and a new section substituted, making other provisions in regard to matters referred to the Supreme Court for hearing and consideration by the Governor in Council; and s. 58 was further amended by changing the order in which the different lists shall be taken up for hearing at the October session of the court.

By 54-55 V. c. 26, sub-sec. (*b*) of s. 52 of The Exchequer Court Act was repealed and another sub-section substituted, extending the jurisdiction of the Supreme Court in appeals from the Exchequer Court and provision was made for entering every appeal from the Exchequer Court on the list for the Province in which the action was tried, instead of placing all such appeals in a separate list as formerly.

By 54-55 V. c. 29, in accordance with " The Colonial Courts of Admiralty Act, 1890," of the United Kingdom, the Exchequer Court was given jurisdiction in Admiralty matters; provision was made for the establishment of Admiralty districts throughout Canada, and the appointment of a local judge for each district; an appeal was given to the Supreme Court from any final judgment, order or decree of a local judge, subject to the provisions of The Exchequer Court Act regarding appeals; and the Maritime Court of Ontario was abolished except as to pending proceedings.

By 55-56 V. c. 29 (The Criminal Code, 1892), the provisions respecting appeals in Criminal cases were re-enacted (see Part LII.), 50-51 V. c. 50 and 51 V. c. 43, which provided for such appeals being repealed.

By 56 V. c. 29, sub-sec. (*b*) of s. 29, which allowed an appeal in all Quebec cases " relating to any fee of office, duty, rent, revenue or any sum of money payable to Her Majesty, or to any title to lands or tenements, annual rents or such like matters or things where the rights in future might be bound," was amended by substituting the words " and other " for the words " or such like "; and the sub-section substituted for sub-sec. 2 was amended in like manner.

By 59 V. c. 14, the Chief Justice of the Court is to be styled " Chief Justice of Canada," and provision is made for an appeal to be heard by four judges by consent of the parties.

By 60-61 V. c. 34, appeals in cases from the Province of Ontario were made subject to a limitation as to the amount in controversy with exceptions similar to those provided in s. 29 for appeals from Quebec. By this Act the Parliament of Canada gave effect to the attempt of the Ontario Legislature to place a limit on appeals from that Province by an Act which the Supreme Court declared *ultra vires*.

II. SUMMARY OF PROCEEDINGS ON APPEAL TO THE SUPREME COURT.

Parts II., III. and IV. of this volume contain the statutes and rules which regulate the practice of the Supreme Court of Canada, to which are added notes of all the decisions of the court since it was organized. For the benefit of solicitors and attorneys practising in the court, the following summary of the proceedings is inserted :—

If a solicitor is instructed to bring an appeal in a case governed by the Supreme and Exchequer Courts Act (R. S. C. c. 135), the first point to be determined (upon which it is often advisable to have counsel's opinion) is: Has the Supreme Court jurisdiction to entertain the appeal? Provided the case is not one in which special leave would be required under 60-61 V. c. 34, relating to Ontario appeals, or if a Quebec case, is of the appealable amount or within the exceptions of section 29 of the Act, both of which will be dealt with hereafter, the jurisdiction depends upon three conditions, each of which has its exceptions.

1. It must have originated in a Superior Court. Section 24 (*a*). The exceptions to this requirement are cases brought in the County Court, s. 24 (*h*); appeals from the North-West Territories, s. 24 (*i*); cases relating to Provincial or Municipal Assessments, s. 24 (*j*); probate cases, s. 24 (*k*), and certain cases from Quebec, s. 29 (2).

2. The judgment to be appealed from must be that of the court of last resort in the Province, ss. 24 (*a*) and 28. The exceptions are Assessment cases, s. 24 (*j*), and appeals from the Court of Review in Quebec, s. 29 (2). By s. 26, sub-section 2, an appeal direct from the court of original jurisdiction can be taken by consent of parties, and by sub-section 3 from the judgment of any Superior Court of any Province except Quebec, by leave of the Supreme Court or a judge thereof.

It must be remembered that the court of last resort is not such court for the particular class of cases to which the one proposed to be appealed may belong, but it is the highest court generally for the Province.

3. Such judgment must be a *final* judgment, ss. 24 (*a*) and 28. The only exceptions in the Act to this requirement are—judgments upon a motion for a new trial, s. 24 (*d*), and decrees or orders in equity suits s. 24 (*e*).

It should be borne in mind also that s. 27 of the Act prohibits an appeal from any order made in the exercise of judicial discretion, except in equity proceedings, and also that although the court has jurisdiction, it will not as a rule entertain an appeal depending on questions of fact or matters of procedure.

If the appeal comes from the Province of Quebec, the amount in controversy, which in these cases means the amount demanded in the action, must be over $2,000, as provided by s. 29, or must come within the provisions of sub-sections (*a*) and (*b*) of that section; so, likewise, if it is an appeal from Ontario, the amount in controversy must be over $1,000, or come within the exceptions provided for by 60-61 V. c. 34. But there are two important distinctions between the Ontario and Quebec appeals. In the Act governing Ontario appeals, the amount in controversy *in the appeal* must be over $1,000, the words in italics not being found in s. 29; the result of that probably is to make the sub-sections in the Ontario Act, providing that the amount demanded shall be the amount in controversy, inoperative, and in these appeals it would have to be the amount recovered. Another distinction is that if a case from Ontario is not appealable under the above mentioned Act, the Court of Appeal for Ontario or the Supreme Court of Canada may grant special leave to appeal.

Having satisfied himself that his case is appealable, or having obtained special leave to appeal, as above indicated, the solicitor must next consider whether or not notice of intention to appeal must be given. See s. 41 of the Act. If necessary, it must be given within 20 days; if no notice is required, or, being required, if notice has been given, the next proceeding is to provide for the security for the costs of the appeal, and application for approval of the security must be made within 60 days from the signing, or entry, or pronouncing of the judgment appealed from. As to whether the time runs from the entry, or pronouncing of the judgment, see notes to s. 40 of the Act. If the application cannot be made within the time, an extension of time should be applied for to the court below or a judge thereof, under s. 42, but the extension can be obtained only under special circumstances. The application to approve of the security can be made either to the court below or a judge thereof, or to the Supreme Court or a judge thereof, and the solicitor, having determined upon which court or judge he shall apply to, prepares a bond in the form given in the appendix, and, if applying to the court below, proceeds according to the practice of that court to have such bond approved; if the application is made in the Supreme Court, he must give four clear days' notice to the opposite party of the application, and send the necessary instructions to his Ottawa agent, who should be appointed for the purpose, if not previously appointed under the requirements of Rule 16; if the bond is in the proper form, and the sureties are satisfactory, the Supreme Court, or the judge to whom the application is made, orders that it be accepted. If security is to be given by a deposit of money in the Supreme Court, an order should be obtained from a judge of the court allowing such deposit to be made; the form of this order will be found in the appendix. The money having been given to the Registrar of the

Court with the necessary fees, it is then deposited by him in the usual way to the credit of the cause.

After the security has been approved of, the appellant has one month within which to settle and print the case. No special rules have been made by the Supreme Court as to the practice to be adopted on settling the case. The statute (section 44) provides that it shall be stated by the parties or, in the event of difference, be settled by the court appealed from or a judge thereof. The appellant's solicitor can send to the solicitor for the respondent a draft of the case and the respondent's solicitor can return it within a reasonable time with such suggestions or alterations as he may think advisable, and the draft can be sent from one to the other until finally signed as agreed upon, or until a difference arises which can be settled only by an application to a judge. Or an agreement can be signed by the solicitors as to what documents, specifying them clearly, the case shall contain. Unnecessary material should be omitted. As to what should be inserted see section 44 of the Act and notes. Upon the appellant's solicitor will then fall the duty of having the case printed. The rules of the court regulating the form and style of the case should be closely followed, and attention is here called to the remarks on this subject under Rule 9. It may happen that the length of the case, or some other circumstance, makes it evident that with reasonable diligence it will not be possible to overtake the printing within the month after security has been allowed. The solicitor for the appellant, to avoid an application on the part of the respondent to dismiss the appeal for want of prosecution (Rule 70), should then apply in the Supreme Court, in Chambers, for further time, giving the usual four clear days' notice of the application to his opponent and filing an affidavit in the Supreme Court in support of his application. When printed, a copy of the case should be submitted to the proper officer of the court below, who, upon being satisfied that it is the case stated by the parties, or settled by the judge, and upon being paid the usual fees, should certify and transmit it to the Registrar of the Supreme Court, with a certified copy of the bond given as security and certified copies of exhibits. (See Rule 10). It may be less expensive and more advantageous to the satisfactory argument of the appeal to obtain from the Supreme Court, in Chambers, an order for the transmission of the original exhibits. Rule 10. The case should be filed in the office of the Registrar of the Supreme Court twenty days before the first day of the session at which it is to be brought on for hearing. At least fifteen days before the first day of the session notice of hearing must be served. (See Rules 11-15).

Each party has in the meantime prepared and printed a concise but complete statement of the facts of the case and the reasons and authorities upon which he intends to rely. This document is called a factum. The factums of both parties should be deposited with the Registrar at least fifteen days before the first day of the session. (Rule 23). As to what the factum should contain and how it should be printed see Rules 24 and 25. The appeal must be inscribed by the appellant for hearing, that is a request must be filed with the Registrar to place it on the list of appeals for hearing, at least fourteen days before the first day of the session at which the appeal is to be heard. (Rule 31). The inscription cannot be made unless the appellant's factum has been deposited. If the respondent has failed to deposit his factum within the time limited by the rule in that behalf, the appellant inscribes *ex parte*. The appeal is then placed on the proper list by the Registrar (see section 58), and will be called by the court when reached.

The above is the procedure in an appeal that is entirely governed by the provisions of the Supreme and Exchequer Courts Act, R. S. C. c. 135. There are certain appeals which are regulated by special acts, namely, appeals in criminal cases, in Exchequer Court cases, in election cases, and in cases under the Winding-up Act. The special provisions respecting these will be found in Part III. of this book. Thus, in criminal appeals, 15 days' notice of intention to appeal must be given to the Attorney-General of the Province; no security is required, and no factums are to be deposited, and notice of hearing, which in the cases dealt with above is to be given under Rule 11 for the next ensuing session of the court, in criminal appeals is given at different times according to the Province from which it comes, as provided by Rule 49. In Exchequer appeals 10 days' notice of appeal is required, and the security, if the appeal is by a subject, is given by a deposit of $50 in court, on which the appeal is immediately inscribed for hearing; if the appeal is by or on behalf of the Crown no deposit is required, but only the notice. In election appeals there is a special procedure provided for by Rules 50, 53-55 inclusive, and 86; the record in these appeals is printed under an order of a judge of the Supreme Court, and consists of so much of the whole record forwarded by the clerk of the Election Court as such order directs. The appeal is inscribed by the Registrar on receipt of the record, and the factums need be deposited only three days before the session at which the appeal is to be heard, and may be dispensed with altogether by order.

In cases under the Winding-up Act, an appeal can be taken only by leave of the Supreme Court or a judge thereof; the amount in controversy must be $2,000 or upwards, to which there are no exceptions; the order having been made, and the security approved, the case then follows the procedure indicated above, in ordinary appeals, and generally the ordinary procedure applies in all the special cases where the special act makes no provision therefor, or contains nothing which would render such procedure inapplicable.

Next, as to the hearing of appeals: The solicitor having an appeal on the list for any term should be careful to obtain a copy of such list, and instruct his agent to see that he has proper notice so as to be present with his counsel, if any, when the appeal is called for hearing. The cases are called in their order on such list, unless by consent of counsel interested a change in the order of hearing is directed by the court, and if counsel for the appellant is not present when the case is called, it is liable to be struck off, and there is great difficulty in getting it restored. Only two counsel on each side as a rule are heard, unless different respondents having different interests choose to be represented separately. The factums should be prepared with a view to the hearing, and should contain pretty full notes of the argument. If authorities are cited which are not in the factum, the court will generally direct that a list of them may be furnished after the argument.

After judgment is delivered the agent for the successful party should apply to the Registrar for an appointment to settle the minutes of the judgment and to tax the costs. The agent drafts the minutes and bill of costs and serves a copy of these papers with the appointment on the agent of the other party. Both agents attend before the Registrar at the time mentioned in the appointment, and the minutes of judgment are settled and the bill taxed by the Registrar, who issues to the agent an allocatur of the costs, and as soon as judgment is entered certifies and transmits it to the proper officer of the court of original jurisdiction, who thereupon makes all proper and necessary entries thereof; and all subsequent proceedings may be taken as if the judgment had been given or pronounced in that court.

PART II.

SUPREME AND EXCHEQUER COURTS ACT

PART II.

R. S. C. c. 135.
THE SUPREME AND EXCHEQUER COURTS ACT.

HER Majesty, by and with the advice and consent of the Senate and House of Commons of Canada, enacts as follows:

Short Title.
1. This Act may be cited as "*The Supreme and Exchequer Courts Act.*" 38 V. c. 11, s. 81.

Interpretation. — "Supreme Court." — "Exchequer Court." — "Judge." — "Judgment." — "Final judgment." — "Appeal." — "The court appealed from."

2. In this Act, unless the context otherwise requires—

(*a*) The expression "the Supreme Court" or "the Court" means the Supreme Court of Canada.

(*b*) The expression "the Exchequer Court" means the Exchequer Court of Canada.

(*c*) The expression "judge" includes the chief justice.

(*d*) The expression "judgment," when used with reference to the court appealed from, includes any judgment, rule, order, decision, decree, decretal order, or sentence thereof; and when used with reference to the Supreme Court, includes any judgment or order of that court.

(*e*) The expression "final judgment" means any judgment, rule, order, or decision, whereby the action, suit, cause, matter, or other judicial proceeding, is finally determined and concluded.

(*f*) The expression "appeal" includes any proceeding to set aside or vary any judgment of the court appealed from.

(*g*) The expression "the court appealed from" means the court from which the appeal is brought directly to the Supreme Court, whether such court is a court of original jurisdiction or a court of appeal. 38 V. c. 11, ss. 2, 5 & 11; 42 V. c. 39, s.9.

See also the Interpretation Act, R. S. C. c. 1.

For the meaning of "final judgment," see notes to s. 24 (*a*), and s. 28. And see s. 28 and notes for meaning of "judicial proceeding. As to what is a "judgment" under sub-sec. (*d*), see judgment of Strong, J., in *Re O'Brien*, 16 Can. S. C. R. at p. 207.

For appeals directly from the court of original jurisdiction, see s. 26, sub-secs. 2 and 3, and notes thereto.

Court continued.

[**3.** The court of common law and equity in and for Canada, now existing under the name of "The Supreme Court of Canada," is hereby continued under such name, and shall continue to be a court of record.]

Section substituted by 50-51 V. c. 16, sch. A. The section originally provided for the continuance also of the Exchequer Court.

By section 101 of the British North America Act, 1867, it is provided that:

"The Parliament of Canada may, notwithstanding anything in this Act, from time to time, provide for the constitution, maintenance, and organization of a general court of appeal for Canada, and for the establishment of any additional courts for the better administration of the laws of Canada."

Under this section the Supreme Court of Canada was organized and established in 1875 by 38 V. c. 11. But it can be said to be in only a limited sense a general court of appeal for Canada, for the existing right of appeal in the various provinces to the Privy Council has been left untouched. Nor can it be called a final court of appeal for Canada, inasmuch as the Privy Council has frequently entertained appeals from its judgments by virtue of the exercise of the royal prerogative. See section 71 and notes. See also Criminal Appeals and notes Part III.

Constitution of court.

[**4.** The Supreme Court shall consist of a chief justice, to be called The Chief Justice of Canada, and five puisné judges, who shall be appointed by the Governor in Council by letters patent under the Great Seal.]

The above was substituted for the corresponding section in R. S. C. c. 135, by 59 V. c. 14. The only change from the former section is the addition of the words "to be called The Chief Justice of Canada."

By an Act of the United Kingdom, passed in 1895 (58-59 V. c. 44), provision was made for the appointment of a judge or retired judge of any British colony, to the Judicial Committee of Her Majesty's Privy Council. Pursuant to this Act His Lordship Sir Henry Strong, Chief Justice of Canada, was, in June, 1896, sworn in a member of the Privy Council and thus became, by the terms of the Act, a member of the Judicial Committee.

Who may be appointed judge.

2. Any person may be appointed a judge of the court who is or has been a judge of a superior court of any of the provinces of Canada, or a barrister or advocate of at least ten years' standing at the bar of any of the said provinces.

Judges from bar of Quebec.

3. Two at least of the judges of the court shall be appointed from among the judges of the Court of Queen's Bench, or of the Superior Court, or the barristers or advocates, of the Province of Quebec.

No other office of profit to be held.

4. No judge of the court shall hold any other office of emolument, either under the Government of Canada or under the government of any province of Canada.

Residence.

5. The judges of the court shall reside at the city of Ottawa, or within five miles thereof. 38 V. c. 11, s. 3, part, and ss. 4 & 10.

Tenure of office.

5. The judges of the court shall hold office during good behaviour, but shall be removable by the Governor-General on address of the Senate and House of Commons. 38 V. c. 11, s. 5.

---

1. Section 7 of *The Supreme and Exchequer Courts Act*, being chapter 185 of the Revised Statutes, as amended by section 57 and schedule A of chapter 16 of the statutes of 1887, is repealed, and the following is substituted therefor:— R.S.C., c. 135, new s. 7.

"**7.** There shall be paid and payable out of the Consolidated Revenue Fund of Canada, the yearly sums following, as and for the salaries of the said judges, that is to say : to the chief justice, the sum of ten thousand dollars, and to each of the puisné judges the sum of nine thousand dollars, which sums shall be paid, free and clear of all deductions whatsoever, by monthly instalments ; the first payment shall be made *pro ratâ* on the first day of the month which occurs next after the appointment of the judge entitled to receive it ; and if any judge resigns his office or dies, he or his executor or administrator shall be entitled to receive such proportionate part of the salary aforesaid as has accrued during the time that he has executed such office since the last payment." Salaries of judges of Supreme Court.

proportionate part of the salary aforesaid as has accrued during the time that he has executed such office since the last payment. 38 V. c. 11, s. 6.

As amended by 50-51 Vic. c. 16, sch. A. The original section contained the words " as judges of both courts " after the word " judges " in the third line, which words were struck out when the Exchequer Court was constituted a separate court and no longer presided over by the Supreme Court judges.

Retiring allowances and how payable.

8. If any judge has continued in the office of judge of [the said court] for fifteen years or upwards, or in the said office and that of judge of one or more of the superior courts, or of the courts of vice-admiralty in any of the provinces of Canada, for periods amounting together to fifteen years or upwards, or becomes afflicted with a permanent infirmity, disabling him from the due execution of his office, and if such judge resigns his office, Her Majesty may, by letters patent under the Great Seal of Canada, reciting such period of office, or such permanent infirmity, grant unto such judge an annuity equal to two-thirds of his salary as such judge at the time of his resignation, to commence immediately after his resignation and to continue thenceforth during his natural life, and to be payable by monthly instalments, and *pro rata* for any period less than a year during such continuance, out of any unappropriated moneys forming part of the Consolidated Revenue Fund of Canada. 38 V. c. 11, s. 7.

As amended by 50-51 V. c. 16, sch. A. The word " Courts " in the second line was changed to " Court."

The qualification for appointment to the Supreme and Exchequer Courts being the same, an Exchequer Court Judge could be appointed to the Supreme Court bench, but there is no provision for his former judicial service being reckoned for retiring allowance under this section.

Oath to be taken.

9. Every judge shall, previously to entering upon the duties of his office as such judge, take an oath in the form following:

Form of oath.

" I,   , do solemnly and sincerely promise and swear that I will duly and faithfully, and to the best of my skill and knowledge, execute the powers and trusts reposed in me as chief justice (*or* as one of the judges) of the Supreme Court of Canada. So help me God." 38 V. c. 11, ss. 8 and 60.

As amended by 50-51 V. c. 16, sch. A. The original section was amended by striking out the words "and of the Exchequer Court" after the word "Court."

Every judge on taking office is also required to take an oath of allegiance to the reigning Sovereign of the United Kingdom in the following form:

"I,   , do sincerely promise and swear that I will be faithful and bear true allegiance to Her Majesty Queen Victoria (*or reigning Sovereign for the time being*) as lawful Sovereign of the United Kingdom of Great Britain and Ireland, and of this Dominion of Canada, dependent on and belonging to the said Kingdom, and that I will defend Her to the utmost of my power against all traitorous conspiracies or attempts whatsoever, which shall be made against Her person, crown and dignity, and that I will do my utmost endeavour to disclose and make known to Her Majesty, Her heirs or successors, all treasons or traitorous conspiracies and attempts which I shall know to be against Her or any of them; and all this I do swear without any equivocation, mental evasion or secret reservation. So help me God."

How administered.

10. Such oaths shall be administered to the chief justice before the Governor-General, or person administering the Government of Canada, in Council, and to the puisné judges by the chief justice, or, in his absence or illness, by any other judge of the court present at Ottawa. 38 V. c. 11, s. 9; 42 V. c. 39, s. 12.

REGISTRAR AND OTHER OFFICERS.

Appointment of Registrar—Clerks and servants.

11. The Governor in Council may, by an instrument under the Great Seal, appoint a fit and proper person, being a barrister of at least five years' standing, to be the registrar of the Supreme Court, and such registrar shall hold office during pleasure, shall reside and keep an office at the city of Ottawa, and shall be paid a salary of two thousand six hundred dollars per annum; and the Governor in Council may, from time to time, appoint such other clerks and servants of the Supreme Court as are necessary, all of whom shall hold office during pleasure. 38 V. c. 11, s. 69.

As amended by 50-51 V. c. 16, sch. A. The original section was amended by striking out the words "and of the Exchequer Court" after the words "Supreme Court" in the 9th line.

By rule 83 the Registrar has been given all the powers and authority of a Judge in Chambers, except in *habeas corpus* and *certiorari* matters, subject to an appeal to a judge. Under the provisions of section 112 of the Act, he also acts as Publisher of the Reports. And by 51 V. c. 37, s. 4, he has the management and control of the library of the court, under the supervision of the Minister of Justice.

The power of the Governor in Council to appoint clerks and servants of the court would seem to be independent of the Civil Service Act.

[**12.** Repealed by 50-51 V. c. 16, sch. B.]

Reporters.

[**13.** The Governor in Council may appoint a reporter and assistant reporter, who shall report the decisions of the Supreme Court, and who shall be paid such salaries respectively as the Governor in Council determines.]

This section was substituted for the original section by 50-51 V. c. 16, sch. A. Under the authority of section 112 the Registrar is the Publisher of the Reports.

Civil Service and Superannuation Acts to apply.

14. The provisions of "The Civil Service Act" and of "The Civil Service Superannuation Act" shall, so far as applicable, extend and apply to such officers, clerks, and servants at the seat of Government. 39 V. c. 26, s. 38.

Sheriff.

15. The sheriff of the county of Carleton, in the Province of Ontario, shall be *ex officio* an officer of the Supreme Court, and shall perform the duties and functions of a sheriff in connection therewith. 40 V. c. 22, s. 3.

As amended by 50-51 V. c. 16, sch. A. The original section has been amended by striking out the words "and of the Exchequer Court" after the words "Supreme Court."

The remuneration of the sheriff for attendance on the Supreme Court is regulated by order-in-council passed on June 7th, 1883.

A form for the sheriff's account for such attendance is given in the appendix.

By general order No. 85, set out in full in Part IV., provision is made for the issue of writs of execution out of the Supreme Court. Forms of writ are given in the order, and a tariff of fees to the sheriff in connection with their execution and for services generally.

BARRISTERS AND ATTORNEYS.

Who may practice as barristers.

16. All persons who are barristers or advocates in any of the Provinces, may practise as barristers, advocates and counsel in the Supreme Court. 38 V. c. 11, s. 76.

As amended by 50-51 V. c. 16, sch. A. The original section was amended by striking out the words "and the Exchequer Court" at the end thereof.

And as solicitors.

17. All persons who are attorneys or solicitors of the superior courts in any of the Provinces, may practise as attorneys, solicitors and proctors in the Supreme Court. 38 V. c. 11, s. 77.

As amended by 50-51 V. c. 16, sch. A. The original section was amended by striking out the words "and Exchequer Court" at the end thereof.

Practitioners to be officers of the court.

18. All persons who may practise as barristers, advocates, counsel, attorneys, solicitors or proctors in the Supreme Court, shall be officers of such [court]. 38 V. c. 11, s. 78.

As amended by 50-51 V. c. 16, sch. A. The original section was amended by striking out the words "or Exchequer Court" after the words "Supreme Court" and by substituting the word "Court" for "Courts respectively" at the end of the section.

For persons entitled to practise, see sections 16 and 17, and see Rule 16 and notes as to the appointment of agents or election of domicile by solicitors and attorneys practising in the Supreme Court.

No roll has to be signed by any barrister or solicitor practising in the Supreme Court of Canada.

THE SUPREME COURT.

SESSIONS AND QUORUM.

Quorum of judges—Judgment may be given by a majority of the judges who have heard the case.

19. [Any five of the judges of the Supreme Court shall constitute a quorum and may lawfully hold the court: Provided always, that it shall not be necessary for all the judges who have heard the argument in any case to be present in order to constitute the court for delivery of judgment in such case, but in the absence of any judge, from illness or any other cause, judgment may be delivered by a majority of the judges who were present at the hearing; and in such case it shall not be necessary for five judges to be present at the delivery of such judgment; and any judge who has heard the case and is absent at the delivery of judgment, may hand his opinion in writing to any judge present at the delivery of judgment, to be read or announced in open court, and then to be left with the registrar or reporter of the court.] 38 V. c. 11, ss. 3 & 12; 42 V. c. 39, s. 18.

The above is the section substituted by the Act 51 V. c. 87, "An Act further to amend 'The Supreme and Exchequer Courts Act,' chapter one hundred and thirty-five of the Revised Statutes of Canada," for sec. 19 of the revised Act, as amended by 50-51 V. c. 16, sch. A.

The section thus substituted has been considered by the court sufficiently wide to enable judgment to be given by a majority of judges in cases in which one of the five judges who constituted the quorum of the court for hearing such cases died before the delivery of judgment.

It is not clear whether or not this section requires a majority of the judges who heard a case argued to be actually present in court to deliver the judgment. It is open to the construction that only one judge need be present, and he may read or announce the opinions of the others and leave them with the registrar or reporter.

The following sub-section was added to s. 19 by 52 V. c. 37:

[" 2: No judge against whose judgment an appeal is brought, or who took part in the trial of the cause or matter, or in the hearing in a court below, shall sit or take part in the hearing of or adjudication upon the proceedings in the Supreme Court; and in any cause or matter in which a judge is unable to sit or take part in consequence of the provisions of this sub-section, any four of the other judges of the Supreme Court shall constitute a quorum and may lawfully hold the court."]

On May 9th, 1894, in the case of *Grant* v. *Maclaren*, a question arose under this sub-section as to the right of Mr. Justice King to hear the case, he having heard the argument before the Supreme Court of New Brunswick, though he took no part in the judgment of that court, and had not presided at the original hearing. The other members of the court (Strong, C.J., and Fournier, Taschereau and Sedgewick, JJ.) were of opinion that he was disqualified, and he withdrew from the bench.

The following proviso was also added to s. 19 by 59 V. c. 14:

["Provided further, that any four judges shall constitute a quorum and may lawfully hold the court in cases where the parties consent to be heard before a court so composed."]

Rule 73 provides that, "If it happens at any time that the number of judges necessary to constitute a quorum for the transaction of the business to be brought before the court is not present, the judge or judges then present may adjourn the sittings of the court to the next or some other day, and so on from day to day, until a quorum shall be present."

Three sessions of appeal yearly.

20. The Supreme Court, for the purpose of hearing and determining appeals, shall hold in each year, at the city of Ottawa, three sessions; the first beginning on the third Tuesday of February, the second on the first Tuesday in May, and the third on the [first] Tuesday in October, in each year; and each of the said sessions shall be continued until the business before the court is disposed of. 42 V. c. 39, s. 16.

By 54-55 V. c. 25, s. 1, the time for the October session was changed from the "fourth" to the "first" Tuesday in October. And see amendment to section 58 as to the order in which appeals are heard in the October session since said amendment.

Power to adjourn.

21. The Supreme Court may adjourn any session from time to time, and meet again at the time appointed for the transaction of business; and notice of such adjournment and of the day fixed for the continuance of such session shall be given by the registrar in the *Canada Gazette*. 38 V. c. 11, s. 14, *part*.

The Court may be convened at any time.

22. The court may be convened at any time by the chief justice, or, in the event of his absence or illness, by the senior puisné judge, in such manner as is prescribed by the rules of court. 38 V. c. 11, s. 14, *part*.

Rule 12 provides for the publication in the *Canada Gazette* of a notice convening the court, and for the form of such notice; see Schedule A appended to the rules.

Rule 73 provides that, "If it happens at any time that the number of judges necessary to constitute a quorum for the transaction of the business to be brought before the court is not present, the judge or judges then present may adjourn the sittings of the court to the next or some other day, and so on from day to day until a quorum shall be present."

JURISDICTION—APPEALS.

Jurisdiction over all Canada.

23. The Supreme Court shall have, hold and exercise an appellate, civil and criminal jurisdiction within and throughout Canada. 38 V. c. 11, s. 15.

Appeal.

24. An appeal shall lie to the Supreme Court,—

From final judgments.

(*a*) From all final judgments of the highest court of final resort now or hereafter established in any Province of Canada, whether such court is a court of appeal or of original jurisdiction, in cases in which the court of original jurisdiction is a superior court;

See p. 27 for remarks and comments on this sub-section, and the decisions of the court respecting the jurisdiction under it.

Upon a special case.

(*b*) From the judgment upon a special case unless the parties agree to the contrary, and the Supreme Court shall draw any inference of fact from the facts stated in the special case which the court appealed from should have drawn;

See notes to (*c*) supra.

Points reserved.

(*c*) From the judgment upon any motion to enter a verdict or non-suit upon a point reserved at the trial;

Where the plaintiff in an action obtained a verdict, which was affirmed by the Supreme Court of Nova Scotia, the defendants appealed to the Supreme Court of Canada, and agreed with the plaintiff, the Government of Nova Scotia becoming a party to such agreement, that the appeal should be decided on the merits, irrespective of the pleadings or any technical defence raised thereon, and limiting the amount in question, the balance being otherwise satisfied. The Supreme Court having affirmed the judgment appealed from, an application for leave to appeal to the Judicial Committee of the Privy Council was refused, on the ground that in deciding the appeal the Supreme Court was not acting in its ordinary jurisdiction as a Court of Appeal, but was acting under the special reference made to it by the agreement. *Halifax and Cape Breton Coal and Railway Co.* v. *Gregory*, Dig. S. C. D. p. 727; 11 App. Cas. 229.

In the *Canadian Pacific Railway Co.* v. *Fleming*, 22 Can. S. C. R. 33, counsel for both parties consented at the trial that the case should be withdrawn from the jury and referred to the full court, with power to draw inferences of fact, and on the law and facts either to assess damages to the plaintiff or enter a judgment of non-suit. The full court having assessed the damages an appeal by the company to the Supreme Court was quashed on the ground that the court appealed from acted under the agreement as a quasi-arbitrator, and its decision, not having been given in the regular course of judicial procedure, was not open to review on appeal.

MOTION FOR NEW TRIAL.

(*d*) From the judgment upon any motion for a new trial;

As amended by 54-55 V. c. 25, s. 2. In this sub-section in R. S. C. c. 135, the appeal was restricted to cases in which the new trial was moved for on the ground that the judge had not ruled according to law, and, as held in *Halifax Street Railway Co.* v. *Joyce*, 17 Can. S. C. R. 709, was applicable to jury cases only.

As to notice of appeal to be given in cases specified in paragraphs (*b*), (*c*) and (*d*), see section 41. In an appeal under paragraph (*d*) notice need only be given where the motion for a new trial is based on the ground that the judge had not ruled according to law.

Since the passing of 32-33 V. c. 29 (P.Q.), the Court of Queen's Bench for Lower Canada has no power to grant a new trial in a criminal case, and the Supreme Court, if satisfied that the judgment of that court in a criminal case is wrong, can only reverse it and order the prisoner to be discharged: *Laliberte* v. *The Queen*, 1 Can. S. C. R. 117. The Court of Queen's Bench can now order a new trial under the Criminal Code.

The Court has no jurisdiction to hear an appeal " from a judgment on a motion for a new trial on the ground that the judge has not ruled according to law," unless the notice required by section 41 has been given: *Vaughan* v. *Richardson*, 17 Can. S. C. R. 703.

Where a new trial has been ordered upon the ground that the answer given by the jury to one of the questions is insufficient to enable the court to dispose of the interest of the parties on the findings of a jury as a whole, no appeal will lie from such order, which is not a final judgment, and cannot be held to come within the exceptions provided for by the Supreme and Exchequer Courts Acts in relation to appeals in cases of new trials. *Barrington* v. *The Scottish Union and National Insurance Co.*, 18 Can. S. C. R. 615.

In an action tried by a judge and jury, the judgment of the Superior Court in review dismissed the plaintiffs' motion for judgment and granted the defendants' motion to dismiss the action.

On appeal to the Court of Queen's Bench, the judgment of the Superior Court was reversed, and the Court set aside the assignment of facts to the jury and all subsequent proceedings, and *suo motu* ordered a *venire de novo* on the ground that the assignment of facts was defective and insufficient and the answers of the jury were insufficient and contradictory.

Held, that the order of the Court of Queen's Bench was not a final judgment and did not come within the exceptions allowing an appeal in cases of new trials, and therefore the appeal would not lie: *The Accident Insurance Co. of North America* v. *McLachlan*, 18 Can. S. C. R. 627.

This and the previous case would be appealable since the amendment to (*d*)

And the same was held in regard to a judgment of the Court of Appeal for Ontario ordering a new trial where the pleadings in the cause had been amended and a new cause of action set up thereby which had never been presented to a jury: *Canadian Pacific Ry. Co.* v. *The Cobban Mfg. Co.*, 22 Can. S. C. R. 132.

Decrees in equity courts.

(*e*) From any judgment, decree, decretal order, or order in any action, suit, cause, matter or other judicial proceeding originally instituted in any superior court of equity in any Province of Canada other than the Province of Quebec, and from any judgment, decree, decretal order, or order in any action, suit, cause, matter or judicial proceeding, in the nature of a suit or proceeding in equity, originally instituted in any superior court in any Province of Canada other than the Province of Quebec;

See also section 26, sub-section 3, and section 27.

Motion to set aside award.

(*f*) From the judgment, rule, order or decision upon any motion to set aside an award, or upon any motion by way of appeal from an award made in any superior court in any of the Provinces of Canada other than the Province of Quebec;

The report of a referee under the Drainage Trials Act of Ontario is not an award from which an appeal will lie under this paragraph: *Township of Harwich* v. *Raleigh*, 18th May, 1895.

Habeas corpus [Certiorari, Prohibition], Mandamus and Municipal by-laws.

(*g*) From the judgment in any case of proceedings for or upon a writ of *habeas corpus*, [*certiorari* or prohibition] not arising out of a criminal charge,—and in any case of proceedings for or upon a writ of *mandamus*,—and in any case in which a by-law of a municipal corporation has been quashed by a rule or order of court, or the rule or order to quash it has been refused after argument. 38 V. c. 11, s. 11, *part, and* ss. 18, 19, 20 *and* 23; 42 V. c. 39, ss. 1, 4 *and* 13.

As amended by 54-55 V. c. 25, s. 2. This sub-section in R. S. C. c. 135, did not provide for cases of *certiorari* and prohibition.

See secs. 31 to 35 and notes thereto, p. 52, as to *habeas corpus* appeals, and s. 36 as to *certiorari*.

PROHIBITION.

The court never refused to hear an appeal in a case of prohibition before the amending Act. See *Poulin* v. *The Corporation of Quebec*, 9 Can. S. C. R. 185; *Chisholm* v. *Kenny*, Dig. S. C. D. p. 539; *Attorney-General* v. *Flint*, 16 Can. S. C. R. 707; *Wallace* v. *O'Toole*, Dig. S. C. D. p. 713; *Molson* v. *Lambe*, 15 Can. S. C. R. 253; and *Godson* v. *City of Toronto*, 18 Can. S. C. R. 36. The jurisdiction as to prohibition applies to appeals from Quebec as well as the other Provinces: *The Montreal Park & Island Railway Co.*, 28 Can. S. C. R. 374.

MANDAMUS.

Before the substitution of sub-sec. 3 of sec. 29 (see p. 47) for the former sub-section, it was held that an appeal would not lie from a judgment of the Court of Review in a case of mandamus: *Danjou* v. *Marquis*, 3 Can. S. C. R. 251; *McDonald* v. *Abbott*, 3 Can. S. C. R. 278. And such an appeal will not lie under the present sub-section where the Court of Review reverses the court of first instance, and it does not appear that an appeal would lie to the Privy Council: *Barrington* v. *The City of Montreal*, 25 Can. S. C. R. 202.

Where the Supreme Court of Nova Scotia made absolute a rule *nisi* for a mandamus to compel a municipal corporation to assess its property for school rates, leaving the merits of the assessment to be decided on the return of the writ, the Supreme Court of Canada held that the granting of the writ was in the discretion of the court below, the exercise of which discretion should not be questioned. *The Queen* v. *The Town of Dartmouth*, 9 Can. S. C. R. 509.

Interlocutory judgments upon proceedings for a writ of mandamus are not appealable under par. (*g*). the word "judgment" therein meaning the final judgment in the case: *Langerin* v. *Les Commissaires d'Ecole de St. Marc*, 18 S. C. R. 599.

MUNICIPAL BY-LAWS.

In an action to recover the combined amount of two business taxes imposed by a municipal by-law, the Court of Queen's Bench affirmed the judgment of the Superior Court, holding the by-law and statute authorizing it *intra vires,* but held that one of the taxes was not authorized by the statute. *Held,* that an appeal would not lie under par. (*g*) from the latter decision: *The Corporation of the City of Sherbrooke* v. *McManamy,* 18 Can. S. C. R. 594.

Where, after the judgment of the Court of Queen's Bench, on an application to quash a by-law, was rendered the by-law was repealed, the Supreme Court refused to entertain an appeal from such judgment, the only matter in dispute being a question of costs: *Moir* v. *The Corporation of the Village of Huntingdon,* 19 S. C. R. 363.

No appeal lies under par. (*g*) from the judgment in an action to set aside a by-law or procès-verbal for irregularities which is not an order of a court quashing or refusing to quash a by-law: *County of Vercheres* v. *Village of Varennes,* 19 Can. S. C. R. 365; *Bell Telephone Co.* v. *The City of Quebec; Quebec Gas Co.* v. *The City of Quebec,* 20 Can. S. C. R. 230; *Dubois* v. *The Corporation of the Village of Ste. Rose,* 21 Can. S. C. R. 65.

But the judgment on a petition to quash a by-law is appealable, being equivalent to the motion or rule to quash of the English practice: *Webster* v. *The City of Sherbrooke,* 24 Can. S. C. R. 52. But not the judgment in an action by a ratepayer contesting the validity of an homologated valuation roll: *McKay* v. *The Township of Hinchinbrooke,* 24 Can. S. C. R. 55. And in this case, the roll having been duly homologated and not appealed against within the delay prescribed by Art. 1061, M. C., the only matter in dispute was a question of costs and the court would not entertain the appeal. *Ibid.*

Where the Court of Queen's Bench has quashed for want of jurisdiction an appeal from a judgment of the Superior Court on a petition to quash a by-law, no appeal lies to the Supreme Court of Canada from its decision: *The City of Ste. Cunegonde de Montreal* v. *Gougeon,* 25 Can. S. C. R. 78.

An appeal will lie under s. 29 (*b*) from the judgment of the Court of Queen's Bench in an action to quash a by-law for the expropriation of land which involves a question of title to land: *Murray* v. *The Town of Westmount,* 27 Can. S. C. R. 579.

[(*h*) And in cases in the Provinces of Nova Scotia, New Brunswick, British Columbia and Prince Edward Island, wherein the sum or value of the matter in dispute amounts to two hundred and fifty dollars or upwards, in which the court of first instance possesses concurrent jurisdiction with a superior court.]

Paragraph (*h*) was added by 50-51 V. c. 16, sch. A, and amended by section 2 of chapter 37 of 51 V., an Act further to amend the Supreme and Exchequer Courts Act, by which British Columbia was added to the other Provinces named in the paragraph.

The jurisdiction of the county courts in the various provinces named in this paragraph is regulated by the following statutes: Nova Scotia: Revised Statutes, 5th series, c. 105, ss. 16, 17, 27, 91. New Brunswick: 45 V. c. 9, ss. 2 & 3, and C. S. N. B. c. 51, s. 51. British Columbia: 48 V. c. 7. Prince Edward Island, 41 V. c. 12.

For extended extracts from these statutes, see Appendix I.

[(*i*) And also by leave of the court or a judge thereof from the decision of the Supreme Court of the North-West Territories, although the matter may not have originated in a superior court.]

By section 7 of the Interpretation Act, paragraph 13, the expression "Province" includes the North-West Territories; and by paragraph 31 of the same Act, the expression "Superior Court" means in the North-West Territories, the Supreme Court of the North-West Territories.

By 49 V. c. 25, s. 2, it is provided that:

"Every Act of the Parliament of Canada, except in so far as otherwise provided in any such Act, and except in so far as the same is, by its terms, applicable only to one or more of the Provinces of Canada, or in so far as any such Act is, for any reason, inapplicable to the Territories, shall, subject to the provisions of this Act, apply and be in force in the Territories."

Further, 50-51 V. c. 16, sch. A, has amended section 58 of the Supreme and Exchequer Courts Act, by inserting therein the words, "North-West Territories," thus providing for the entry of appeals from the Territories on the list of appeals to be heard.

Under these provisions an appeal would lie from the Supreme Court of the North-West Territories, so that this amendment has been made to extend a jurisdiction already given. The word "Court" in this paragraph meaning the Supreme Court of Canada (see section 2, paragraph (*a*), Supreme and Exchequer Courts Act), the leave to appeal must be obtained from that court or judge thereof when an appeal is sought in a case which has not originated in the Supreme Court of the North-West Territories. But when a case has originated in the last mentioned court, the leave may be granted by either the Supreme Court of Canada or a judge thereof, or by the Supreme Court of the Territories or a judge thereof, as in other cases to which section 46 of the Supreme and Exchequer Courts Act is applicable.

By an ordinance of the North-West Territories, an appeal is given from the decision of the Court of Revision for adjudicating upon assessments for school rates to the Supreme Court. In *Angus* v. *Calgary School Trustees*, 16 Can. S. C. R. 716, an appeal from the Supreme Court affirming the decision of the Court of Revision was quashed for want of jurisdiction, the case not having originated in a Superior Court. But such an appeal would now lie either under the above par. (*i*) or par. (*j*) of s. 24.

[(*j*) From the judgment of any court of last resort created under provincial legislation to adjudicate concerning the assessment of property for provincial or municipal purposes, in cases where the person or persons presiding over such court is or are appointed by provincial or municipal authority and the judgment appealed from involves the assessment of property at a value of not less than ten thousand dollars;]

Paragraph (*j*) was added to section 24 by 52 V. c. 37.

By the Ontario Assessment Act, 55 V. c. 48, as amended by 58 V. c. 47, a ratepayer who is dissatisfied with the decision of the Board of Revisors as to his assessment, may appeal to the County Court Judge of the District. If the assessment in dispute exceeds a certain amount, the judge may associate with him for the hearing of the appeal the two County Court judges from the nearest adjoining districts, and in such case the three judges form the Court of Appeal. The Supreme Court quashed, for want of jurisdiction, an appeal from the judgment of a court composed of three County Court judges on an assessment under the said Act, holding that the "persons presiding over such court" were not appointed by provincial or municipal authority, the appointment of County Court judges being in the gift of the Federal Government: *City of Toronto* v. *The Toronto Railway Co.*, 27 Can. S. C. R. 640.

["(*k*) From any judgment on appeal from a case or proceeding instituted in any Court of Probate in any of the Provinces of Canada, other than the Province of Quebec, save and except where the matter in controversy does not exceed five hundred dollars."]

Paragraph (*k*) was added by 52 V. c. 37.

Before the passing of this Act it was held that an appeal would not lie from a judgment of the Supreme Court of Nova Scotia in a case originally instituted in the Court of Wills and Probate, which was not a Superior Court within the meaning of s. 24 (*a*): *Beamish* v. *Kaulbach*, 3 Can. S. C. R. 704. The only appeal under this paragraph is *Lamb* v. *Cleveland*, 19 Can. S. C. R. 78.

REQUIREMENTS TO GIVE JURISDICTION.

1. The first essential to give jurisdiction is that the case shall have originated in a Superior Court, if not coming within the exceptions in paragraphs (h), (i), (j) and (k) of section 24.

See *Beamish* v. *Kaulbach*, 3 Can. S. C. R. 704, in which the cause originated in the Court of Wills and Probate of Lunenburg, Nova Scotia.

Mayor v. *The Corporation of the City of Three Rivers*, Dig. S. C. D. p. 422, No. 26, followed in *Mayor, etc., of Terrebonne* v. *The Sisters of the Providence Asylum*, Ibid. p. 434, No. 43, in which the action originated in the Circuit Court of the Province of Quebec.

The Queen v. *Nevins*, Ibid. p. 427, No. 33, in which the proceedings originated in a conviction by a justice of the peace, and had been brought by *certiorari* before the Court of Queen's Bench for Manitoba.

C. P. Railway Co. v. *Therese*, 16 Can. S. C. R. 606, in which the original proceeding was an order by a Judge in Chambers, for payment out of court of money deposited in expropriation proceedings under the Railway Act.

Angus v. *Calgary School Trustees*, 16 Can. S. C. R. 716, where the proceedings originated in a judgment of the Court of Revision for adjudicating upon assessments for school rates in the North-West Territories. But see remarks on this case under s. 24 (i), p. 26.

An appeal will lie when the case was originally instituted in the Superior Court of Quebec, though the judgment appealed from has held that it should have been brought in the Circuit Court and the appeal results in such judgment being affirmed: *Blachford* v. *McBain*, 19 Can. S. C. R. 42.

See *McGugan* v. *McGugan*, 21 Can. S. C. R. 267, per Taschereau, J., where the original proceeding was an order by a judge of the High Court of Justice for Ontario to tax the costs of plaintiff's solicitor under R. S. O. (1887) c. 147, s. 42, which allows such order to be made by a judge of the High Court or County Court under certain circumstances.

But where the first proceeding in a cause was by petition to a judge of the Supreme Court of Nova Scotia, under section 454 of the Charter of the City of Halifax, for the removal of a building erected upon or close to the line of the street without the certificate of the city engineer for the location of the line having been first obtained, it was held that an appeal would lie: *City of Halifax* v. *Reeves*, 23 Can. S. C. R. 340.

Cases originating in a county court or other court of inferior jurisdiction, subject to the exceptions provided for by paragraphs (h), (i), (j) and (k), would not be appealable to the Supreme Court, although they might be appealable to the highest Court of Appeal of the Province.

2. The appeal must come from the highest court of final resort in a Province, pursuant to the provisions of s. 24 (*a*). The latter section is supplemented by section 26, which is as follows:

"**26.** Except as otherwise provided in this Act, or in the Act providing for the appeal, no appeal shall lie to the Supreme Court but from the highest court of last resort having jurisdiction in the Province in which the action, suit, cause, matter or other judicial proceeding was originally instituted, whether the judgment or decision in such action, suit, cause, matter or other judicial proceeding was or was not a proper subject of appeal to such highest court of last resort:

" 2. Provided, that an appeal shall lie directly to the Supreme Court from the judgment of the court of original jurisdiction, by consent of parties:

" 3. Provided, also, that an appeal shall lie to the Supreme Court by leave of such court, or a judge thereof, from any judgment, decree, decretal order, or order made or pronounced by a superior court of equity, or made or pronounced by any judge in equity or by any superior court in any action, cause, matter or other judicial proceeding in the nature of a suit or proceeding in equity, and from the final judgment of any superior court of any province, other than the Province of Quebec, in any action, suit, cause, matter or other judicial proceeding originally commenced in such superior court, without any intermediate appeal being had to any intermediate court of appeal in the province. 38 V. c. 11, s. 11, part, and s. 27; 42 V. c. 39, ss. 5, 6 and 7."

It will be observed that this section 26 refers to, and its sub-sections provide for, certain exceptions to the general rule, which will be treated of in the notes to that section.

In *Keily* v. *Sullivan*, 1 Can. S. C. R. 1, it was held that the Supreme Court of Judicature of Prince Edward Island is the court of last resort in that province. In that case it was contended that the Lieutenant-Governor in Council constituted a court of error and appeal.

In *Danjou* v. *Marquis*, 3 Can. S. C. R. 251, it was held that the appeal in cases of mandamus was restricted to the highest court of final resort in the province, and that an appeal would not lie from any court in the Province of Quebec but the Court of Queen's Bench.

See also *Macdonald* v. *Abbott*, 3 Can. S. C. R. 278, in which the appeal was quashed for want of a proper certificate under section 46 that security for costs had been given by the appellant, but two of their lordships reaffirmed the ruling in *Danjou* v. *Marquis* that an appeal would not lie from a judgment of the Court of Review. But see now, sub-sec. 3 of s. 29, as amended by 54-55 V. c. 25, and remarks thereon, p. 47.

Where by an Act of the Legislature of Quebec the decision of the Superior Court in a certain class of cases is made final, no appeal lies from the judgment of the Court of Queen's Bench quashing an appeal to that court for want of jurisdiction: *City of Ste. Cunegonde de Montreal* v. *Gougeon*, 25 Can. S. C. R. 78.

3. The appeal must be from a final judgment—paragraph (*a*) section 24, which allows an appeal.

"(*a*) From all final judgments of the highest court of final resort now or hereafter established in any Province of Canada, whether such court is a court of appeal or of original jurisdiction, in cases in which the court of original jurisdiction is a superior court;"

Section 28 further provides as follows:

"Except as provided in this Act or in the Act providing for the appeal an appeal shall lie only from final judgments in actions, suits, causes, matters and other judicial proceedings originally instituted in the Superior Court of the Province of Quebec, or originally instituted in a superior court in any of the Provinces of Canada other than the Province of Quebec."

A rule setting aside a judgment obtained against a defendant insolvent, who had neglected to plead his discharge before judgment, as he might have done, and who the court held was estopped from setting it up afterwards to defeat the execution, is a final judgment, from which an appeal will lie: *Wallace* v. *Bossom*, 2 Can. S. C. R. 488. But see *Schroeder* v. *Rooney*, Dig. S. C. D. p. 403, No. 6, in which it was doubted if an appeal lay from a judgment dealing with an order made by the judge of first instance setting aside a judgment for fraud.

An order made by a court in the exercise of the summary jurisdiction which a superior court has over its immediate officers, on an application by a third party to the court to compel the prothonotary to pay over interest received by him, is an order from which an appeal will lie: *Wilkins* v. *Geddes*, 3 Can. S. C. R. 203.

An order making absolute a rule *nisi* obtained by respondent to confirm his rank and precedence as Queen's Counsel, was held an order from which an appeal would lie: *Lenoir* v. *Ritchie*, 3 Can. S. C. R. 575.

In an action instituted in the Superior Court of the Province of Quebec against ten defendants, the declaration claimed an administration of certain property and demanded a *partage* of all the real estate described in the declaration in which the plaintiff claimed an undivided share. Three of the defendants demurred, except as to two lots of land in which they acknowledged that the defendant had an undivided share. The Superior Court sustained the demurrers and the judgment was affirmed by the Court of Queen's Bench for Lower Canada (appeal side). *Held*, that the judgment of the Court of Queen's Bench finally determined and put an end to the appeal, which was a judicial proceeding within the meaning of section 9, of the Supreme and Exchequer Courts Act, 1876, s.-s. 2, and was a final judgment from which an appeal would lie.

"The result is, that though an appeal cannot be taken from a court of first instance directly to this court until there is a final judgment, yet whenever a Provincial Court of Appeal has jurisdiction, this court can entertain an appeal from its judgment finally disposing of the appeal, the case being in other respects a proper subject of appeal." *Per* Strong, J., delivering the judgment of the court. *Chevalier* v. *Cuvillier*, 4 Can. S. C. R. 605.

This case was followed in *Shields* v. *Peak*, 8 Can. S. C. R. 579. The declaration in that case contained, in addition to the common counts, a count alleging fraud against the defendant under The Insolvent Act of 1875. The defendant pleaded that the contract under which the alleged cause of action arose was made in England and not in Canada. The judgment on a demurrer to that plea was held to be a final judgment in a judicial proceeding, and appealable to the Supreme Court of Canada.

Where a judgment of the Court of Appeal (P. Q.) declared plaintiff entitled to a balance on a building contract, but remitted the case to the Superior Court to enable experts to decide what amount should be deducted for defective work, *Held*, that this judgment was a final judgment from which an appeal would lie; and that although on an appeal from a final judgment an appellant may have the right to impugn an interlocutory judgment rendered in the cause, yet he loses this right if he voluntarily and without reserve acts upon such interlocutory judgment: *Shaw* v. *St. Louis*, 8 Can. S. C. R. 385.

Where a capias had issued under Art. 798, of the C. C. P. (P. Q.) and the prisoner petitioned to be discharged under Art. 819, C. C. P., which petition was dismissed after issue joined on the pleadings under Art. 820, C. C. P., and the judgment of dismissal affirmed by the Court of Queen's Bench for Lower Canada, *Held*, that the judgment was a final judgment in a judicial proceeding within the meaning of section 28, Supreme and Exchequer Courts Act, and therefore appealable: *Mackinnon* v. *Keroack*, 15 Can. S. C. R. 111.

A judgment on an interpleader issue at the instance of a sheriff under the procedure in Ontario is a final judgment from which an appeal will lie: *Whiting* v. *Hovey*, 14 Can. S. C. R. 515. And so is a judgment on an interpleader issue between landlord and tenant when the landlord claims a lien on the lessee's goods for rent: *Lynch* v. *Seymour*, 15 Can. S. C. R. 341.

But an appeal will not lie from a judgment on a demurrer which does not finally put an end to any part of an action: *Kandick* v. *Morrison*, 2 Can. S. C. R. 12; *Reid* v. *Ramsay*, Dig. S. C. D. 420, No. 21; *Bank B. N. A.* v. *Walker*, Ibid. p. 425, No. 30; *Roblee* v. *Rankin*, 11 Can. S. C. R. 137; *Shaw* v. *Canadian Pacific Ry. Co.*, 16 Can. S. C. R. 703.

Nor, although it has jurisdiction, will the court entertain an appeal from a judgment or order dealing with a mere matter of procedure: *Gladwin* v. *Cummings*, Dig. S. C. D. p. 426, No. 32; *Dawson* v. *Union Bank*, Ibid. p. 428, No. 35; *O'Donohoe* v. *Beatty*, 19 Can. S. C. R. 356; *South Colchester* v. *Valade*, 24 Can. S. C. R. 622; *Ferrier* v. *Trepannier*, 24 Can. S. C. R. 86; *Arpin* v. *The Merchants Bank*, 24 Can. S. C. R. 142. *Williams* v. *Leonard*, 26 Can. S. C. R. 406. Nor when the appeal depends on mere questions of fact: *Arpin* v. *The Queen*, 14 Can. S. C. R. 736; *Titus* v. *Colville*, 18 Can. S. C. R. 709; *Schwersenski* v. *Vineberg*, 19 Can. S. C. R. 243; *Bickford* v. *Hawkins*, 19 Can. S. C. R. 362; *Welland Election Case*, 20 Can. S. C. R. 376. Especially when it is the second appellate court before which the case has come. *Warner* v. *Murray*, 19 Can. S. C. R. 720. *Demers* v. *Montreal Steam Laundry Co.*, 27 Can. S. C. R. 537.

But the court may reverse on questions of fact even against the concurrent findings of two courts below. *North British & Mercantile Ins. Co.* v. *Tourville*, 25 Can. S. C. R. 177; *Lefeunteum* v. *Beaudoin*, 28 Can. S. C. R. 89.

In cases tried by a judge without a jury, the appellate court may deal with questions of fact as fully as the trial judge, there being a difference in this respect between jury and non-jury cases: *Phoenix Ins. Co.* v. *McGhee*, 18 Can. S. C. R. 61.

Nor will an appeal lie for the purpose of deciding a mere question of costs: *Moir* v. *The Village of Huntingdon*, 19 Can. S. C. R. 363; *McKay* v. *Hinchinbrooke*, 24 Can. S. C. R. 55. But where there has been a mistake upon some matter of law or of principle, which the party appealing has an actual interest in having reviewed, and which governs or affects the costs, he is entitled to the benefit of correction by appeal: *Archbald* v. *deLisle*, 25 Can. S. C. R. 1.

In an appeal from Quebec an order dissolving an interim injunction was held not a final judgment from which an appeal would lie: *Stanton* v. *Canada Atlantic Ry. Co.*, Dig. S. C. D. p. 430, No. 37. And the same was held in respect to a judgment of the Supreme Court of Nova Scotia, affirming an *ex parte* order granted to the plaintiff in an action of trespass restraining the defendants from digging trenches and laying pipes: *Kearney* v. *Dickson*, Dig. S. C. D. p. 431, No. 38.

A judgment of the Supreme Court of New Brunswick making absolute a rule for attachment for contempt, the object of which is to bring the party into court to enable him to purge his contempt if he can, is not a final judgment: *Ellis* v. *Baird*, 16 Can. S. C. R. 147. But a decision of the Court of Appeal for Ontario in a case of constructive contempt was held a final judgment in an action or suit under s. 24 (*a*) and also " in a matter or other judicial proceeding " within the meaning of s. 26: *In re O'Brien*, 16 Can. S. C. R. 197. But see *Ellis* v. *The Queen*, 22 Can. S. C. R. 7, in which it was held that contempt of court is a criminal matter as to which this appeal is governed by s. 68. The same case decided that a decision adjudging the party guilty of contempt but deferring sentence, was not a final judgment from which an appeal would lie.

A petition was presented by the owner of land to the Divisional Court to have a judgment allowing a mechanic's lien set aside as a cloud on his title, and the petitioner was allowed to defend the action for lien on terms. A judgment dismissing the petition for non-compliance with such terms was held not a final judgment: *Virtue v. Hayes, In re Clarke*, 16 Can. S. C. R. 721.

And a judgment of the Court of Queen's Bench for Lower Canada, quashing a writ of appeal from the decision of the Court of Review on the ground that it had been issued *de plano*, and not in accordance with the provisions of Art. 1116 C. C. P., was not final: *Ontario & Quebec Ry. Co. v. Marcheterre*, 17 Can. S. C. R. 141.

No appeal lies from interlocutory judgments in proceedings for a writ of mandamus: *Langevin v. Les Commissaires d'Ecole pour la Municipalité de St. Marc*, 18 Can. S. C. R. 599.

A judgment ordering a new trial on the ground that the answer of the jury to one of the questions submitted is insufficient to enable the Court to dispose of the whole case, is not a final judgment: *Barrington v. The Scottish Union & National Ins. Co.*, 18 Can. S. C. R. 615. Nor is an order for a *venire de novo* on the ground that the assignment of facts was defective and insufficient and the answers of the jury insufficient and contradictory: *Accident Ins. Co. v. McLachlan*, 18 Can. S. C. R. 627. Nor a judgment of an appellate court ordering a new trial where the pleadings in the cause had been amended since the verdict and a new cause of action thereby set up which had never been presented to a jury: *Canadian Pacific Ry. Co. v. The Cobban Mfg. Co.*, 22 Can. S. C. R. 132.

A judgment of the Court of Queen's Bench, reversing the decision of the Superior Court which quashed on petition a seizure before judgment, and ordering the petition contesting the seizure to be proceeded with at the hearing of the main action, is not appealable: *Molson v. Barnard*, 18 Can. S. C. R. 622.

Nor a judgment of the Supreme Court of the North-West Territories, affirming the refusal of a Judge in Chambers to set aside a writ served out of the jurisdiction on the ground that defendant was not subject to the process of the court, and if he was the writ was not in proper form: *Martin v. Moore*, 18 Can. S. C. R. 634.

A judgment confirming a judge's order on return of a summons, allowing plaintiffs to enter judgment on a specially indorsed writ, is not a final judgment: *Rural Municipality of Morris v. London and Canadian Loan and Agency Co.*, 19 Can. S. C. R. 434. Nor is a judgment confirming an order which perpetually restrains parties from proceeding with an action against a bankrupt but reserves liberty to apply: *Maritime Bank of Canada v. Stewart*, 20 Can. S. C. R. 105.

A judgment refusing an application to be admitted an attorney is not a final judgment: *In re Cahan*, 21 Can. S. C. R. 100, per Taschereau and Patterson, JJ. Nor is the judgment on application for an order to tax costs under R. S. O. (1887) c. 147, s. 42: *McGugan* v. *McGugan*, 21 Can. S. C. R. 267, per Ritchie, C.J., and Taschereau, J. Nor a judgment of the Court of Appeal for Ontario affirming the decision of the Divisional Court on appeal from the report of a taxing officer on a reference to tax costs. Per Taschereau, J., in *McDougall* v. *Cameron*, 21 Can. S. C. R. 379.

But where the plaintiff in an action died before judgment and respondent petitioned to be allowed to continue the suit as legatee, under a will which was contested on the ground that the will was revoked by a later one, a judgment holding the later will void and allowing the suit to be continued was held to be a final judgment and appealable: *Baptist* v. *Baptist*, 21 Can. S. C. R. 425.

A judgment of the Court of Queen's Bench on a petition for leave to intervene in a cause is interlocutory only and not appealable: *Hamel* v. *Hamel*, 26 Can. S. C. R. 17. And so is a judgment affirming the refusal of the trial judge to grant a trial by jury: *Demers* v. *The Bank of Montreal*, 27 Can. S. C. R. 197.

For English cases as to distinction between final and interlocutory judgments, see Annual Practice 1897-8, pp. 1072-1074; also Wilson's Judicature Acts, 6th edition, p. 445; *In re Riddell, ex parte Earl of Strathmore*, 20 Q. B. D. 512.

4. Appeals in cases from Ontario and Quebec are subject to a limitation as to the amount in controversy except in certain specified cases. See p. 50.

Further jurisdiction — Criminal cases — Exchequer courts — Maritime Court, Ont.—Election cases—Insolvency.

25. The court shall also have jurisdiction,—

(*a*) In appeals in criminal cases as hereinafter provided;

(*b*) In appeals from the Exchequer Court;

*(*c*) In appeals from the Maritime Court of Ontario as provided in "*The Maritime Court Act*";

(*d*) In appeals from the court or judge as provided in "*The Dominion Elections Act*"; and—

(*e*) In appeals from the court or judge as provided in "*The Winding-up Act*."

* The Maritime Court of Ontario was abolished by 54-55 V. c. 29, and the jurisdiction in Admiralty cases was vested in the Exchequer Court of Canada in accordance with The Colonial Courts of Admiralty Act, 1890 (Imp.).

34   SUPREME AND EXCHEQUER COURTS ACT.

1. Criminal appeals are now regulated by The Criminal Code, 1892, Part LII.

2. Exchequer appeals are regulated by sections 51 to 53 both inclusive of 50-51 V. c. 16.

3. Election appeals. Paragraph (*d*) is an error. It should have read " as provided in the Dominion Controverted Elections Act." See sections 50, 51 & 54 of that Act.

4. Appeal under " The Winding-up Act," R. S. C. c. 129, ss. 74, 75 & 76.

All these appeals are dealt with in a subsequent part of the present volume, but it must be borne in mind that the general provisions of the Supreme and Exchequer Courts Act and the procedure thereunder apply to such appeals, unless the special Act relating to any particular class of appeals otherwise provides, or its provisions are inconsistent with such application.

Appeals to be from court of last resort.

26. Except as otherwise provided in this Act, or in the Act providing for the appeal, no appeal shall lie to the Supreme Court but from the highest court of last resort having jurisdiction in the Province in which the action, suit, cause, matter or other judicial proceeding was originally instituted, whether the judgment or decision in such action, suit, cause, matter or other judicial proceeding was or was not a proper subject of appeal to such highest court of last resort:

Appeal by consent.

2. Provided, that an appeal shall lie directly to the Supreme Court from the judgment of the court of original jurisdiction, by consent of parties:

Appeal per saltum by leave of court or judge.

3. Provided also, that an appeal shall lie to the Supreme Court by leave of such court, or a judge thereof, from any judgment, decree, decretal order, or order made or pronounced by a superior court of equity, or made or pronounced by any judge in equity, or by any superior court in any action, cause, matter or other judicial proceeding in the nature of a suit or proceeding in equity, and from the final judgment of any superior court of any Province other than the Province of Quebec, in any action, suit, cause, matter or other judicial proceeding originally commenced in such

superior court, without any intermediate appeal being had to any intermediate court of appeal in the Province. 38 V. c. 11, s. 11, *part, and* s. 27; 42 V. c. 39, ss. 5, 6 & 7.

"Except as otherwise provided in this Act." These exceptions are cases respecting municipal or provincial assessments, s. 24 (*f*). Judgments of the Court of Review, Quebec, s. 29 (2), and appeals *per saltum* under the above sub-sections 2 and 3.

"Or in the Act providing for the appeal." In criminal cases an appeal lies from the judgment of any division of the High Court of Justice for Ontario; in election cases from the judgment of the judges trying an election petition; and in Admiralty cases from the judgment of a local judge of the Exchequer Court for an Admiralty district.

The final words of s. 26 apply to cases in which the court of last resort has taken jurisdiction and given judgment on the merits: *Blachford* v. *McBain*, 19 Can. S. C. R. 42, in which the Court of Queen's Bench held that the action was improperly brought in the Superior Court, which judgment was affirmed on appeal. In *Ste. Cunegonde* v. *Gougeon*, 25 Can. S. C. R. 78, it was held that no appeal would lie from a judgment of the Court of Queen's Bench quashing an appeal to that court for want of jurisdiction.

Sub-section 2 does not apply to Quebec appeals; see s. 29. And by its terms sub-section 3 does not apply to such appeals.

For decisions as to appeals being restricted to judgments of the highest court of last resort, see notes to s. 24 (*a*), p. 28.

By 54-55 V. c. 25, an important exception is made to the principle of this section and of s. 24 (*a*) by allowing appeals from judgments of the Court of Review in Quebec.

The provisos in this section contain exceptions to the general rule laid down by the Act that appeals must come from the highest court of last resort.

With respect to appeals provided for by special Acts criminal appeals come from the court of last resort having jurisdiction in such matters, election appeals from the trial judge, exchequer appeals from the Exchequer Court.

Special circumstances should be shown to induce the Supreme Court or judge thereof to grant leave to appeal *per saltum* under sub-section 3.

In *Schultz* v. *Wood* from Manitoba, 6 Can. S. C. R. 585, an appeal was allowed from the judgment of the judge who heard the cause without any appeal to the full court, it being shown that there were then only two judges on the bench in Manitoba, the chief justice, who was plaintiff in the cause, and the judge from whose decree the appeal was brought.

In *Bank of B. N. A.* v. *Walker*, Dig. S. C. D. p. 671, No. 8, an appeal direct was allowed under the circumstances of that case.

But in *Sewell* v. *British Columbia Towing Co.*, Dig. S. C. D. p. 670, No. 7, the circumstances disclosed were not considered sufficient to justify an appeal direct.

In *Moffat* v. *The Merchants Bank*, 11 Can. S. C. R. 46, leave to appeal direct was given on the ground that the Court of Appeal for Ontario would be bound by a decision in a similar case, the effect of which the appellant sought to avoid. See *Canada Company* v. *Kyle, infra.*

In *Langtry* v. *Dumoulin,* 13 Can. S. C. R. 258, leave to appeal direct was allowed, although the Court of Appeal had refused permission to appeal to that court. The suit was one brought against D. as rector of St. James' Cathedral, Toronto, with respect to certain lands. The churchwardens, upon judgment being given against D. by the Chancery Division of the High Court of Justice, applied to the Court of Appeal for Ontario for leave to appeal to that court, D. refusing to allow his name to be used for that purpose. This application was refused, the court holding that the churchwardens had no interest in the lands or revenues.

In a case which came by consent to the Supreme Court from the court of original jurisdiction, the judge in equity of New Brunswick, the judgment of the Supreme Court was reversed by the Judicial Committee, whose judgment was made an order of the Supreme Court and certified to the court below. The judge in equity having subsequently for the purpose of carrying out the judgment so certified to the court below, made an order which the appellant alleged to be erroneous, he was allowed under the circumstances to appeal direct without going to the full court in New Brunswick: *Lewin* v. *Howe,* 14 Can. S. C. R. 722.

In *The Canada Company* v. *Kyle,* 15 Can. S. C. R. 188, from Ontario, decided 21st March, 1887, it was sought to appeal directly from the judgment on further consideration of the trial judge, there having been no intermediate appeal either to the Divisional Court or the Provincial Court of Appeal. It was held, by Strong, J., 1. That section 6, of the Supreme Court Amendment Act of 1879, authorized an order being made in any proper case, as well when the proceeding in the court below was an action at law as where it was a suit in equity. 2. That the section applied to a case where it was sought to appeal directly from the judgment of the judge who tried the case (without a jury) no recourse having been had to the jurisdiction of the Divisional Court of Ontario, under the practice prevailing in Ontario, the judgment of the judge at the trial being in effect the judgment of the Divisional Court, and an appeal directly from a judgment such as the one in question to the Court of Appeal of Ontario, being according to the general course of practice. But 3. That the foundation of an application under section 6, must be some reasonable ground of appeal, and it was not a sufficient reason for allowing an appeal directly to the Supreme Court, that the Court of Appeal for Ontario had already decided the abstract point of law in dispute, and the proposed appellant asserted that that court would adhere to its previous decision, although subsequent cases in England had since decided the point otherwise. In *Moffatt* v. *The Merchants Bank, supra*, leave to appeal direct was given, because the Court of Appeal had not only decided the same legal question which the appellant sought to raise, but had decided it upon the same actual state of facts and virtually upon the same evidence oral and documentary.

In *Attorney-General* v. *The Vaughan Road Co.*, leave to appeal *per saltum* was given by the Registrar in May, 1892, on it appearing that the Court of Appeal for Ontario had really decided the merits of the appeal by its judgment on an application for an injunction.

On December 22nd, 1894, application was made to the Registrar, sitting as a Judge in Chambers, for leave to appeal *per saltum*. The action in the case was brought to obtain from defendant, formerly clerk of the municipality (plaintiffs) the books and papers in his possession as such clerk. Judgment was given at the trial directing the books and papers to be given up with $5 damages and High Court costs. This judgment was affirmed by the Divisional Court and leave to appeal to the Court of Appeal (special leave being necessary), was refused. The Registrar refused the application as all the judges before whom the case had come had declared the defence to be without merits as to the matters in issue, and no special circumstances had been shown to justify a further appeal. The decision of the Registrar was subsequently affirmed by a Judge in Chambers, and by the full court: *Bartram* v. *The Village of London West*, 24 Can. S. C. R. 705.

On January 13th, 1896, an application for leave to appeal *per saltum* was made to the Registrar sitting as a Judge in Chambers in a case of *Lewis* v. *The City of London*, based on the ground that it had, in effect, been already decided by the Court of Appeal in another case of *Lewis* (the same appellant) v. *Alexander*. The Registrar refused to make the order inasmuch as, though the two cases might have been identical as to the facts, the questions of law were not the same, and to allow the appeal *per saltum* they must be identical in both respects.

The application for leave to appeal *per saltum* must be made within the time limited by s. 40 for bringing appeals to the Supreme Court: *Stewart* v. *Skulthorpe*, Dec., 1894, and *Roberts* v. *Donovan*, June, 1895. Leave was refused by the Registrar in these cases for being too late under s. 40.

The decision of a judge on an application for leave to appeal *per saltum* is not subject to an appeal to the full court. See *Ex parte Stevenson* [1892] 1 Q. B. 394; *Re Central Bank of Canada*, 17 Ont. P. R. 395.

No appeal from orders made in exercise of judicial discretion—Exception.

27. No appeal shall lie from any order made in any action, suit, cause, matter or other judicial proceeding made in the exercise of the judicial discretion of the court or judge making the same; but this exception shall not include decrees and decretal orders in actions, suits, causes, matters or other judicial proceedings in equity, or in actions or suits, causes, matters or other judicial proceedings in the nature of suits or proceedings in equity instituted in any superior court. 42 V. c. 39, s. 2.

But see section 30; and section 61, as to rules for new trials.

A decision in a case of constructive contempt of court is not a matter of judicial discretion under this section: *In re O'Brien*, 16 Can. S. C. R. 197.

But an order for discharge of bail on a writ of capias, for failure to enter special bail as required by rule of court is, and no appeal lies from a judgment affirming such order: *Scammell* v. *James*, 16 Can. S. C. R. 593.

Nor from a judgment on a petition by an owner of land to vacate a mechanic's lien as a cloud upon his title: *Virtue* v. *Hayes; In re Clarke*, 16 Can. S. C. R. 721.

An order on return of a summons to show cause, allowing judgment to be entered on a specially indorsed writ, is made in the exercise of judicial discretion, and no appeal lies from a judgment affirming it: Per Patterson, J., in *Rural Municipality of Morris* v. *London and Canadian Loan and Agency Co.*, 19 Can. S. C. R. 434. Nor, likewise, from a judgment affirming an order to perpetually restrain plaintiff from proceeding with an action against a bankrupt. Per Patterson, J., in *Maritime Bank* v. *Stewart*, 20 Can. S. C. R. 105. Nor from a judgment on an order for taxation of costs under R. S. O. (1887) c. 147, s. 42: *McGugan* v. *McGugan*, 21 Can. S. C. R. 267, per Taschereau and Patterson, JJ.

In a suit for the removal of executors and trustees under a will, the decision of a Court of Equity as to items in the trustees' account is an exercise of judicial discretion within the meaning of this section: *Grant* v. *Maclaren*, 23 Can. S. C. R. 310.

A refusal to amend the pleadings in an action is also an exercise of judicial discretion under s. 27: *Williams* v. *Leonard*, 26 Can. S. C. R. 406.

And so is an application to re-open the pleadings in a cause after judgment by default for want of appearance has been entered: *O'Donohoe* v. *Bourne*, 27 Can. S. C. R. 654.

Appeals from final judgments in cases specified.

28. Except as provided in this Act or in the Act providing for the appeal, an appeal shall lie only from final judgments in actions, suits, causes, matters and other judicial proceedings originally instituted in the Superior Court of the Province of Quebec, or originally instituted in a superior court in any of the Provinces of Canada other than the Province of Quebec. 42 V. c. 39, s. 3.

See section 24 and notes.

"Except as provided in this Act." The Act allows an appeal from other than final judgments in the following cases: Judgments on motion for a new trial s. 24 (d). Decrees or orders in equity s. 24 (e) and appeals *per saltum* s. 26 (3).

An appeal is allowed in cases not originating in a Superior Court; in County Court cases, s. 24 (h); in cases from the North-West Territories, s. 24 (i); in Assessment cases, s. 24 (j); in Probate cases, s. 24 (k); and in cases from the Province of Quebec, s. 29 (2).

"Or in the Act providing for the appeal." In election cases an appeal lies from the decision of a judge on preliminary objections which, if allowed, dispose of the petition. In Admiralty cases there is an appeal from the judgment of a local judge.

In what cases appeal shall lie in Quebec.

29. No appeal shall lie under this Act from any judgment rendered in the Province of Quebec in any action, suit, cause, matter or other judicial proceeding, wherein the matter in controversy does not amount to the sum or value of two thousand dollars, unless such matter, if less than that amount,—

Validity of Act or ordinance.

(a) Involves the question of the validity of an Act of the Parliament of Canada, or of the Legislature of any of the provinces of Canada, or of an ordinance or Act of any of the councils or legislative bodies of any of the Territories or Districts of Canada; or—

Fees to the Crown, title to property, etc.

(b) Relates to any fee of office, duty, rent, revenue or any sum of money payable to Her Majesty, or to any title to lands or tenements, annual rents [and other] matters or things where the rights in future might be bound:

By 56 V. c. 29, s. 1, the concluding portion of sub-section (*b*) was amended by changing the words "or such like matters and things where the rights in future might be bound" to "and other matters and things," etc.

An opposition filed under the provisions of Arts. 484 and 487 C. C. P., for the purpose of vacating a judgment by default is a "judicial proceeding" under this section: *Turcotte* v. *Dansereau*, 26 Can. S. C. R. 578. And so is an opposition to a seizure under execution: *King* v. *Dupuis*, 28 Can. S. C. R. 388.

No appeal shall lie when the "matter in controversy does not amount to the sum or value of two thousand dollars."

But an exception to this is made by section 74 of the Act in the class of cases mentioned in sections 72 & 73, which provide for certain controversies between the Dominion of Canada and any province, or between provinces, and for determining cases in which the validity of an Act of the Parliament of Canada or of the Legislature of the province may be called in question. Section 74 provides that these sections shall apply "whatever is the matter in dispute."

In *Ayotte* v. *Boucher*, 9 Can. S. C. R. 460, it was held, that although the amount claimed by the declaration was made to exceed $2,000 by including interest which had been barred by prescription, the appeal would lie.

In *McCorkill* v. *Knight*, Dig. S. C. D. p. 694, No. 116, the appellant was allowed to show by affidavit that the matter in dispute was over $2,000.

And where the matter in dispute was the ownership of bank shares, it was held that their actual, and not their par value at the time the action was instituted, should determine the right to appeal under this section, and that such actual value could be established by affidavit. *Muir* v. *Carter*; *Holmes* v. *Carter*, 16 Can. S. C. R. 473.

But where a motion to quash an appeal was supported by an affidavit that the amount in controversy was insufficient, which was met by a counter affidavit that it was over the required sum, the court dismissed the motion, but made the appellant pay the costs. *Dreschel* v. *Auer Incandescent Light Mfg. Co.*, 28 Can. S. C. R. 268.

In *Champoux* v. *Lapierre*, Dig. S. C. D. p. 426, No. 31, it was held, that when an opposition was filed to a seizure under a judgment for less than $2,000, the question of jurisdiction was governed by the amount of the judgment and not by the value of the property seized, although such value exceeded $2,000.

See also *Bourget* v. *Blanchard*, Dig. S. C. D. p. 423, No. 27: *Gendron* v. *McDougall*, Ibid, p. 429, No. 36.

But in *King* v. *Dupuis*, 28 Can. S. C. R. 388, where goods to the value of $3,000 were seized under execution on a judgment for less than $1,000 an appeal was entertained from the judgment on an opposition to the seizure.

When the only question involved was the personal obligation of the respondent in a hypothecary action to pay a sum of $165.82, for a church rate imposed on an immovable by the levy of a fixed sum, the payment of which was to be made by two annual instalments, it was held, that the value of the immovable could not affect the right of appeal, and that the appeal would not lie. *Bank of Toronto* v. *Le Curé et les Marguilliers, etc., de la Paroisse de la Nativité*, 12 Can. S. C. R. 25.

Where, in an action on a life insurance policy, the appellants claimed the whole amount, $3,000, and the respondent one-half, as *commune en biens*, the court below awarded half the sum to each. It was held that only $1,500 was in controversy, and the appeal would not lie. *Labelle* v. *Barbeau*, 16 Can. S. C. R. 390. And where the total value of the property in question on an appeal was $3,000, but the appellant admitted that respondent only claimed a half interest, the appeal was quashed. *Hood* v. *Sangster*, 16 Can. S. C. R. 723.

An appeal was heard from the judgment in an action to set aside an award for less than $2,000 on an expropriation of land under the Railway Act, though either interest or costs would have to be added to bring it up to that amount. *Quebec, etc., Railway Co.* v. *Mathieu*, 19 Can. S. C. R. 426. In this case the Registrar, on an application to approve security, had held that interest could be added but not costs.

Real estate valued at over $11,000, was sold, subject to a mortgage with right of *remere* for a year. The vendor having assigned creditors for the sum of $1,880 brought action to have the sale set aside as made in fraud of creditors. On appeal from a judgment dismissing such action, it was held that as appellants' claim was under $2,000, and they did not represent the creditors as a body, the case was not appealable. *Flatt* v. *Ferland*, 21 Can. S. C. R. 32.

Plaintiff, in an action, claimed, 1. Rescission of a building contract. 2. $1,000 damages. 3. $545 for value of bricks in possession of defendant. The Superior Court dismissed the claim for damages, but granted the other conclusions. The Court of Queen's Bench dismissed the action. On appeal to the Supreme Court, it was held that the building for which the contract had been made having been completed since the action was brought, only the claim for $545 and the costs was in controversy, and the appeal would not lie. *Cowen* v. *Evans*, 22 Can. S. C. R. 328.

An opposition *afin de conserver* for $24,000 on proceeds of a sale under execution of a judgment for $1,129 was contested, but maintained by the Court of Queen's Bench, and the *opposant* collocated *au marc de livre* on $930, the proceeds of the sale. It was held that an appeal would not lie to the Supreme Court from this judgment, the pecuniary interest of appellant, who contested the opposition, being less than $2,000. *Kinghorn* v. *Laruc,* 22 Can. S. C. R. 347.

In an action by an agent for $1,471.07 for balance of accounts as *negotiorum gestor* of his principal against the latter's executors, there was a plea of compensation for $3,416 and interest. Replication, that this sum was paid by a *dation en paiement* of immovables, and answer that the transaction was not a giving in payment but a giving of security. The Court of Queen's Bench held that defendants had been paid by the *dation en paiement,* and owed a balance of $1,154 to plaintiff. *Held,* that the defendants' interest affected by this judgment was more than $2,000, over and above the plaintiff's claim, and they had a right of appeal to the Supreme Court. *Hunt* v. *Taplin,* 24 Can. S. C. R. 36.

Where appellant proved a claim of $920 against an insolvent estate, and contested a collocation of respondent's claim for $2,044.66, he was held not to be entitled to appeal to the Supreme Court from a judgment against him, although his contestation might result in restoring to the estate a sum of over $2,000. *Lachance* v. *La Société de Prets et de Placements de Québec,* 26 Can. S. C. R. 200.

In an opposition filed for the purpose of vacating a judgment by default there is an appeal if the amount due for principal and interest at the time it is filed exceeds $2,000. *Turcotte* v. *Dansereau,* 26 Can. S. C. R. 578.

In an action *en declaration de paternité,* plaintiff claimed an allowance of $15 per month until the child (then four years and nine months old) should attain the age of ten years, and $20 per month thereafter "until such child should be able to support and provide for himself." The Court of Queen's Bench held that under ordinary circumstances such allowance would cease at the age of fourteen. *Held,* that the demand must be understood to be for allowances only until the child was fourteen years of age, and that the case was not appealable even if more than $2,000 might, under certain contingencies, become involved as a consequence of the said judgment. *Macdonald* v. *Galivan,* 28 Can. S. C. R. 258.

The first exception to the rule that the amount in controversy must be $2,000 is in cases involving the validity of an Act of Parliament or a Legislature.

The constitutional validity of an Act may come before the court on a reference from the Governor-General in Council under s. 37.

In an action against a municipal corporation for repayment of business taxes imposed by by-law, both the by-law and the statute authorizing it were claimed to be *ultra vires.* The Superior Court held both valid, and the Court of Queen's Bench affirmed the judgment as to the statute, but held the by-law not authorized. An appeal was taken by the municipality from the latter decision, and there was no cross-appeal. The majority of the judges of the Supreme Court held that no question as to the validity of the Act of the Legislature was raised, and as less than $2,000 was in controversy, and no future rights involved, the appeal was quashed. *City of Sherbrooke* v. *McManamy*, 18 Can. S. C. R. 594.

Sub-section (*b*) excepts cases relating to any fee of office, etc., "and other matters or things where the rights in future might be bound."

The matter relating to the fee of office must be that really in controversy in the suit, and not something merely collateral thereto. *Chagnon* v. *Normand*, 16 Can. S. C. R. 661. The clause does not give jurisdiction in a case in which the action was for penalties under the Quebec Election Act (R. S. Q. Art. 429), though the effect of the judgment may be to disqualify the appellant from holding office under the Crown for seven years. *Ibid.*

An action by a school mistress for a sum due her as fees collected by the School Commissioners under C. S. L. C. c. 15, s. 68, does not relate to a fee of office. *Lariviere* v. *School Commissioners of Three Rivers*, 23 Can. S. C. R. 723.

Prior to the amendment substituting "and other matters or things" for "such like matters or things" it was held that the words "where rights in future might be bound" should be read as qualifying all the words in this sub-section. If, for instance, a fee of office is claimed, but the right to it is denied by the defendant, the case is appealable. But if, in an action for a fee of office, the defendant pleads payment, the case is not appealable if under $2,000. *Per* Taschereau, J., in *Bank of Toronto* v. *Le Curé, etc., de 'a Paroisse de la Na'ivité*, 25 Can. S. C. R. 12. This ruling was afterwards applied in the following cases:

An appeal was refused in a case similar to one of contract for payment of a sum by certain instalments to an amount of $170.20 in all, as not coming within the words "rights in future" as used in the Act. *Per* Gwynne, J., in *Beaubien* v. *Bernatchez*, Dig. S. C. D. p. 433, No. 41.

In an action brought against the collector of customs at Montreal to recover the sum of $222.80, the difference of duty between 20 and 30 per cent. *ad valorem* on the value of certain importations, *Held*, that the case came within the statute and was appealable, although it was contended that by a recent amendment to the tariff it was declared that for the future, goods of the kind should be subject to a duty of 30 per cent., and that therefore appellant's future rights could not be affected. *Darling* v. *Ryan*, Dig. S. C. D. p. 435, No. 44.

In this case the court was of opinion that the vested right of appeal in the plaintiff was not taken away by the Act changing the rate of duty.

In *Wheeler* v. *Black*, M. L. R. 2 Q. B. 159, it was held, *per* Cross, J., that a question of servitude is a question involving future rights within the meaning of the Act. The appeal was entertained and disposed of by the Supreme Court, 14 Can. S. C. R. 242. But in *Wineberg* v. *Hampson*, 19 Can. S. C. R. 369, the Supreme Court held that the fact that a question of servitude arose in the action would not give it jurisdiction. In *Chamberland* v. *Fortier*, 23 Can. S. C. R. 371, it was held that the judgment in an *action negatoire* to have a servitude declared non-existent, bound future rights.

By a *proces-verbal* made by a municipal council, one R. was ordered to improve a portion of road fronting his land. On his refusal to do the work, the council had it performed at a cost of $200, for which amount they sued R. *Held*, per Fournier, Henry and Gwynne, JJ. (Strong and Taschereau, JJ., dissenting, and Ritchie, C.J., expressing no opinion on the point), that the charge or servitude imposed on R. was in its nature permanent, and had necessarily the effect of affecting the future rights of R. in the free enjoyment of his property and the case was therefore appealable. *Reburn* v. *La Corporation de la Paroisse de Ste. Anne du Bout de L'Isle*, 15 Can. S. C. R. 92.

Where the plaintiff by the conclusion of his declaration sought to recover back from the defendants, a building society, a sum of $810, part of a sum considerably over $2,000 paid by plaintiff under protest to obtain a release of certain mortgages, *Held*, by Tessier, J., that no appeal would lie, although to settle the contention between the parties it might be necessary to consider their respective rights under the mortgages which were originally given for a large sum. Mr. Justice Tessier having reserved to the defendants their right to apply to the Supreme Court for leave, the application was renewed before the Registrar and refused, and on appeal to Henry, J., the decision of the Registrar was affirmed. *Ouimet* v. *La Societe de Construction Permanente de des Artisans*, 1 Mar. 1888.

In an action for $1,333.36, balance of one of several payments of $2,000, each payable yearly while security given by plaintiff for defendants remained in the hands of the Government, defendants pleaded that the security had been released. The Court of Queen's Bench gave judgment for the amount claimed, and a judge of that court allowed an appeal on the ground that future rights were bound by the judgment. The Supreme Court quashed the appeal, holding that if future rights were bound they did not relate to any of the matters specified in sub-section (*b*). *Gilbert* v. *Gilman*, 16 Can. S. C. R. 189.

Future rights may be bound by the judgment in an action by a municipal corporation to recover the amount of a special assessment for a drain along the property of the defendants. *Les Ecclesiastiques de St. Sulpice de Montreal* v. *The City of Montreal*, 16 Can. S. C. R. 399. And see *Stevenson* v. *The City of Montreal*, 27 Can. S. C. R. 187.

Plaintiffs had, by statute, the exclusive right to maintain a toll bridge over a river, being bound to rebuild in case it was destroyed or became impassable, and in the meantime to maintain a ferry across the river, for which they might collect tolls. The bridge having been carried away by ice, defendant built a temporary bridge across the river, though a ferry was maintained by plaintiffs, who brought an action claiming $1,000 damages and demolition of defendant's bridge. It was held that an appeal would lie from the judgment in such action, as future rights might be bound. *Galarneau* v. *Gilbault*, 16 Can. S. C. R. 579.

Future rights could not be bound by the judgment in an action for payment of a business tax, holding that the by-law imposing it was not authorized by statute. *City of Sherbrooke* v. *McManamy*, 18 Can. S. C. R. 594.

Nor by a judgment setting aside for irregularity a municipal by-law defining who were to be liable for the rebuilding and maintenance of a bridge. *County of Vercheres* v. *The Village of Varennes*, 19 Can. S. C. R. 365.

The court held that no title to lands nor future rights were in question on appeal from a judgment condemning defendants to complete within a certain time works and drains in a lane separating the properties of the parties to prevent water entering plaintiff's house on the slope below. *Wineberg* v. *Hampson*, 19 Can. S. C. R. 369.

Pending an action for $1,000 for calls on the stock of the plaintiff company, the latter was put in liquidation under the Winding-Up Act. An appeal from the judgment, dismissing the action was refused, the amount in controversy being less than $2,000, and no future rights being involved. *Dominion Salvage and Wrecking Co.*, v. *Brown*, 20 Can. S. C. R. 203.

The obligation of a municipality under a by-law to keep a road in repair, is not "future rights" under sub-section (b). *Dubois* v. *Le Village de Ste. Rose*, 21 Can. S. C. R. 65.

Plaintiff was entitled to an allowance of $200 per month under a will. An appeal was refused from the judgment in an action for a monthly instalment, there being no future rights to be bound. *Rodier* v. *Lapierre*, 21 Can. S. C. R. 69.

"Annual rents" in sub-section (b) mean ground rents (*rentes foncieres*), and not annuities or other like charges or obligations. *Ibid.*

A judgment of the Court of Queen's Bench, that an injunction does not lie to prevent encroachment on land by an adjoining proprietor, where there has been no legal *bornage*, and that the proper remedy is by an action *en bornage*, does not put in issue a title to lands where rights in future might be bound. *Emerald Phosphate Co.* v. *The Anglo-Continental Guano Works*, 21 Can. S. C. R. 422.

A judgment in an action to vacate a sheriff's sale of an immovable is appealable under sub-section (b). *Lefeuntun* v. *Veronneau*, 22 Can. S. C. R. 203.

In an *action negatoire* to have a servitude claimed by defendant declared non-existent, it was held that an appeal would lie from the judgment, as the controversy related to matters where rights in future might be bound. *Chamberland* v. *Fortier*, 23 Can. S. C. R. 371.

A school mistress sued for $1,243 as fees due her under C. S. L. C. c. 15, s. 68, collected by the school commissioners while she was in their employ, which had ceased when the action was brought. An appeal from the judgment dismissing her action was refused, the court holding that the matter in controversy did not relate to a fee of office under section 29 (b), and if it did no rights in future would be bound. *Laririere* v. *School Commissioners for the City of Three Rivers*, 23 Can. S. C. R. 723.

An action by one of two adjoining owners of land, to have a line run by a surveyor under an agreement between the owners, declared to be the true line, was held to involve a question relating to a title to lands, and also matters or things where rights in future might be bound. *McGoey* v. *Leamy*, 27 Can. S. C. R. 193.

The two following cases have dealt with the effect of the amendment in sub-section (b), making it read "other matters or things where the rights in future might be bound."

In *O'Dell* v. *Gregory*, 24 Can. S. C. R. 661, it was held that the words "other matters or things" mean rights of property analogous to titles to lands, etc., and not personal rights; that "title" means a vested right of title already acquired, though the enjoyment may be postponed, and that the right of a married woman to an annuity under her marriage contract, in case she should become a widow, is not a right in future which would authorize an appeal in an action by her husband for *separation de corps*, in which, if judgment went against her, the right to the annuity would be forfeited.

This was followed in *Raphael* v. *Maclaren*, 27 Can. S. C. R. 319, holding that sub-section (b) does not include future rights merely pecuniary in their nature, which do not affect rights to or in real property, or rights analogous to interests in real property.

In an action to quash a by-law passed for the expropriation of land, the controversy relates to a title to land, and an appeal lies from the judgment therein, although the amount in controversy may be less than $2,000. *Murray* v. *The Town of Westmount*, 27 Can. S. C. R. 579. So, likewise, in an action to revindicate a strip of land admitted to have been encroached upon by the erection of a building extending beyond the boundary line, and for demolition and removal of the walls and eviction of defendant. *Delorme* v. *Cusson*, 28 Can. S. C. R. 66.

Cases not originating in superior court.

"2. Where the matter in controversy involves any such question, or relates to any such fee of office, duty, rent, revenue or sum of money payable to Her Majesty, or to any such title to lands or tenements, annual rents or other matters or things where rights in the future might be bound, or amounts to or exceeds the sum or value of two thousand dollars, there shall be an appeal from judgments rendered in the said Province, although such action, suit, cause, matter or judicial proceeding may not have been originally instituted in the Superior Court:

Courts appealed from.

" 3. Provided that such appeals shall lie only from the Court of Queen's Bench, or from the Superior Court in review in cases where, and so long as, no appeal lies from the judgment of that Court when it confirms the judgment rendered in the Court appealed from, which by the law of the Province of Quebec are appealable to the Judicial Committee of the Privy Council:

Amount in controversy.

"4. Whenever the right to appeal is dependent upon the amount in dispute, such amount shall be understood to be that demanded and not that recovered, if they are different."

Sub-section 2 in R. S. C. c. 135, merely provided that the appeals mentioned in the previous part of the section should lie only from the Court of Queen's Bench. It was repealed, and the present sub-sections substituted, by 54-55 V. c. 25, s. 3, which was amended by 56 V. c. 29, s. 2, by changing the words " such like " before matters or things in the fourth line of sub-section 2, to the word " other."

Sub-section 3 contains an important departure from the principle provided in s. 24 (a), that appeals shall come only from the court of last resort in the Province, by allowing appeals from the Court of Review under the conditions specified. By sub-section 4, Parliament for the first time fixes a mode of determining the amount in controversy in these cases.

In *Hurtubise* v. *Desmarteau*, 19 Can. S. C. R. 562, it was held that this amendment did not apply to a case in which the judgment of the Court of Review was delivered on the day the Act came into force.

And it did not apply to a case which was argued before the Court of Review and taken *en delibere* the day it came into force, the judgment not being given until a month later. *Couture* v. *Bouchard*, 21 Can. S. C. R. 281.

In *Williams* v. *Irvine*, 22 Can. S. C. R. 108, the case was standing for judgment in the Court of Review before the Act was passed, and it was held not to apply. Mr. Justice Fournier was of opinion that it would not cover any case instituted before its passage.

Williams v. *Irvine* was followed in the cases of *Cowen* v. *Evans*, *Mitchell* v. *Trenholme* and *Mills* v. *Limoges*, reported together in 22 Can. S. C. R. 331.

These cases were decided on the principle of *Taylor* v. *The Queen*, 1 Can. S. C. R. 65, in which it was held that no appeal would lie from the judgment signed, entered or pronounced prior to January 11th, 1876, the day on which the Act constituting the court came into force.

The amending Act does not authorize an appeal from a judgment of the Court of Review in case of mandamus where the judgment of the Superior Court is reversed and there is an appeal to the Court of Queen's Bench. *Barrington* v. *The City of Montreal*, 25 Can. S. C. R. 202.

An appeal from the Court of Review is only given in a case which is appealable as of right to the Judicial Committee of the Privy Council, and it follows that in such appeals, the amount in controversy must be £500 sterling, the amount required to give an appeal in Quebec cases to the Judicial Committee, though in cases from the Court of Queen's Bench only $2,000 is necessary. *Per* Gwynne and Patterson, JJ., in *Couture* v. *Bouchard*, 21 Can. S. C. R. 281.

In *Dufresne* v. *Guerremont*, 26 Can. S. C. R. 216, it was held that interest could not be added to the amount demanded in the action to bring it up to the sum of £500, and that in such appeals it is the amount demanded that determines the right to appeal. This decision was followed in *Citizens' Light and Power Co.* v. *Parent*, 27 Can. S. C. R. 316.

If the Court of Review increases the damages allowed by the Superior Court, the judgment of the latter is not "confirmed," and no appeal lies. *Simpson* v. *Palliser*, Oct., 1898.

Then by sub-section 4 the amount demanded, and not that recovered, is to determine the amount in controversy on the appeal.

Prior to this enactment there was no statutory mode of determining the amount in controversy, but the first time the question came before the court in *Joyce* v. *Hart*, 1 Can. S. C. R. 321, it was held, that in determining the sum or value in dispute in cases of appeal by a defendant the proper course was to look at the amount for which the declaration concludes, and not at the amount of the judgment.

In *Levi* v. *Reed*, 6 Can S. C. R. 482, the plaintiff obtained in the Superior Court a judgment for $1,000 damages. The defendant thereupon appealed to the Court of Queen's Bench, and the plaintiff did not cross-appeal for an increase of damages, but contended that the judgment for $1,000 should be confirmed. The Court of Queen's Bench reduced the damages to $500. The plaintiff then appealed to the Supreme Court of Canada. In this case also the court held that for determining the matter in controversy the amount for which the declaration concluded, should be looked at, and the ruling in *Joyce* v. *Hart* was affirmed and approved.

This rule was uniformly acted upon by the court until 1888, when the Judicial Committee of the Privy Council held, in *Allan* v. *Pratt*, 13 App. Cas. 780, an appeal in a Quebec case, that the amount of the judgment, and not what was claimed by the declaration, should be looked at to determine the sum in dispute, and the Supreme Court followed that ruling until the present sub-section 2 was enacted in 1891.

Thus, in *Monette* v. *Lefebvre*, 16 Can. S. C. R. 387, it was held that where the plaintiff acquiesced in the judgment of the court of first instance by not appealing therefrom, and such judgment was reversed on appeal by the defendant to the Court of Queen's Bench, the amount in controversy on an appeal by plaintiff from the latter judgment to the Supreme Court was determined by the judgment of the court of first instance, and not the amount claimed in the declaration.

The Supreme Court has held that it had no jurisdiction to hear an appeal under s. 29, where the amount in controversy had not been established by the judgment appealed from. *Ontario and Quebec Railway Co.* v. *Marcheterre*, 17 Can. S. C. R. 141.

In an action for $10,000 damages the Superior Court gave judgment for plaintiff for $2,000. Defendant appealed to the Court of Queen's Bench where the amount was reduced. *Held*, that on an appeal by the plaintiff from the latter judgment the amount in controversy as regarded him was that awarded by the Superior Court, and he had a right to appeal. *Cossette* v. *Dun*, 18 Can. S. C. R. 222.

And in an action to recover $800 and interest, where judgment was given against the defendant for more than $2,000, he was held entitled to an appeal. *Dawson* v. *Dumont*, 20 Can. S. C. R. 709.

The following cases have been decided under the Act determining the amount in controversy by the amount demanded:

Where the plaintiff in an action for more than $2,000, obtained a judgment at first instance for less than that amount, and did not take a cross-appeal on an appeal by defendant to the Court of Queen's Bench, where such judgment was reversed, he was entitled to appeal to the Supreme Court. *Laberge* v. *Equitable Life Assurance Society*, 24 Can. S. C. R. 59.

Art. 2311, R. S. Q., which is identical with sub-section 4, applies to appeals to the Judicial Committee of the Privy Council. *Dufresne* v. *Guévremont*, 26 Can. S. C. R. 216.

Interest cannot be added to the amount demanded, though claimed in the declaration, to bring it up to £500 sterling, and give a right to appeal from the Court of Review. *Ibid.*

In *Citizens' Light and Power Co.* v. *Parent*, 27 Can. S. C. R. 316, the declaration demanded more than £500, and there was a right

50 SUPREME AND EXCHEQUER COURTS ACT.

of appeal from the Court of Review though the judgment granted only $2,000.

APPEALS FROM ONTARIO.

In 1881 the Legislature of the Province of Ontario by section 43 of the Ontario Judicature Act which has been re-enacted in the Revised Statutes for 1887 and 1897, limited the appeals to the Supreme Court from that Province to cases where more than $1,000 was in dispute, with certain exceptions.

In *Forristal* v. *McDonald*, Dig. S. C. D. p. 422, No. 25, the Supreme Court of Canada intimated that it considered this section unconstitutional and *ultra vires* of the Ontario Legislature, and an appeal was allowed although the matter in controversy was less than $1,000 and leave to appeal had been refused by the Court of Appeal for Ontario. Several appeals have since then been allowed as a matter of right and heard by the Supreme Court, notwithstanding the objection that the cases were not appealable under this section.

In *Clarkson* v. *Ryan*, 17 Can. S. C. R. 251, the Act was held *ultra vires* of the Legislature.

By 60-61 V. c. 34, the Parliament of Canada enacted substantially the same provisions for limiting Ontario appeals. Section 1 of that Act, which has the peculiar title, considering that it relates almost entirely to proceedings in the Supreme Court of Canada, of " An Act respecting the Supreme Court of Ontario and the Judges thereof " is as follows:

Aurora
Markham
32 S.C.R. 457

1. *No appeal shall lie to the Supreme Court of Canada from any judgment of the Court of Appeal for Ontario, except in the following cases:—*

(a) Where the title to real estate or some interest therein is in question;   *30 S.C.R. 304   28 SCR 258 & 268.*

(b) Where the validity of a patent is affected;   *21 SCR 398*
31 SCR 7.

(c) Where the matter in controversy in the appeal exceeds the sum or value of one thousand dollars, exclusive of costs;

(d) Where the matter in question relates to the taking of an annual or other rent, customary or other duty or fee, or a like demand of a general or public nature affecting future rights;   *26 SC*
5 OLR 703   32 SCR 194

(e) In other cases where the special leave of the Court of Appeal for Ontario or of the Supreme Court of Canada to appeal to such last-mentioned court is granted;

32 SCR 480
39 CLJ 110
28 SCR 444
31 SCR 385
30 SCR 186

(f) Whenever the right to appeal is dependent upon the amount in dispute, such amount shall be understood to be that demanded, not that recovered, if they are different.   *31 SCR 7*
28 SCR 447
28 SCR 481

It will be observed that by sub-section (c) the amount in controversy *in the appeal* must exceed $1,000, which will probably render sub-section (f) inoperative as the words "in the appeal" will probably be held to mean the amount as determined by the judgment appealed from, and (c) being the earlier clause will over-ride the other when they are repugnant. Section 29 of the Act, relating to Quebec appeals, does not contain these words.

Another variance between this Act and sec. 29 consists in the power given by sub-section (c) to grant special leave to appeal in cases that would not be appealable under any of the other sub-sections. It will no doubt be necessary, to induce the court to grant such leave, to show that the case is one of public interest or that it is of special importance. The principles upon which special leave is granted by the Judicial Committee of the Privy Council are no doubt those which will be observed by the courts in proceeding under this clause.

The application for special leave must be made to the Court of Appeal or to the Supreme Court of Canada. In other proceedings of a like nature in the Supreme Court the application may be made to a judge as, for instance, for leave to appeal *per saltum* or to appeal in proceedings under the Winding-Up Act. As leave must be applied for within sixty days from the date of judgment, or such further time as may be allowed under section 42 of the Act, it will not often be convenient to apply to the Supreme Court.

Three cases under this Act have come before the court up to this time (May session, 1898). In *Bain* v. *Anderson*, February session, 1898, the amount of the judgment appealed from was less than $1,000, but the court did not pronounce on the question of jurisdiction, having decided to dismiss the appeal.

In *Fisher* v. *Fisher*, 28 Can. S. C. R. 494, special leave was refused, the court holding that the fact of the decision in the case being of special importance to benefit insurance companies and persons insured therein, was not a ground for granting the leave. *Told, Royal Templars v. Hargrove 3, SCR 386*

In *Jermyn* v. *Tew*, 28 Can. S. C. R. 497, the appeal was quashed, and it was held that no title to real estate or interest therein was in question on an appeal from the judgment in an action to set aside a second mortgage for over $1,000, where the first mortgage had been foreclosed pending the proceedings, and the appellant could only benefit by succeeding in his appeal to the extent of receiving some $270, the balance due on the proceeds of sale.

Certain matters excepted.

30. Nothing in the three sections next preceding shall in any way affect appeals in Exchequer cases, cases of rules for new trials and cases of *mandamus, habeas corpus* and municipal by-laws. 42 V. c. 39, s. 11.

Cases of rules for new trials, *habeas corpus* and municipal by-laws form exceptions to the general rule enunciated in section 28, one of the excepted sections, that only final judgments may be appealed from.

The nature of the provisions of the excepted sections prevent them from applying to Exchequer cases, in which the appeals are regulated by secs. 51 and 52 of The Exchequer Court Act.

Sections 27 and 29 do not, by their terms, apply to cases of mandamus, and though s. 28 is also excepted, yet the appeal in such cases can only be from final judgments: *Langevin* v. *School Commissioners of St. Marc*, 18 Can. S. C. R. 599.

The appeals in cases of rules for new trials is given by s. 24 (*d*). In cases of mandamus, *habeas corpus* and municipal by-laws, by. s. 24 (*g*). And secs. 31 to 35 also relate to *habeas corpus* appeals.

HABEAS CORPUS APPEALS.

Extradition.

31. No appeal shall be allowed in any case of proceedings for or upon a writ of *habeas corpus* arising out of any claim for extradition made under any treaty. 39 V. c. 26, s. 31, *part*.

HABEAS CORPUS.

Concurrent jurisdiction in habeas corpus matters.

32. Every judge of the court shall have concurrent jurisdiction with the courts or judges of the several provinces, to issue the writ of *habeas corpus ad subjiciendum*, for the purpose of an inquiry into the cause of commitment in any criminal case under any Act of the Parliament of Canada, but such judge shall not have such jurisdiction in *habeas corpus* matters arising out of any claim for extradition made under any treaty:

Appeal to the court.

2. If the judge refuses the writ or remands the prisoner, an appeal shall lie to the court. 38 V. c. 11, s. 51; 39 V. c. 26, s. 31, *part*.

Powers of the court in such cases.

33. In any *habeas corpus* matter before a judge of the Supreme Court, or on any appeal to the Supreme Court in any *habeas corpus* matter, the court or judge shall have the same power to bail, discharge or commit the prisoner or person, or to direct him to be detained in custody or otherwise to deal with him as any court, judge or justice of the peace having jurisdiction in any such matters in any Province of Canada. 39 V. c. 26, s. 29.

Prisoner need not be present in court.

34. On any appeal to the Supreme Court in any *habeas corpus* matter, it shall not be necessary, unless the court otherwise orders, for any prisoner or person on whose behalf such appeal is made, to be present in court; but the prisoner or person shall remain in the charge or custody to which he was committed or had been remanded, or in which he was at the time of giving the notice of appeal, unless at liberty on bail, by order of a judge of the court which refused the application, or of a judge of the Supreme Court; but the Supreme Court may, by writ or order, direct that such prisoner or person shall be brought before it. 39 V. c. 26, s. 30.

When such appeals shall be heard.

35. An appeal to the Supreme Court in any *habeas corpus* matter shall be heard at an early day, whether in or out of the prescribed sessions of the court. 39 V. c. 26, s. 28.

APPEALS IN MATTERS OF *HABEAS CORPUS* NOT ARISING OUT OF A CRIMINAL CHARGE.

The jurisdiction in matters of *habeas corpus* not arising out of a criminal charge is given by section 24, paragraph (*g*), Supreme and Exchequer Courts Act.

No security for costs is required in proceedings for or upon a writ of *habeas corpus*. See s. 46, sub-sec. 2. The first proceeding, therefore, in the Supreme Court in a *habeas corpus* appeal is the filing of the case, which must be done within 60 days from the pronouncing of the judgment, there being nothing to exempt such appeals from the operation of sec. 40: See *In re Smart*, 16 Can. S. C. R. 396.

The Registrar, acting as a judge in Chambers, has no authority to grant writs of *habeas corpus* or adjudicate upon the return thereof. See General Order 83.

Rule 12 provides for the convening of the court for the purpose of disposing of *habeas corpus* matters. The other rules specially applicable are 46, 47, 48 and 49, which see.

An appeal will not lie when at the time of bringing it the appellant is at large: *Fraser* v. *Tupper*, Dig. S. C. D. p. 421, No. 24.

Costs are not given, as a general rule, in *habeas corpus* matters, *in favorem libertatis*: *In re Johnson*, Dig. S. C. D. p. 677, No. 41.

But when the appeal has been brought, after the appellant was at large, and for the purpose of trying the question of costs, it was dismissed with costs: *Fraser* v. *Tupper*, Dig. S. C. D. p. 421, No. 24.

APPEALS IN MATTERS OF *HABEAS CORPUS* ARISING OUT OF A CRIMINAL CHARGE.

Section 24 (*g*) only allows an appeal in proceedings for or upon a writ of *habeas corpus* not arising out of a criminal charge. Section 32 gives a judge of the Supreme Court jurisdiction to issue the writ to inquire into the cause of commitment in any criminal case under an Act of the Parliament of Canada, and sub-sec. 2 provides for an appeal to the court in case the judge refuses the writ or remands the prisoner.

In these cases there is no appeal except from the judge of the Supreme Court: *In re Boucher*, Dig. S. C. D. p. 325, No. 2.

In a case of commitment by a coroner for murder, an application for a writ of *habeas corpus* was refused by Strong, J., on the ground that it was not a commitment in a criminal case " under an Act of the Parliament of Canada," the Act 32-33 V. c. 20 not creating the offence of murder but only defining the punishment: *In re Poitvin*, Dig. S. C. R. p. 327, No. 3. The writ cannot be issued in a case of murder, which is a common law offence : *In re Sproule*, 12 Can. S. C. R. 140, per Strong, J.

A judge of the Supreme Court will not assume appellate jurisdiction by issuing a writ of *habeas corpus* in a matter which has been disposed of on appeal to the Appellate Court of the Province: *In re Boucher*, *supra*.

Nor where a conviction has been regular and made by a court in the unquestionable exercise of its authority and acting within its jurisdiction, the only objection being that the magistrate erred on the facts and that the evidence did not justify the conclusion which he arrived at as to the guilt of the prisoner, will the Supreme Court or a judge thereof, go behind the conviction and inquire into the merits of the case by the use of a writ of *habeas corpus*, and thus act as a Court of Appeal from the magistrate's decision. *In re Trepannier*, 12 Can. S. C. R. 111.

Although the judge may grant the writ and discharge the prisoner, the court, notwithstanding sub-section 2 of section 32, may still exercise the jurisdiction inherent in every Superior Court, of inquiring into and judging of the regularity or abuse of its process, and if necessary of setting aside a writ improvidently issued. *In re Sproule*, 12 Can. S. C. R. 140. And an application to the court to quash a writ of *habeas corpus* as improvidently issued, may be entertained in the absence of the prisoner. *Ibid*.

After a conviction for felony by a court having general jurisdiction over the offence charged, a writ of *habeas corpus* is an inappropriate remedy. *Ibid*.

If the record of a Superior Court, produced on an application for a writ of *habeas corpus*, contains the recital of acts requisite to confer jurisdiction it is conclusive and cannot be contradicted by extrinsic evidence. *Ibid.*

The jurisdiction of the judge of the Supreme Court in these cases is limited to an inquiry into the cause of imprisonment as disclosed by the warrant of commitment. *Ex parte Macdonald*, 27 Can. S. C. R. 683.

CERTIORARI.

Writ of Certiorari.

36 A writ of *certiorari* may, by order of the court or a judge thereof, issue out of the Supreme Court, to bring up any papers or other proceedings had or taken before any court, judge or justice of the peace and which are considered necessary with a view to any inquiry, appeal or other proceeding had or to be had before the court. 39 V. c. 26, s. 34.

This section provides for the issue of a writ of *certiorari*, by order of the court or a judge. But it must be considered necessary with a view to any inquiry, appeal or other proceeding had or to be had before the court. Therefore, a judge cannot order the issue of such a writ in any proceeding before him in a *habeas corpus* matter. Nor does the section authorize the court to issue a writ of *certiorari* in such proceedings. To do so would be to assume appellate jurisdiction over the inferior court. *In re Trepannier*, 12 Can. S. C. R. 111.

This decision was followed by Mr. Justice Patterson on an application for a writ of *habeas corpus* in April, 1890. *Re Arabin alias Ireda.*

Writ of *certiorari* moved for to bring up papers from the Supreme Court of British Columbia, the Chief Justice of that court having made an order staying execution on the judgment of the Supreme Court of Canada, certified to the court below in the usual way, on the ground that an appeal was being proceeded with to the Privy Council. Motion refused. *Sewell v. British Columbia Towing Co.*, Dig. S. C. D. p. 675, No. 31.

SPECIAL CASES REFERRED TO THE COURT.

Governor may refer matters for opinion.

"**37**. Important questions of law or fact touching provincial legislation, or the appellate jurisdiction as to educational matters vested in the Governor in Council by '*The British North America Act*, 1867,' or by any other Act or law, or touching the constitutionality of any legislation of the Parliament of Canada, or touching any other matter with reference to which he sees fit to exercise this power, may be referred, by the Governor in Council, to the Supreme Court for hearing or consideration; and the court shall thereupon hear and consider the same:

"2. The court shall certify to the Governor in Council, for his information, its opinion on questions so referred, with the reasons therefor, which shall be given in like manner as in the case of a judgment upon an appeal to the said court; and any judge who differs from the opinion of the majority shall in like manner, certify his opinion and his reasons:

"3. In case any such question relates to the constitutional validity of any Act which has heretofore been or shall hereafter be passed by the Legislature of any Province, or of any provision in any such Act, or in case, for any reason, the Government of any Province has any special interest in any such question, the Attorney-General of such Province, or, in the case of the North-West Territories, the Lieutenant-Governor thereof, shall be notified of the hearing, in order that he may be heard if he thinks fit:

"4. The court shall have power to direct that any person interested, or, where there is a class of persons interested, any one or more persons as representatives of such class, shall be notified of the hearing upon any reference under this section, and such persons shall be entitled to be heard thereon:

"5. The court may, in its discretion, request any counsel to argue the case as to any interest which is affected and as to which counsel does not appear, and the reasonable expenses thereby occasioned may be paid by the Minister of Finance and Receiver-General out of any moneys appropriated by Parliament for expenses of litigation:

"6. The opinion of the court upon any such reference, although advisory only, shall, for all purposes of appeal to Her Majesty in Council, be treated as a final judgment of the said court between parties:

"7. General rules and orders with respect to matters coming within the jurisdiction of the court under this section may be made in the same manner and to the same extent as is provided by this Act, with respect to other matters within its jurisdiction, and, in particular, such rules and orders as to the judges making them seem best for the investigation of questions of fact involved in any reference thereunder."

Substituted by 54-55 V. c. 25, s. 4, for section 37 of R. S. C. c. 135, which, as well as the corresponding section of 38 V. c. 11, merely provided for a reference by the Governor-General in Council, which the judges of the Supreme Court should consider and certify their opinion thereon in writing, not giving any reasons.

In a report to His Excellency on the advisability of a reference to the court to determine the validity of The Jesuits' Estates Act of Quebec, the late Sir John Thompson, Minister of Justice, refers to these proceedings as follows: "The provision which confers that power on your Excellency was undoubtedly intended to enable the Governor-General to obtain an opinion from the Supreme Court of Canada in relation to some order which his government might be called on to make, or in relation to some action which his officers might be called on to adopt. For the guidance of your Excellency, or of your officers, the provision may be a valuable one, but, used as a means of solving legal problems in which the Government of Canada has no direct concern, however much they may interest or excite the public mind, as the petitioner seems to propose, or used to compel an adjudication on private rights and interests, it would be perverted, the undersigned humbly submits, into an arbitrary and inquisitorial power, anticipating and interfering with the ordinary course of justice. Used in that manner it would become in time a means of depriving the provincial courts of their functions to a considerable extent, as every important and influential interest affected by legislation would seek the opinion of the Supreme Court of Canada by application to the Governor in Council to have such opinion obtained, and the provincial courts would be in a great degree bound by the opinions so pronounced, however inadequately the parties concerned might have been represented. The rights of parties concerned would be practically concluded without their having had the opportunity which the laws of the respective provinces give them of submitting those rights voluntarily for decision in the mode, and on the proof, which may seem best adapted to elicit a thorough investigation. If the parties interested did not take part in such inquiries before the Supreme Court of Canada, the *ex parte* decision on their rights would be an unsatisfactory method of disposing of the questions involved; if they did participate, under the compulsion of the proceeding by which the government in sending the question to the court had actually acted as a plaintiff, in calling them to the bar of the tribunal, the Supreme Court would, to that extent, be turned into a court of first instance, instead of being what Parliament declared it should be, a court of appeal.

"Those whose rights are in any way affected by legal questions should, unless some interest on the part of the government being involved a different course is necessary, be permitted to raise and discuss such questions in the form, at the time, and before the tribunal of their own choice, without being hampered by an opinion certified by the highest tribunal or an *ex parte* argument, it may be, or, at any rate, without the presentation of facts and testimony which may have an important influence on the decision which should be arrived at, and which are presented in the course of ordinary legal proceedings.

* * * * * * *

"It may be safely concluded, therefore, that the object and scope of the enactment are not to obtain a settlement by this summary procedure of legal questions even of great public interest, or to obtain an adjudication upon private rights, but solely to obtain advice which is needed by the Crown in affairs of administration. This being the case, your Excellency might, not inappropriately, give to the petitioner an answer like that which was given on the 13th December, 1872, by the Registrar of Her Majesty's Privy Council to a request that the opinion of the Judicial Committee might be obtained as to the validity of a statute of New Brunswick. In that answer it was stated that Her Majesty could not be advised to refer to a committee of the Council in England a question which Her Majesty had no authority to determine and on which the opinion would not be binding on the parties. Indeed, there seems much reason to doubt, both from this authority, and from general principles, that the decision of the Supreme Court on such a reference would be binding on any parties or on any interests involved. It would simply advise your Excellency as to the opinions entertained by the members of the court." 12 Legal News, pp. 286-7.

And see 24 Am. Law Rev. 369, as to the like proceedings in the United States.

The view of Sir John Thompson would perhaps be modified by the extended provisions of the present section, but it is confirmed in one respect by the remarks of Mr. Justice Taschereau in his judgment on the reference respecting Provincial Fisheries, 26 Can. S. C. R. 444, at p. 539, namely: "Our answers are merely advisory, and we have to say what is the law as heretofore judicially expounded, not what is the law according to our opinion. We determine nothing. We are mere advisers, and the answers we give bind no one, not even ourselves."

In his judgment on the reference as to the validity of the Manitoba Public Schools Act, 22 Can. S. C. R. 577, Taschereau, J., doubted the authority of Parliament to provide for these proceedings, as by the B. N. A. Act only a *Court of Appeal* for the Dominion can be established.

The following cases were referred to the court under the corresponding section of 38 V. c. 11: *In re New Brunswick Penitentiary*, April, 1880; *In re Canada Temperance Act '78 and County of Perth*, Dig. S. C. D. p. 105, No. 3; *In re Canada Temperance Act '78 and County of Kent*, Dig. S. C. D. p. 106, No. 4: " *The Thrasher Case*," Dig. S. C. D. p. 480, No. 12.

The question of the validity of the Liquor License Act, 1883, and Amending Act, Dig. S. C. D. p. 509, was not submitted under this section, but under section 26 of 47 V. c. 32.

The case of *The Manitoba Railway Crossings*, as to the validity of the Act of the Legislature of that Province, 50-51 V. c. 29 was referred under s. 37 of R. S. C. c. 135.

In all the above cases the judges gave no reasons but merely certified their opinions to the Governor in Council, following in this respect the practice of the Judicial Committee when dealing with cases referred by the Crown for advice. See Macpherson, 149.

Under the present section the following cases have been referred to the court, the reasons of the judges being published in the respective reports:

In re Statutes of Manitoba relating to Education, 22 Can. S. C. R. 577; *In re Provincial Jurisdiction to pass Prohibitory Liquor Laws*, 24 Can. S. C. R. 170; *In re Provincial Fisheries*, 26 Can. S. C. R. 444; and *In re Criminal Code, Bigamy Sections*, 27 Can. S. C. R. 461.

In the case of the *Manitoba Schools Act*, 22 Can. S. C. R. 577, the court requested Mr. Christopher Robinson, Q.C., to argue the appeal on behalf of the Province. In the Prohibition case in 24 Can. S. C. R. 170, it directed the Brewers and Distillers' Association of Ontario to be notified, and counsel appeared for them at the hearing.

Report upon Private Bill or Petition.

38. The Supreme Court, or any two of the judges thereof, shall examine and report upon any private bill or petition for a private bill presented to the Senate or House of Commons, and referred to the court under any rules or orders made by the Senate or House of Commons. 38 V. c. 11, s. 53.

The bill to incorporate the Christian Brothers, in 1876, is the only one referred under this section.

PROCEDURE IN APPEALS.

PERFECTING APPEALS.

Proceedings in Appeals.

39. Proceedings in appeals shall, when not otherwise provided for by this Act, or by the Act providing for the appeal, or by the general rules and orders of the Supreme Court, be as nearly as possible in conformity with the present practice of the Judicial Committee of Her Majesty's Privy Council. 38 V. c. 11, s. 24.

The practice of the Judicial Committee will be found in Macpherson's Practice of the Privy Council and Lattey's Privy Council Practice. See notes to section 53 for practice of the Judicial Committee on applications to dismiss for want of prosecution. See also Appendix.

When appeals shall be brought.

[**40.** Except as otherwise provided, every appeal shall be brought within sixty days from the signing or entry or pronouncing of the judgment appealed from.]

This section has been substituted by 50-51 V. c. 16, sch. A, for section 40 as it stood in chapter 135 of the Revised Statutes, which limited the time to thirty days.

Appeals otherwise provided for, are:

(*a*) Criminal appeals. See Criminal Code, 1892, s. 750.

(*b*) Exchequer Court appeals, including Admiralty cases. See 50-51 V. c. 16, s. 51, and 54-55 V. c. 29, s. 14.

(*c*) Election appeals. See Dominion Controverted Elections Act, section 51.

(*d*) Appeals under the Winding-up Act. See section 74, subsection 4 of chapter 129, R. S. C.

This section 40 has taken the place of the provision of the original Supreme and Exchequer Courts Act of 1875, section 25, that every appeal, other than an Election appeal, "shall be brought within thirty days from the signing, or entry or pronouncing of the judgment appealed from." In 1879, the section was passed giving an appeal to the Supreme Court, by leave of the court or a judge, from the court of original jurisdiction without an intermediate appeal to the Appellate Court of the Province (excepting the Province of Quebec). Section 6 of the Supreme Court Amendment Act of 1879, similar to sub-section 3 of section 26 of chapter 135, R. S. C.

In appeals from the Province of Quebec the time runs in every case from the pronouncing of the judgment.

In other appeals, where any substantial matter remains to be determined before the judgment can be entered, the time for appealing runs from the entry of the judgment. Where nothing remains to be settled, as for instance in the case of the simple dismissal of a bill, or where no judgment requires to be entered, the time for appealing runs from the pronouncing of the judgment. *O'Sullivan* v. *Harty*, 13 Can. S. C. R. 431; *Walmsley* v. *Griffith*, 13 Can. S. C. R. 434; *Martley* v. *Carson*, 13 Can. S. C. R. 439; *News Printing Co.* v. *Macrae*, 26 Can. S. C. R. 695; *Martin* v. *Sampson*, 26 Can. S. C. R. 707.

SUPREME AND EXCHEQUER COURTS ACT.   61

Section 40 applies to appeals *per saltum*. See notes to s. 26, p. 35; and to *habeas corpus* appeals. *In re Smart*, 16 Can. S. C. R. 396.

In *Taylor* v. *The Queen*, 1 Can. S. C. R. 65, it was held that an appeal would not lie from a judgment signed, entered or pronounced before the Act constituting the Supreme Court came into force. And see the cases referred to under sub-sec. 3 of sec. 29, where it was held that the Act allowing appeals from the Court of Review in Quebec did not refer to cases pending when it was passed.

The delay prescribed by section 40 is not suspended during the vacations of the Court established by Rules 74 and 75. *News Printing Co.* v. *Macrae*, 26 Can. S. C. R. 695.

By Rule 130 of the English Bankruptcy Act, no appeal can be brought from an order of the Court after 21 days from the time such order is signed, entered or otherwise perfected. *Held*, that an order of the Bankruptcy Divisional Court is "perfected" when it is signed by the Registrar and sealed with the seal of the Court, though it may not be placed on file until some days later. *Re Helsby*, 42 W. R. 218.

Notice of appeal in cases specified.

41. No appeal upon a special case, or from the judgment upon a motion to enter a verdict of non-suit upon a point reserved at the trial, or from the judgment upon a motion for a new trial, upon the ground that the judge has not ruled according to law, shall be allowed, unless notice thereof is given in writing to the opposite party, or his attorney of record, within twenty days after the decision complained of, or within such further time as the court appealed from, or a judge thereof, allows: 38 V. c. 11, s. 21.

The cases referred to are those specified by paragraphs (*b*), (*c*) and (*a*) of section 24. "Within 20 days after the decision complained of" would exclude the day upon which the decision is rendered and include the last of the 20 days, unless the last of such days should happen to fall on a holiday. See rule 72 and notes.

There are other cases in which notice of appeal has to be given:

(*a*) Criminal appeals—Notice of appeal has to be served on Attorney-General for the proper Province within 15 days after the affirmance of conviction, or such further time as the Supreme Court or a judge thereof allows. Criminal Code, 1892, sec. 750. See Criminal Appeals.

(*b*) In Exchequer appeals, including appeals in Admiralty cases, notice of the setting down of the appeal must be given within 10 days. 50-51 V. c. 16, s. 51.

62   SUPREME AND EXCHEQUER COURTS ACT.

If the appeal is on behalf of the Crown a preliminary notice takes the place of a deposit under the Act. Section 53. See Exchequer Appeals.

(c) Election appeals—Notice of setting down an appeal for hearing must be given within three days. Dominion Controverted Elections Act, section 51, sub-section 3. See Election Appeals.

The notice is not an initiation of the appeal, and cannot be set aside before the security has been given : *Smith* v. *Smith*, 11 Ont. P. R. 6. And see as to effect of notice *Reg.* v. *McGanley*, 22 Ont. P. R. 259; *Ex parte Saffrey*, 5 Ch. D. 365.

The Supreme Court or a judge thereof has no power to extend the time for giving notice of appeal, but only " the court appealed from or a judge thereof."

The giving of the notice is a condition precedent (*Vaughan* v. *Richardson*, 17 Can. S. C. R. 703), which must be shewn to have been complied with before the appeal could be allowed, but when the notice has been given, either within the twenty days or within the extended time fixed by a judge under this section, the appellant would be obliged to bring his appeal within the sixty days from the entry or pronouncing of the judgment or to apply under section 42 for an extension.

The "special case" mentioned in section 41 has no reference to the case prepared, under Cons. Rule 413, for an appeal to the Court of Appeal for Ontario. Therefore, the latter Court overruled an objection to a bond for security for costs of an appeal to the Supreme Court on the ground that notice should have been given under said section, it being contended that every appeal from that court is on a "special case." *Draper* v. *Radenhurst*, 14 Ont. P. R. 376.

Where a new trial is asked because the trial judge should have withdrawn the case from the jury, it is a motion "upon the ground that the judge has not ruled according to law," and notice of appeal must be given. *Rowlands* v. *The Canada Southern Railway Co.*, 13 Ont. P. R. 93.

Allowance of appeal in special cases on terms.

42. Provided always, that the court proposed to be appealed from, or any judge thereof, may, under special circumstances, allow an appeal, notwithstanding that the same is not brought within the time hereinbefore prescribed in that behalf; but in such case, the court or judge shall impose such terms as to security or otherwise as seems proper under the circumstances; but the provisions of this section shall not apply to any appeal in the case of an election petition. 38 V. c. 11, s. 26.

The judgment of the Court of Appeal in plaintiff's favour was pronounced on March 5th, 1889. On March 16th defendant's solicitors wrote to their clients suggesting an appeal, but received no instructions until April 2nd. On April 3rd, an application was made under sec. 42 to extend the time for appealing. The only explanation given for the delay was the production of a telegram to the solicitors from an officer of the defendant company, giving instructions to appeal, and suggesting that the matter had been overlooked by another officer. The court held that these were not "special circumstances," under this section, and the application was refused. *Rowlands* v. *The Canada Southern Railway Co.*, 13 Ont. P. R. 93.

Approving of the security is a mode of allowing the appeal. *Fraser* v. *Abbott*, Dig. S. C. D. p. 695, No. 125; *The Queen* v. *Taylor*, 1 Can. S. C. R. 65; *Walmsley* v. *Griffith*, 13 Can. S. C. R. 434; *Vaughan* v. *Richardson*, 17 Can. S. C. R. 703; *News Printing Co.* v. *Macrae*, 26 Can. S. C. R. 695.

When a judge of the court below has made an order allowing the security he is *functus officio*, and the appeal is then subject to the jurisdiction of the Supreme Court. Orders made in the cause by the court below after the allowance of the security will be disregarded by the Supreme Court. *Lakin* v. *Nuttall*, 3 Can. S. C. R. 691; *Walmsley* v. *Griffith*, Dig. S. C. D. p. 697, No. 129; *Starrs* v. *Cosgrave Brewing and Malting Co.*, *Ibid.* p. 697, No. 130.

The power of allowing an appeal under special circumstances is given by this section 42 only to the court below or a judge thereof. Therefore if an application be made to the Supreme Court or a judge thereof under section 46, it should be made within the sixty days given by section 40. *Walmsley* v. *Griffith*, Dig. S. C. D. p. 699, No. 134.

The Court of Appeal for Ontario has held that no appeal lies to that court from a judgment of a judge of that court extending the time for appealing. *Neill* v. *Travellers' Ins. Co.*, 9 Ont. App. R. 54; *Re Central Bank of Canada*, 17 Ont. P. R. 395.

Wherever power is given to a legal authority to grant or refuse leave to appeal, the decision of that legal authority is final and conclusive. *Ex parte Stevenson*, 3 Times L. R. 486.

There would seem to be no power in either court to extend the time for bringing an appeal under "the Dominion Controverted Elections Act."

As to what are "special circumstances" within the meaning of this section see authorities cited on page 1116 of the Annual Practice, 1897, and in Wilson's Judicature Acts, 6th edition, page 446. Most of the cases will also be found in Maclennan's Judicature Act, 2nd edition, pages 696-698, notes to Order 2 of the Court of Appeal of Ontario. See also *Langdon* v. *Robertson*, 12 Ont. P. R. 139, approving of *Sievewright* v. *Leys*, 9 Ont. P. R. 200; *re Gabourie, Casey* v. *Gabourie*, 12 Ont. P. R. 252; *Platt* v. *Grand Trunk Railway Co.*, 12 Ont. P. R. 380.

No uniform rule can be deduced from the cases, but if any rule can be laid down it seems to be, that to do justice in the particular case is above all other considerations, as was said in *re*

Gabourie, supra. In *re Manchester Economic Building Society,* 24 Ch. D. 488, in which application for special leave to appeal was made after the expiration of the time fixed, Brett, M.R., says, at p. 497: "I know of no rule other than this, that the court has power to give the special leave, and exercising its judicial discretion, is bound to give the special leave, if jurisdiction requires that that leave should be given."

Proceedings requisite to bring cases into Supreme Court—When error is alleged.

43. No writ shall be required or issued for bringing any appeal in any case to or into the Supreme Court, but it shall be sufficient that the party desiring so to appeal shall, within the time herein limited in the case, have given the security required and obtained the allowance of the appeal:

2. Whenever error in law is alleged, the proceedings in the Supreme Court shall be in the form of an appeal. 38 V. c. 11, ss. 16 and 28.

See notes to preceding section.

But notice of appeal must be given in certain cases. See section 41 and notes.

The proceedings subsequent to the allowance of the security are governed by the Supreme Court Rules, when not provided for specially by the Act.

Appeal to be on a special case.

44. The appeal shall be upon a case to be stated by the parties or, in the event of difference, to be settled by the court appealed from, or a judge thereof; and the case shall set forth the judgment objected to and so much of the pleadings, evidence, affidavits and documents as is necessary to raise the question for the decision of the court. 38 V. c. 11, s. 29.

Rule 1 of the Supreme Court says the first proceeding in appeal in the Supreme Court shall be the filing of a case pursuant to this section. The case must be certified under the seal of the court appealed from. But see remarks under Rule 1.

The case cannot be filed unless it contains the formal judgment of the court appealed from. *Reid* v. *Ramsay,* Dig. S. C. D. p. 420, No. 21; *Kearney* v. *Kean, Ibid,* p. 672, No. 14; *Wallace* v. *Souther, Ibid,* p. 672, No. 15.

In one case from British Columbia it was ordered that the Registrar should be at liberty to file the case as received without the formal order, the appellant within six weeks to attach the formal order to the case and copies. *Bank of B. N. A.* v. *Walker*, Dig. S. C. D. p. 673, No. 17.

It ought also to contain the formal judgment order or decree of the court of original jurisdiction. *Wright* v. *Huron*, Dig. S. C. D. p. 673, No. 20. This Rule has been consistently followed, and the Registrar directed not to file a case that does not contain this order.

And Rule 2 provides that in addition to the proceedings mentioned in the section, the case shall invariably contain a transcript of all the opinions or reasons for their judgment delivered by the judges of the court or courts below, or an affidavit that such reasons cannot be procured, with a statement of the efforts made to procure the same.

In practice a certificate of the prothonotary has usually been accepted in lieu of the affidavit in cases from the Province of Quebec, but the court has several times called attention to the insufficiency of such certificate where it has only excused the absence of reasons for judgment in the Court of Queen's Bench, and is silent as to those in the Superior Court. It has been observed, too, that reasons have been afterwards published in the reports in a case appealed to the Supreme Court which has not been furnished with them.

By Rule 3 it is required that the case shall also contain a copy of any order which may have been made by the court below or any judge thereof enlarging the time for appealing.

Rule 4 provides for the remitting of the case to the court below, in order that it may be made more complete by the addition thereto of further matter. See notes to sections 63, 64 and 65, as to amendments.

The Registrar will not tax the costs of printing any immaterial documents which an appellant inserts in a case, or allows to be inserted without protest. The appellant should apply to a judge of the Supreme Court in Chambers for an order to dispense with unnecessary printing, but such application should not be made until the case has been settled, as provided by the above section. *Carrier* v. *Bender*, Dig. S. C. D. p. 674, No. 22.

The case should not contain matter that was not before the court of original jurisdiction. *Lionais* v. *The Molsons Bank*, 10 Can. S. C. R. 526; *Montreal Loan and Mortgage Co.* v. *Fauteaux*, Dig. S. C. R. p. 20, No. 11; *Exchange Bank of Canada* v. *Gilman*, 17 Can. S. C. R. 108.

Where, after the institution of proceedings in an appeal, judges of the court below filed documents with the prothonotary purporting to be additions to their respective opinions, such documents were improperly allowed to form part of the case on appeal, and could not be considered by the appellate court. *Per* Taschereau, J., in *Mayhew* v. *Stone*, 26 Can. S. C. R. 58.

The case should be filed within one month after the security required by the Act shall have been allowed, otherwise the respondent may move to dismiss, pursuant to section 53 of the Act. (Rule 5.)

But the Supreme Court or a judge thereof may extend the time. (Rules 42 and 70.)

The case must be accompanied by a certificate under the seal of the court below stating that the appellant has given proper security to the satisfaction of the court whose judgment is appealed from or of a judge thereof, and setting forth the nature of the security to the amount of $500, as required by the 46th section of the Act, and a copy of any bond or other instrument by which security may have been given must be annexed to the certificate. (Rule 6.) See *McDonald* v. *Abbott*, 3 Can. S. C. R. 278. And see notes to section 46 and Rule 6.

Rules 7, 8 and 9 provide for the printing of the case and regulate its style, size, number of copies to be printed and deposited, etc.

And Rule 10 provides that, together with the case, certified copies of all original documents and exhibits used in evidence in the court of first instance, are to be deposited with the Registrar, unless their production be dispensed with by order of a judge of the Supreme Court; and it provides also for the transmission of the originals by order of the Supreme Court or a judge thereof.

In practice this rule is generally complied with by printing as part of the case all the material exhibits; and where this cannot be done without great expense, for instance, where account books, plans, etc., or models or other articles, have been filed, an order to transmit the originals should be applied for.

An application to amend a case should be made to a judge in Chambers and not to the court. *Aetna Ins. Co.* v. *Brodie*, Dig. S. C. D. p. 673, No. 18. But no application should be made with respect to the contents of a case, or to dispense with printing any part of it, until it has been settled between the parties, or by a judge of the court below, pursuant to the statute. *Carrier* v. *Bender*, Dig. S. C. D. p. 674, No. 22.

These rules as to printing do not apply to election appeals, which are specially regulated by Rules 50 to 55, inclusive; nor do they apply to criminal appeals and appeals in matters of *habeas corpus*, which may be heard on a written case. (Rule 47.)

Transmission of case by clerk of the court appealed from.

45. The clerk or other proper officer of the court appealed from shall, upon payment to him of the proper fees and the expenses of transmission, transmit the case forthwith after such allowance to the Registrar of the Supreme

Court, and further proceedings shall thereupon be had according to the practice of that court. 38 V. c. 11, s. 30.

"Forthwith after such allowance" refers to the allowance of the appeal, but by Rule 5 of the Supreme Court the appellant has a month in ordinary cases in which to have his case transmitted. This time was especially granted to enable him to have his case printed and transmitted.

The word "forthwith" in statutes and Rules of Court must be construed with reference to the objects of the provision and the circumstances of the case. *Ex parte Lamb*, 19 Ch. D. 169; *Maxwell v. Scarfe*, 18 O. R. 529.

The case to be transmitted must be a printed case, and no manuscript record or original documents should be forwarded to the Registrar of the Supreme Court (except in election appeals, criminal appeals, or appeals in matters of *habeas corpus*), unless the Supreme Court or a judge thereof so orders. See notes to preceding section.

SECURITY AND STAYING EXECUTION.

Security to be given—Exceptions.

46. No appeal shall be allowed until the appellant has given proper security, to the extent of five hundred dollars, to the satisfaction of the court from whose judgment he is about to appeal, or a judge thereof, or to the satisfaction of the Supreme Court, or a judge thereof, that he will effectually prosecute his appeal and pay such costs and damages as may be awarded against him by the Supreme Court:

2. This section shall not apply to appeals [by or on behalf of the Crown] in election cases, in cases in the Exchequer Court, in criminal cases, or in proceedings for or upon a writ of *habeas corpus*. 38 V. c. 11, s. 31; 42 V. c. 39, s. 14.

This section is taken from section 31 of the Supreme and Exchequer Courts Act of 1875, as amended by section 14 of the Supreme Court Act of 1879, which reads as follows :

"31. No appeal shall be allowed (except only the case of appeal in proceedings for or upon a writ of *habeas corpus*) until the appellant has given proper security to the extent of five hundred dollars to the satisfaction of the court from whose judgment he is about to appeal, or a judge thereof, or to the satisfaction of the Supreme Court or a judge thereof, that he will effectually prosecute his appeal and pay such costs and damages as may be awarded *in case the judgment appealed from be affirmed*; Provided that this section shall not apply to appeals in election cases, for which special provision is hereinafter made."

The words in italics have been omitted in the section of the revised statute, which excepts also Exchequer and criminal appeals, as well as election and *habeas corpus* appeals. (Sub-section 2.)

For form of bond for security see Appendix.

As to security in election appeals, see section 51 of the Dominion Controverted Elections Act.

The security in Exchequer appeals is provided for by sections 51 and 53 of chapter 16 of 50-51 V.

Application for special leave to appeal under "The Winding-up Act" must be made to a judge of the Supreme Court of Canada, while the security has to be given in some of these appeals (those from the District of Keewatin) according to the practice of the court below, the words "the court" in line 9 of sub-section 4 of section 74 of that Act referring, apparently, to the court below. But in appeals provided for by section 76, the security may be given under section 46 of the Supreme and Exchequer Courts Act to the satisfaction either of the court below or a judge thereof, or of the Supreme Court or a judge thereof.

There is no power to dispense with the security required by section 46, or to admit an appeal *in forma pauperis*. *Fraser* v. *Abbott*, Dig. S. C. D. p. 695, No. 125. And in *Dominion Cartridge Co.* v. *Cairns*, Sedgewick, J., refused an application for a certified copy of the record without payment of the court fees, on the ground of the applicant's poverty.

On appeal from an order of a judge of the Supreme Court of New Brunswick in Chambers, discharging the bail to the sheriff on an arrest under a writ of capias, it was held that as the bail, the only parties really interested in the appeal, were not before the court, and not entitled to the benefit of the bond for security for costs given by the plaintiff in the action, the appeal must be quashed for want of proper security. *Scammell* v. *James*, 16 Can. S. C. R. 593.

And where an appeal was brought from the refusal of the Supreme Court of Nova Scotia to admit the appellant as an attorney, there was no person interested in opposing the application or the appeal and no security for costs was given. *Held*, that the court had no jurisdiction to entertain the appeal. *In re Cahan*, 21 Can. S. C. R. 100.

Per Ritchie, C.J., and Taschereau, J.—Except in the cases specially provided for, no appeal can be heard by this court unless the security for costs has been given as provided by section 46 of the Supreme and Exchequer Courts Act. *Ibid.*

The appellant is not a necessary party to the bond, but if made a party he should sign it. *Robertson* v. *Harris*, 14 Ont. P. R. 373, *per* Osler, J.A.

As a municipality has the ordinary right of suing and being sued, it can, as incident to such right, properly join in a bond for security under this section given in a suit in which it was a party. *London and Canadian Loan and Agency Co.* v. *Morris*, 1 West. L. T. 215, *per* Taylor, C.J.

The bond should not provide for security for anything but the costs of the appeal, as required by section 46. Thus, where the condition of the bond was that appellants should " effectually prosecute their said appeal and pay such costs and damages as may be awarded against them by the Supreme Court of Canada, and shall pay the amounts by said judgments respectively directed to be paid, either as a debt or for damages or costs or the part thereof as to which the said judgments may be affirmed if they or either of them be affirmed only as to part, and all damages awarded against the said the Bank of Hamilton on such appeal," the Registrar refused to approve of it. *Bank of Hamilton* v. *Halstead*, April, 1897.

And a bond conditioned to pay costs " in case the appeal should be dismissed," was refused in *Bazinet* v. *Gadomy*, February, 1892. No such condition is attached to the security by section 46, and a respondent is not obliged to accept it.

In *Laine* v. *Beland*, February, 1896, a bond was refused for a similar defect.

An objection to the form of a bond should be by application in Chambers to dismiss. *Union Bank* v. *Whitman*, 16 Can. S. C. R. 410.

The application to the court below or a judge thereof to have the security allowed must be made within the sixty days limited by section 40, subject to the right to make an application under section 42.

In every appeal the time within which an application may be made to the Supreme Court or a judge thereof, is limited to the sixty days, unless the time is extended by a judge of the court below. See *Walmsley* v. *Griffith*, Dig. S. C. D. p. 670, No. 6. Even when the appeal comes direct from the court of original jurisdiction under sub-section 3 of section 26.

The approval of the security is a mode of allowing the appeal, and after such approval has been given and appeal allowed, the court below ceases to have any jurisdiction over the case, except under the provisions relating to the stay of execution (sec. 47 *et seq.*); and any order thereafter made by the court below will be disregarded by the Supreme Court. *Lakin* v. *Nuttall*, 3 Can. S. C. R. 691; *Walmsley* v. *Griffith*, Dig. S. C. D. p. 697, No. 129; *Starrs* v. *Cosgrave Brewing and Malting Co.*, Ibid, p. 697, No. 130.

When the order of the provincial court granting leave to appeal made no provision as to costs in case of dismissal for want of prosecution (" effectually prosecute his appeal ") the Judicial Committee of the Privy Council held that the said court had power to correct the omission in its order. *Milson* v. *Carter*, 69 L. T. 735.

When an appeal from the Court of Queen's Bench for Lower Canada has been regularly allowed, and the case is before the Supreme Court, the Superior Court has no power to suspend by injunction, proceedings on the appeal. *McManamy v. The City of Sherbrooke*, 13 Legal News, 290.

An application in the Supreme Court to have the security allowed should be made in Chambers, and not to the full court, and should be on notice, stating the nature of the security. A copy of the bond should be served with the notice, and the original filed in the Registrar's office.

Where an application had been made to a judge in Chambers and refused, the court refused to entertain a similar application. *McNab v. Wagler*, Dig. S. C. D. p. 699, No. 133.

But it is no bar to an application to the Supreme Court or a judge thereof that a similar application has been made to the court or a judge below and refused. *Ontario and Quebec Railway Co. v. Marcheterre*. 17 Can. S. C. R. 141. This is not an infringement of the rule that where a judge has discretionary power the exercise of his discretion is final, since the allowance of the appeal is a matter of right, and not of discretion, where the requirements as to jurisdiction are fulfilled.

The court has no discretion to increase the amount of security on appeal to the Supreme Court of Canada fixed by this section at $500, although there may be a number of respondents all in different interests. *Per* Osler, J.A., *Archer v. Severn*, 12 Ont. P. R. 472.

In *Wheeler v. Black*, M. L. R. 2 Q. B. 159, it was held by Cross, J., of the Court of Queen's Bench, (P.Q.), after consultation with the other members of that court, that personal security is sufficient, and that the sureties need not justify on real estate.

As to the effect of the bond in staying execution in certain cases, see section 47.

The security required to obtain a stay of execution may be given by the same instrument whereby the security under section 46 is given. (Section 47, sub-section 2.) But this only applies when the security is approved by the court below or a judge thereof. In an application in the Supreme Court the bond cannot be so encumbered.

In an application to a judge of the Court of Appeal the object of the bond was not only to secure payment of the costs which might be awarded by the Supreme Court of Canada under section 46, but also, under section 47 (c), to procure a stay of execution of the judgment appealed from as to the costs thereby awarded against the appellant. The condition was " shall effectually prosecute the said appeal and pay such costs and damages as may be awarded against the appellant by the Supreme Court of Canada, and shall pay the amount *by the said mentioned judgment* directed to be paid either as a debt or for damages or costs," etc. *Held*, that this did not cover the costs awarded against the appellant by the judgment appealed from, as in strictness the language refers to the judgment of the Supreme Court. *Robinson* v. *Harris*, 14 Ont. P. R. 373.

By sub-section 30 of section 7 of the Interpretation Act, it is provided that, "The expression 'sureties' means sufficient sureties, and the expression 'security' means sufficient security, and whenever these words are used, one person shall be sufficient therefor, unless otherwise expressly required."

As a rule there is no *viva voce* examination of sureties on an application in the Supreme Court for approval of a bond under section 46, though it has been permitted in some cases. If the respondent has not had sufficient time to satisfy himself as to the sureties the hearing on the application will be enlarged to enable him to do so, and if necessary, both parties will be permitted to file affidavits in respect to the sufficiency of the security. *Union Fire Ins. Co.* v. *Shoolbred*, May 28th, 1889.

Where security is given by deposit of money into court certain fees are payable under the tariff, namely, one per cent. on the amount of the deposit, and $2 for the order.

The order allowing such deposit should specify clearly its purpose, and state that it was given to the satisfaction of a judge. A form of order is given in the Appendix.

Execution stayed—Exceptions—If the judgment orders delivery of documents or personalty—Or execution of conveyance—If the court appealed from is one of appeal—If the judgment directs sale, etc., of realty—If the judgment directs payment of money as a debt, etc.—As to instrument for giving such security.

47. Upon the perfecting of such security, execution shall be stayed in the original cause, except in the following cases:—

(*a*) If the judgment appealed from directs an assignment or delivery of documents or personal property, the execution of the judgment shall not be stayed, until the things directed to be assigned or delivered have been brought into court, or placed in the custody of such officer or receiver as the court appoints, nor until security has been given to the satisfaction of the court appealed from, or of a judge thereof, in such sum as the court or judge directs, that the appellant will obey the order or judgment of the Supreme Court;

(*b*) If the judgment appealed from directs the execution of a conveyance or any other instrument, the execution on the judgment shall not be stayed, until the instrument has been executed and deposited with the proper officer of the court appealed from, to abide the order or judgment of the Supreme Court;

(c) If the court appealed from is a court of appeal and such assignment or conveyance, document, instrument, property or thing, as aforesaid, has been deposited in the custody of the proper officer of the court in which the cause originated, the consent of the party desiring to appeal to the Supreme Court, that it shall so remain to abide the judgment of the Supreme Court, shall be binding on him, and shall be deemed a compliance with the foregoing requirements of this section;

(d) If the judgment appealed from directs the sale or delivery of possession of real property, chattels real or immovables, the execution of the judgment shall not be stayed until security has been entered into to the satisfaction of the court appealed from, or a judge thereof, and in such amount as the said last mentioned court or judge directs, that during the possession of the property by the appellant he will not commit, or suffer to be committed, any waste on the property,—and that if the judgment is affirmed, he will pay the value of the use and occupation of the property from the time the appeal is brought until delivery of possession thereof,—and also, if the judgment is for the sale of property and the payment of a deficiency arising from the sale, that the appellant will pay the deficiency;

(e) If the judgment appealed from directs the payment of money, either as a debt or for damages or costs, execution thereof shall not be stayed, until the appellant has given security to the satisfaction of the court appealed from, or of a judge thereof, that if the judgment or any part thereof is affirmed, the appellant will pay the amount thereby directed to be paid, or the part thereof as to which the judgment is affirmed, if it is affirmed only as to part, and all damages awarded against the appellant on such appeal;

2. Provided that in any case in which execution may be stayed on the giving of security under this section, such

security may be given by the same instrument whereby the security prescribed in the next preceding section is given. 38 V. c. 11, s. 32.

Fiat to sheriff when security is perfected—If the court appealed from is one of appeal—Proviso; as to poundage.

48. When the security has been perfected and allowed, any judge of the court appealed from may issue his fiat to the sheriff, to whom any execution on the judgment has issued, to stay the execution, and the execution shall be thereby stayed, whether a levy has been made under it or not; and if the court appealed from is a court of appeal, and execution has been already stayed in the case, such stay of execution shall continue without any new fiat, until the decision of the appeal by the Supreme Court: Provided always, that upon any judgment appealed from, on which any execution is issued before the judge's fiat to stay the execution is obtained, no poundage shall be allowed against the appellant, unless a judge of the court appealed from otherwise orders. 38 V. c. 11, s. 33.

Money levied and not paid over before fiat to be repaid.

49. If, at the time of the receipt by the sheriff of the fiat, or of a copy thereof, the money has been made or received by him but not paid over to the party who issued the execution, the party appealing may demand back from the sheriff the amount made or received under the execution, or so much thereof as is in his hands not paid over, and in default of payment by the sheriff, upon such demand, the party appealing may recover the same from him in an action for money had and received, or by means of an order or rule of the court appealed from. 38 V. c. 11, s. 35.

Perishable property.

50. If the judgment appealed from directs the delivery of perishable property, the court appealed from, or a judge thereof, may order the property to be sold and the proceeds to be paid into court, to abide the judgment of the Supreme Court. 38 V. c. 11, s. 36.

As to staying proceedings under section 47, see cases cited in Maclennan's Judicature Act, 2nd edition, pages 701-2, decided under the R. S. O. 1887, c. 38, s. 27, relating to appeals to the Court of Appeal of Ontario, which section is substantially the same as the above section, 47.

In England it is provided by Order 58, Rule 16, that "an appeal shall not operate as a stay of execution or proceedings, under the decision appealed from, except so far as the court appealed from, or any judge thereof, or the Court of Appeal may order." But a stay of execution for the payment of money or costs, under section 47, will be given to an appellant as a matter of right upon giving the security prescribed by that section.

On an appeal to the Court of Appeal for Ontario, the appellant had deposited money in court as security for costs and obtained a stay of execution. His appeal being dismissed he was allowed to deposit a further sum of $500 as security under section 46 for an appeal to the Supreme Court, and it was held that the stay of execution operated in respect of the further appeal, and a new order was not necessary. *Agricultural Ins Co. of Watertown* v. *Sargent*, 16 Ont. P. R. 297.

DISCONTINUANCE OF PROCEEDINGS.

Discontinuing proceedings.

51. An appellant may discontinue his proceedings by giving to the respondent a notice entitled in the Supreme Court and in the cause, and signed by the appellant, his attorney or solicitor, stating that he discontinues such proceedings; and thereupon the respondent shall be at once entitled to the costs of and occasioned by the proceedings in appeal; and may, in the court of original jurisdiction, either sign judgment for such costs or obtain an order from such court, or a judge thereof, for their payment, and may take all further proceedings in that court as if no appeal had been brought. 38 V. c. 11, s. 39.

The respondent should file the notice of the discontinuance in the office of the Registrar of the Supreme Court, and obtain an appointment to tax the costs of the proceedings in appeal.

CONSENT TO REVERSAL OF JUDGMENT.

Consent to reversal.

52. A respondent may consent to the reversal of the judgment appealed against, by giving to the appellant a notice entitled in the Supreme Court and in the cause, and signed by the respondent, his attorney or solicitor, stating that he consents to the reversal of the judgment; and thereupon the court, or any judge thereof, shall pronounce judgment of reversal as of course. 38 V. c. 11, s. 40.

Unless such notice provides that the appellant shall have costs, they will not be included in the judgment.

DISMISSAL FOR DELAY.

Dismissal for delay to proceed.

53. If an appellant unduly delays to prosecute his appeal, or fails to bring the appeal on to be heard at the first session of the Supreme Court, after the appeal is ripe for hearing, the respondent may, on notice to the appellant, move the Supreme Court, or a judge thereof in Chambers, for the dismissal of the appeal; and such order shall thereupon be made as the said court or judge deems just. 38 V. c. 11, s. 41.

Rule 5 of the Supreme Court provides, that if the appellant does not file his case in appeal with the Registrar, within one month after the security required by the Act shall be allowed, he shall be considered as not duly prosecuting his appeal, and the respondent may move to dismiss. The time may be extended by the Supreme Court or a judge thereof. (Rules 42 and 70.)

But any unreasonable delay will expose the appellant to a motion to dismiss. And if the motion be granted by a judge in Chambers in the reasonable and proper exercise of his discretion the court will not interfere. *Whitfield* v. *The Merchants Bank*, Dig. S. C. D. p. 681, No. 66; *Winnipeg* v. *Wright*, 13 Can. S. C. R. 441. In *Whitfield* v. *The Merchants Bank*, it was held that respondent not being ready to proceed was no excuse for delay on the part of the appellant.

And such a motion should be made in the first instance to a judge in Chambers. *Martin* v. *Roy, Ibid,* p. 682, No. 69.

In election appeals it was formerly considered that motions to dismiss for want of prosecution must be made to the court: *North York Election Case*, Dig. S. C. D. p. 682, No. 71; but in the *Halton Election Case,* 19 Can. S. C. R. 557, the court referred such a motion to a judge in Chambers, and since then the Registrar has heard them. *Chicoutimi and Saguenay Election Case,* Dig. S. C. D. p. 682, No. 72.

Rule 44 provides that unless an appeal is brought on for hearing by the appellant within one year next after the security shall have been allowed, it shall be held to have been abandoned without any order to dismiss being required, unless the Supreme Court or a judge thereof shall otherwise order.

See Rule 70 and notes for other cases relating to the granting or refusing an extension of time for the prosecution of appeals.

As section 39, Supreme and Exchequer Courts Act, provides that proceedings in appeals shall, when not otherwise provided for, be as nearly as possible in conformity with the present practice of the Judicial Committee, it may be as well to refer to the practice of the Judicial Committee bearing on the dismissal of appeals for want of prosecution. By the present practice of the Judicial Committee of the Privy Council, the Registrar or other proper officer having the custody of records in any court from which an appeal is brought, is directed to send a transcript of the record with all possible despatch to the Registrar of the Privy Council; the appellant or his agent must within six calendar months from the arrival of the transcript and the registration of it in all matters brought by appeal from colonies and plantations east of the Cape of Good Hope or from the Territories of the East India Company, and within three months in all matters brought by appeal from any other part of Her Majesty's Dominions abroad, apply for the printing of the transcript, and in default the appeal is to stand dismissed without further order. *Order of the 13th June*, 1853. (See Appendix.) This order, says Macpherson (Prac. P. C. p. 96), has practically superseded the rule requiring the petition of appeal to be filed within a year and day. "The Judicial Committee would always," he adds, "have granted leave to appeal upon a proper case being made, even after the lapse of a year and a day from the judgment." And at p. 99, he says: "Even when an appeal stands dismissed for want of prosecution, it is sometimes restored upon cause shown, proper terms being of course imposed. Indeed the Privy Council have gone a great way in excusing unintentional laches, in one case restoring a case after it had been dismissed for want of prosecution during ten years." See Macpherson, chapter 5, beginning page 94, "On Dismissal of Appeals before Hearing," for practice of the Judicial Committee generally in dealing with delays in prosecuting appeals.

Following this practice, when an order was made by the Registrar, sitting as a Judge in Chambers, directing an appeal to stand dismissed if the case was not filed within a certain delay, he afterwards vacated the order and granted a further extension, the excuse for the failure to comply with it being that the appellant's solicitor, owing to an infectious illness in his family, had been kept in quarantine, and prevented from preparing the case. *Foran* v. *Handley*, Mar. 1892.

PARTIES.

DEATH OF PARTIES.

Case of death of one of several appellants.

54. In the event of the death of one of several appellants, pending the appeal to the Supreme Court, a suggestion may be filed of his death, and the proceedings may, thereupon, be continued at the suit of and against the surviving appellant, as if he were the sole appellant; but such suggestion, if untrue, may be set aside on motion made to the Supreme Court, or a judge thereof in Chambers. 38 V. c. 11, s. 42.

Of sole appellant or of all the appellants.

55. In the event of the death of a sole appellant, or of all the appellants, the legal representative of the sole appellant, or of the last surviving appellant, may, by leave of the court or a judge, file a suggestion of the death, and that he is such legal representative, and the proceedings may thereupon be continued at the suit of and against such legal representative as the appellant; and if no such suggestion is made, the respondent may proceed to an affirmance of the judgment, according to the practice of the court, or take such other proceedings as he is entitled to; and such suggestion, if untrue, may, on motion, be set aside by the court or a judge thereof. 38 V. c. 11, s. 43.

Of one of several respondents.

56. In the event of the death of one of several respondents, a suggestion may be filed of such death, and the proceedings may be continued against the surviving respondent; but such suggestion, if untrue, may, on motion, be set aside by the court or a judge thereof. 38 V. c. 11, s. 44.

Of sole respondent or of all the respondents.

57. In the event of the death of a sole respondent, or of all the respondents, the appellant may proceed, upon giving one month's notice of the appeal and of his intention to continue the same, to the representative of the deceased party, or if no such notice can be given, then upon such notice to the parties interested as a judge of the Supreme Court directs. 38 V. c. 11, s. 45.

These provisions relate only to the contingency of the death of a party to the appeal. But Rule 36 supplements these sections by providing as follows: "In any case not already provided for by the Act, in which it becomes essential to make an additional party to the appeal, either as appellant or respondent, and whether such proceeding becomes necessary in consequence of the death or insolvency of any original party, or from any other cause, such additional party may be added to the appeal by filing a suggestion as nearly as may be in the form provided for by section 43 [now 55] of the Act."

Rules 37 and 38 provide a mode of setting aside such suggestion, and of trying any question of fact arising out of it.

In the event of the death of a party interested in an appeal between the hearing of the appeal and the delivery of judgment, the judgment of the Supreme Court will be entered *nunc pro tunc* as of the date of hearing. *Merchants' Bank* v. *Smith*, Dig. S. C. D. p. 688, No. 102; *Merchants' Bank* v. *Keefer*, Ibid, p. 688, No. 103; *Ontario and Quebec Railway Co.* v. *Philbrick*, Ibid, p. 688, No. 104.

As a general rule the appeal must be heard on the "case" as transmitted to the court.

In an appeal from Quebec, where it was sought to add a party as co-respondent on the ground that he had obtained from the respondents a notarial assignment of all their interest in the suit, made prior to the hearing of the case by the Court of Appeal of the Province, the Supreme Court held that the application to add the assignee should have been made at the earliest opportunity to the court below, and was not one the Supreme Court should be called upon to decide. *Dorion* v. *Crowley*, Dig. S. C. D. p. 694, No. 120.

But where a party has been improperly joined, as co-plaintiff or co-defendant, the Supreme Court will order him to be struck out of the record. *Caldwell* v. *Stadacona F. & L. Ins. Co.*, 11 Can. S. C. R. 212.

And where a party was, by the judgment of the court, made liable for the costs of the appeal, although he had in fact not been a party to such appeal, nor interfered in the appeal by depositing a factum, or appearing by counsel at the argument, the judgment was amended by the court. *Long* v. *Hancock* (not reported).

And where parties, other than those on the record, have an interest entitling them to prosecute an appeal in the name of the plaintiff on the record, the Supreme Court will permit them to do so, on such terms as may seem just. *Langtry* v. *Dumoulin*, 13 Can. S. C. R. 258.

Where a party was not in the case as originated, but received notice of appeal, and was represented by counsel at the hearing, he was allowed to tax his costs of the appeal. *Hogaboom* v. *Receiver-General*, December, 1897.

Where the unsuccessful party to a suit died after verdict and before judgment on a rule for a new trial, and judgment *nunc pro tunc* as of a day prior to his death was entered by order of a judge, and a suggestion of the death entered on the record, the court refused to quash an appeal by his executors. *Muirhead* v. *Shireff*, 14 Can. S. C. R. 735.

But where, in an action against a railway conductor for damages on account of personal injuries caused by negligence of the defendant, the plaintiff died between the verdict of nonsuit and the judgment of the full court granting a new trial, a suggestion of his death being entered on the record, an appeal by the defendant against his executors was quashed, it being held that an entirely new cause of action had arisen under C. S. N. B. c. 86, the equivalent in New Brunswick of Lord Campbell's Act, the original cause of action being entirely gone, and incapable of being revived. *White* v. *Parker*, 16 Can. S. C. R. 699.

Sections 54 to 57 of the Supreme and Exchequer Courts Act provide for the practice to be followed in case of the death of parties to an appeal pending in the Supreme Court. And by 52 V. c. 37, ss. 3 and 4, provision is made whereby an appeal may be taken by or against the legal representatives of a party to an action who has died before delivery of judgment in the court below. Those sections are as follows:

DEATH OF PARTY BEFORE JUDGMENT.

[*3. In the event of the death of a sole plaintiff or defendant before the judgment of the court in which an action or an appeal is pending is delivered, and if such judgment is against the deceased party, his legal representatives, on entering a suggestion of the death, shall be entitled to proceed with and prosecute an appeal in the Supreme Court of Canada, in the same manner as if they were the original parties to the suit.*]

[*4. In the event of the death of a sole plaintiff or sole defendant before the judgment of the court in which an action or an appeal is pending is delivered, and if such judgment is in favor of such deceased party, the other party, upon entering a suggestion of the death, shall be entitled to prosecute an appeal to the Supreme Court of Canada against the legal representatives of such deceased party, provided that the time limited for appealing shall not run until such legal representatives are appointed.*]

ENTRY OF CAUSES.

Entry of appeals on list and order of hearing.

58. The appeals set down for hearing shall be entered by the registrar of the court, on a list, divided into three parts, and to be numbered and headed as follows: "Number one, Maritime Provinces cases"; "Number two, Quebec cases"; "Number three, Ontario cases": and the registrar shall enter all appeals from the Provinces of Nova Scotia, New Brunswick and Prince Edward Island on part numbered one, and all appeals from the Province of Quebec on part numbered two, and all appeals from the Provinces of Ontario, Manitoba and British Columbia [and from the North-West Territories] on part numbered three, in the order in which they are respectively received; and such appeals shall be heard and disposed of in the order in which they are so entered, unless otherwise ordered by the court. 42 V. c. 39, s. 15.

[Provided that, at the October sittings of the court, the appeals entered on part numbered two shall be first heard, then those entered on part numbered three, and finally those entered on part numbered one.]

This proviso was added by 54-55 V. c. 25 s. 5, after the time for the October session was changed from the fourth to the first Tuesday in that month.

Order of Cases on Lists "One" and "Three."

[In the list "Number one, Maritime Provinces cases," and "Number three, Ontario cases," mentioned in the fifty-eighth section of "*The Supreme and Exchequer Courts Act,*" the court may, by order, direct in what order the cases from the different provinces shall be entered.]

52 V. c. 37 s. 5. The order that has been adopted pursuant to this section is to put cases from the most distant province at the head, and those from the nearest province at the foot of the respective lists. Thus, in list No. 1 the order would be 1, Prince Edward Island; 2, Nova Scotia, and 3, New Brunswick cases; and in list No. 3, British Columbia, North-West Territories, Manitoba and Ontario.

Entry of Exchequer Court Appeals,

[Every appeal from the Exchequer Court set down for hearing before the Supreme Court of Canada shall be entered by the registrar on the list for the Province in which the action, matter or proceeding, the subject of the appeal, was tried or heard by the Exchequer Court,—or if such action, matter or proceeding was partly heard or tried in one Province and partly in another, then on such list as the registrar thinks most convenient for the parties to the appeal.]

54-55 V. c. 26, s. 9. Prior to this enactment Exchequer Court appeals were entered in a separate list and were generally the last cases argued.

It has been the practice to give election appeals precedence, as required by the spirit of the provisions relating to such appeals.

And appeals in *habeas corpus* proceedings, when heard at a regular session are generally entered before the ordinary cases.

No appeal can be set down for hearing which has not been filed twenty clear days before the first day of the session. (Rule 31 as amended by Rule 80). Nor unless the appellant's factum has been deposited in the proper time. But if the respondent fails to deposit his factum in the proper time the appellant may inscribe the appeal for hearing *ex parte*. (Rule 27.) Such inscription *ex parte* may be set aside upon an application to a Judge in Chambers sufficiently supported by affidavits. (Rule 28.)

The Registrar should be requested to inscribe the appeal for hearing by præcipe filed in his office.

JUDGMENTS.

Quashing proceedings in certain cases.

59. The Supreme Court may quash proceedings in cases brought before it, in which an appeal does not lie, or whenever such proceedings are taken against good faith. 38 V. c. 11, s. 37.

When an appeal is quashed for want of jurisdiction, the court may order the taxation and payment of costs. *Beamish* v. *Kaulbach*, Dig. S. C. D. p. 677, No. 44.

A motion to quash should be made to the court, and not to a Judge in Chambers, and should be made at the earliest convenient moment.

In *The Queen* v. *Nevins*, Dig. S. C. D. p. , No. 33, although the objection was taken by the court, the appellant was allowed costs.

But when the objection to the jurisdiction is taken at the hearing by the court, as a general rule no costs will be given. *Major* v. *The Corporation of Three Rivers*, Ibid, p. 422, No. 26; *Champoux* v. *Lapierre*, Dig. S. C. D. p. 426, No. 31; *Gendron* v. *McDougall*, Ibid. p. 429, No. 36; *Bank of Toronto* v. *Le Curé, etc., of the Parish of The Nativity*, Ibid, p. 432, No. 40; *Domville* v. *Cameron*, Ibid, p. 421, No. 23. In this last case the appeal was heard *ex parte*, the respondent not appearing.

When the objection to the jurisdiction is taken by the respondent in his factum, and the motion made to the court at the earliest convenient time, the general costs of the appeal will be given, and a counsel fee as on motion to quash. *Danjou* v. *Marquis*, 3 Can. S. C. R. 251; Dig. S. C. D. p. 414, No. 11; *Reid* v. *Ramsay*, Ibid. p. 420, No. 21; *McGowan* v. *Mockler*, Ibid. p. 421, No. 22; *Le Maire, etc., de Terrebonne* v. *Les Sœurs de la Providence*, Ibid p. 434, No. 43.

On a motion to quash, a fee of $25 may be allowed, according to discretion of the Registrar, subject to be increased by order of the court or a judge. In *Danjou* v. *Marquis* (*supra*), the fee was increased to $75. In *McGowan* v. *Mockler* (*supra*), the fee was increased to $50. In *Haggart* v. *Brampton*, December, 1897, $30 was taxed.

Appeal may be dismissed or judgment given.

60. The Supreme Court may dismiss an appeal, or give the judgment, and award the process or other proceedings which the court, whose decision is appealed against, should have given or awarded. 38 V. c. 11, s. 38, *part*.

Section 53 provides for the dismissal of an appeal by the Supreme Court or a judge thereof for delay.

New trial may be ordered.

61. On any appeal the court may, in its discretion, order a new trial, if the ends of justice seem to require it, although such new trial is deemed necessary upon the ground that the verdict is against the weight of evidence. 43 V. c. 34, s. 4.

This section establishes an exception to section 27. See also section 24, paragraph (*d*), and section 30.

When the court below, in the exercise of its discretion, has ordered a new trial on the ground that the verdict is against the weight of evidence, the Supreme Court will not entertain the appeal. *Eureka Woolen Mills* v. *Moss*, 11 Can. S. C. R. 91.

COSTS.

Payment of costs.

62. The Supreme Court may, in its discretion, order the payment of the costs of the court appealed from, and also of the appeal, or any part thereof, as well when the judgment appealed from is varied or reversed as where it is affirmed. 38 V. c. 11, s. 38, *part*.

This is taken from the latter part of section 38 of the Supreme and Exchequer Courts Act of 1875, but that section read "as well when the judgment appealed from is reversed as where it is affirmed." It has been thought necessary or advisable to provide specially for the case where the judgment is varied.

Section 79 of the Supreme and Exchequer Courts Act of 1875, provided that the judges of the Supreme Court or any five of them might, from time to time, make general rules and orders, among other things, "for fixing the fees and costs to be taxed and allowed to and received and taken by * * * the officers of the said courts."

SUPREME AND EXCHEQUER COURTS ACT.   83

By section 32 of the Supreme Court Amendment Act of 1876, it was provided that the judges of the Supreme Court or any five of them might, under the 79th section of the Act of 1875, from time to time make general rules and orders for awarding and regulating costs in the Supreme and Exchequer Courts in favor of and against the Crown as well as the subject.

These provisions of section 79 of the Act of 1875, and section 32 of the Act of 1876, were consolidated in section 109 of the Revised Act.

Rule 57 provides that costs in appeal between party and party shall be taxed pursuant to the tariff of fees contained in Schedule D to the orders.

This tariff has been amended in certain particulars by Rules 81 & 82.

The court has not thought it advisable to regulate costs between solicitor and client. The Registrar does not tax such costs. *Boak* v. *Merchants Marine Ins. Co.*, Dig. S. C. D. p. 677, No. 45.

The general rule has been to allow costs to the successful party, even when an appeal has been quashed for want of jurisdiction. But not when the objection to the jurisdiction has been taken by the court itself. See notes to section 59.

Where an appeal was allowed on an objection taken for the first time on the argument of the appeal before the Supreme Court, no costs were given. *Canada Southern Ry. Co.* v. *Norvell*, Dig. S. C. D. p. 34, No. 5.

In an appeal from Quebec, where an objection that the action had been prescribed was taken by the appellant (defendant) for the first time on the argument of the appeal, the court held that it was bound to give effect to the objection, but the appeal was allowed without costs in any of the courts. *Dorion* v. *Crowley*, Dig. S. C. D. p. 709, No. 12.

The uniform practice has been not to give costs where the court has been equally divided. Dig. S. C. D. p. 676, No. 39.

In *habeas corpus* appeals and criminal appeals, as a general rule no costs are given. *In re G. R. Johnson*, Dig. S. C. D. p. 677, No. 41; and p. 329, No. 5.

But where an appeal in a *habeas corpus* matter has been proceeded with after the discharge of the prisoner and for the mere purpose of obtaining a decision on the question of costs, the appeal was dismissed with costs. *Fraser* v. *Tupper*, Dig. S. C. D. p. 421, No. 24.

Rule 58 provides that the court or a judge may direct a fixed sum for costs to be paid in lieu of directing the payment of costs to be taxed.

In interlocutory applications not provided for in the tariff (schedule D) costs have usually been fixed, in pursuance of this order.

Section 35 of the Supreme Court Amendment Act of 1876 provided, that an order in either the Supreme Court or the Exchequer Court for payment of money, whether for costs or otherwise, might be enforced by the same writs of execution as a judgment in the Exchequer Court.

This section was introduced into the Revised Statute as section 107. Now, by chapter 16 of 50 & 51 V., sch. A, the following section is substituted: "An order in the Supreme Court for payment of money, whether for costs or otherwise, may be enforced by such writs of execution as the court prescribes." General Order 85 provides for such writs.

By section 108 of the Revised Act, it is provided, that no attachment as for contempt shall issue in the Supreme Court for non-payment of money only.

Writs of execution have never been issued from the Supreme Court of Canada to enforce payment of the costs of appeal. Payment of such costs must be enforced by process from the courts below. But a writ of execution may be issued in an election appeal for the costs of the appeal. In *North Ontario Case (Wheler* v. *Gibbs*), February, 1881, a *fi. fa.* goods was issued for such costs.

But with respect to costs of the court below in an election case, see section 54 of the Dominion Controverted Elections Act, and Election Appeals, *post*, Part II.

For interlocutory costs, a writ of execution may be obtained from the Supreme Court.

As to distraction of costs, it has been held that where distraction has not been asked for by the pleadings, or by the factum, it should be asked for when judgment is rendered. If not then asked for, any subsequent application must be made to the court upon notice to the other side. *Letourneux* v. *Dansereau*, Dig. S. C. D. p. 677, No. 46. But since the new code of procedure came into force in Quebec distraction is allowed in every case, unless expressly withheld.

When no one appears on behalf of appellant when an appeal is called for hearing and counsel for respondent asks for the dismissal of the appeal, it will be dismissed with costs. Dig. S. C. D. and cases cited, p. 681, No. 65.

See further, Rule 57 and notes, for the practice relating to costs generally, and the taxation and enforcement of payment of costs.

AMENDMENTS.

Necessary amendments may be made.

63. At any time during the pendency of an appeal before the Supreme Court, the court may, upon the application of any of the parties, or without any such application, make all such amendments as are necessary for the purpose of determining the appeal, or the real question or controversy between the parties, as disclosed by the pleadings, evidence or proceedings. 43 V. c. 34, s. 1.

At whose instance.

64. Any such amendment may be made, whether the necessity for the same is or is not occasioned by the defect, error, act, default or neglect of the party applying to amend. 43 V. c. 34, s. 2.

Conditions of amendment.

65. Every amendment shall be made upon such terms as to payment of costs, postponing the hearing or otherwise, as to the court seems just. 43 V. c. 34, s. 3.

As to amending a record by adding a plea of justification under writ, in an action against sheriff for seizing logs under writ of replevin, see *Swim* v. *Sheriff*, Dig. S. C. D. p. 142, No. 14.

As to amending pleadings in action brought by a corporation against defendant for selling without license contrary to bylaws, see *Piche* v. *City of Quebec*, Dig. S. C. D. p. 497, No. 6.

Appeal refused from an interlocutory judgment of the court below refusing motion for leave to file new pleas. *Dawson* v. *Union Bank*, Dig. S. C. D. p. 428, No. 35.

Amending Case.

As to what the "case" should contain, see section 44, and notes.

Rule 4 of the Supreme Court provides that the court, or a judge thereof, may order the case to be remitted to the court below, in order that it may be made more complete by the addition thereto of further matter.

If the formal order or judgment of the court below has not been made part of it, the case cannot be received by the Registrar, and if received, the court may order the appeal to stand over till perfected. *Kearney* v. *Kean*, Dig. S. C. D. p. 672, No. 14.

In one appeal the court ordered the appeal to be placed at the foot of the list for hearing, to permit the rule of the court below to be added, counsel for respondent consenting. *Wallace* v. *Souther*, Ibid. p. 672, No. 15.

In an appeal from British Columbia, where the case contained no formal order or judgment of the court below, over-ruling demurrers, upon application of the agent for appellant's solicitors, the agent of respondent's solicitors consenting, it was ordered that the Registrar be at liberty to file the case as received, without the formal order, and that the appellants might attach within six weeks from that date the said formal order to the case and copies. *Bank of B. N. A.* v. *Walker*, Dig. S. C. D. p. 673, No. 17.

Where it appeared on the argument of the appeal that the decree of the court of first instance was not in the case, the argument was allowed to proceed on counsel undertaking to have decree added before judgment given. *Wright* v. *Huron,* Dig. S. C. D. p. 673, No. 20.

An application to amend the " case " should be made to a Judge in Chambers and not to the court. *Aetna Ins. Co.* v. *Brodie,* Dig. S. C. D. p. 673, No. 18.

Where the judge of the court below had certified that the examination of one D. was made part of the case *quantum valeat,* the Supreme Court remitted the case to the court below, to be settled in accordance with the statute and practice, holding that it should appear clearly whether the examination did or did not properly form a part of the case. *McCall* v. *Wolff,* Dig. S. C. D. p. 673, No. 19.

Where it appeared that certain papers which a judge of the court below had directed should form part of the case had been incorrectly printed, the Registrar was directed to remit the case to the court below to be corrected. *Parker* v. *Montreal City Passenger Railway Co.,* Dig. S. C. D. p. 674, No. 24.

Amending Judgment.

When it is clear that by oversight or mistake an error has occurred in its judgment, the court has power of its own motion to amend its judgment to make it conform to the intention of the court, and the principles upon which it was based. *Rattray* v. *Young,* Dig. S. C. D. p. 692, No. 110; *Penrose* v. *Knight, Ibid.* p. 689, No. 108; *Smith* v. *Goldie, Ibid.* p. 689, No. 109.

A motion to amend must not be practically a motion to reverse the judgment of the court. *Reeves* v. *Gerriken, Ibid.* p. 689, No. 106.

When the judgment is amended to conform to the intention of the court, the judgment will be made to read *nunc pro tunc.* *Smith* v. *Goldie, Ibid.* p. 689, No. 109.

When a new trial had been ordered by the Supreme Court, on the ground that an important question had not been submitted to or answered by the jury, a motion to set aside the judgment and re-open the hearing, supported by affidavits stating that as a matter of fact such question had actually been answered by the jury, was refused with costs, the court holding that it was bound by the case as transmitted, and as forming the material upon which the hearing was based. *Providence Washington Ins. Co.* v. *Gerow,* 14 Can. S. C. R. 731.

INTEREST.

Interest to be allowed.

66. If on appeal against any judgment, the Supreme Court affirms such judgment, interest shall be allowed by the court for such time as execution has been delayed by the appeal. 38 V. c. 11, s. 34.

The question of the allowance of interest, for time judgment has been stayed by the appeal, is one which the court will dispose of on its own motion. *McQueen* v. *The Phoenix Mutual Fire Ins. Co.*, Dig. S. C. D. p. 688, No. 99.

In an appeal from New Brunswick it was held that interest should be allowed on the principal sum from last day of next term after verdict. *Clark* v. *Scottish Imperial Ins. Co.*, *Ibid.* p. 688, No. 100.

By 50-51 V. c. 16, s. 33, the Exchequer Court, in adjudicating upon any claim against the Crown on a contract in writing shall not allow any interest thereon unless the same has been stipulated for by a written agreement. In *The Queen* v. *McLean*, Dig. S. C. D. p. 399, No. 6, the Supreme Court held the suppliant not entitled to interest on a claim for damages for breach of a contract in writing. In *St. Louis* v. *The Queen*, 25 Can. S. C. R. p. 665, interest was allowed against the Crown, but the question of the suppliant's right to it was not argued. It is now settled, by *The Queen* v. *Henderson*, 28 Can. S. C. R. 425, that in cases from the Province of Quebec interest will be allowed where the claim against the Crown is not founded upon a contract in writing. In that case it was for the price of goods delivered to and used by the Crown. As to the other Provinces, the question is still open.

In a case before the Exchequer Court for return of duties improperly imposed, judgment was given against the claimants. This was afterwards affirmed by the Supreme Court, but reversed by the Privy Council, and judgment ordered to be entered for the suppliant for the amount claimed and costs. On the case coming again before the Exchequer Court judgment was entered for the principal sum only, interest being refused, and an appeal was taken to the Supreme Court for the interest. In the meantime the Crown presented a petition to the Judicial Committee of the Privy Council, praying for a declaration that the claimants were not entitled to interest under their Lordships' judgment. The petition was dismissed, their Lordships stating that interest having been claimed, and the question not having been argued in any of the courts, it should be allowed. The Crown thereupon consented, under section 52 of the Act, to the judgment of the Exchequer Court being reversed on the appeal to the Supreme Court. *Toronto Railway Co.* v. *The Queen*, Oct. 1897.

CERTIFICATE OF JUDGMENT.

Judgment to be carried out by the court below:

67. The judgment of the Supreme Court in appeal shall be certified by the Registrar of the court to the proper officer of the court of original jurisdiction, who shall thereupon make all proper and necessary entries thereof; and all subsequent proceedings may be taken thereupon as if the judgment had been given or pronounced in the said last-mentioned court. 38 V. c. 11, s. 46.

68 & 69. [These sections, which related to criminal appeals were repealed by chapter 50 of 50-51 V., which substituted other provisions, and these have been re-enacted by The Criminal Code, 1892. See Criminal Appeal, *post*, Part III.]

70. [Relating to appeals from the Exchequer Court has been repealed by chapter 16 of 50-51 V., which has substituted Code, 1892. See Exchequer Appeals *post*, Part. III.]

JUDGMENT FINAL AND CONCLUSIVE.

Judgment to be final—Saving H. M. prerogative.

71. The judgment of the Supreme Court shall, in all cases, be final and conclusive, and no appeal shall be brought from any judgment or order of the Supreme Court to any court of appeal established by the Parliament of Great Britain and Ireland, by which appeals or petitions to Her Majesty in Council may be ordered to be heard: saving any right which Her Majesty may be graciously pleased to exercise by virtue of her royal prerogative. 38 V. c. 11, s. 47.

Compare this section with the provisions making the judgment of the Supreme Court final in criminal appeals, and taking away any appeal to the Privy Council in such appeals. See Part III. Criminal Appeals. Many of the cases in which application has been made to the Judicial Committee of the Privy Council for leave to appeal, with the result in each case, have been noted in the Dig. S. C. D. p. 887.

For other cases appealed to the Privy Council since the issue of the Digest, see Canadian Appeals by C. H. Masters and vols. 13 to 23 inclusive of the Supreme Court Reports.

A party wishing to appeal to the Privy Council does not apply to the Supreme Court for leave to appeal. The court has held that it has no power to entertain such an application. Dig. S. C. D. p. 695, No. 122.

The usual practice is to apply to the Registrar of the Supreme Court for a certified copy of the case, factums, judgment and reasons of the judges. The Judicial Committee has held that it will not entertain any application for leave to appeal, unless the final judgment of the Supreme Court has been drawn up and entered. *Pion v. North Shore Ry. Co.* After obtaining the certified copy of the papers, the proceedings before the Judicial Committee are by petition and affidavit. See Macpherson, Privy

Council Practice, page 22, *et seq.*, and Lattey's Privy Council Practice, page 32, *et seq.*

If leave to appeal is granted, the Registrar of the Supreme Court is directed by order of the Privy Council to send the necessary papers to the Registrar of the Privy Council.

In several appeals recently allowed the Judicial Committee has accepted the papers already certified by the Registrar as sufficient, and has dispensed with the transmission of any others, the documents transmitted by the Registrar, in obedience to the order, being the same as those furnished to the appellant and laid by him before the Judicial Committee.

If he wishes to do so, the appellant may print the record before it is transmitted to England, but he must be careful to comply with the rules of the Judicial Committee regulating the size of type, style, etc. These rules will be found on page 68, appendix to Macpherson's Privy Council Practice, 2nd ed. See also appendix to this volume. The type used for the Privy Council is pica, a size not much used in this country, most of our statutes, reports, etc., being printed in small pica, which is also the type required for cases and factums in the Supreme Court. If the record is not printed at all, or not printed in accordance with the rules of the Judicial Committee, the printing must be done in London.

In Lattey's Handibook on Privy Council Practice it is stated, page 3: "One great objection to the record being printed abroad is, that a successful appellant is unable to recover the cost of printing from the respondent, whilst if the record is printed in England such charges are always included in the solicitor's bill, and are allowed on taxation."

The order in appeal of the Privy Council is given to the solicitor of the successful party. If it reverses the judgment of the Supreme Court it should, on motion, be made an order of that court (*Lewin* v. *Wilson*, 14 Can. S. C. R. 722), be entered on the records of the court and then certified to the court below. If the judgment of the Supreme Court be affirmed it is not necessary to have the order of the Privy Council made an order of the Supreme Court. It is sufficient to make it an order of the court of original jurisdiction.

The application to make an order of the Privy Council an order of the Supreme Court may be made in Chambers.

SPECIAL JURISDICTION OF SUPREME AND EXCHEQUER COURTS.

Powers to be exercised with consent of Provincial Legislatures.

72. When the Legislature of any Province of Canada has passed an Act agreeing and providing that the Supreme

Court and the Exchequer Court, or the Supreme Court alone, as the case may be, shall have jurisdiction in any of the following cases, that is to say:—

First. Of controversies between the Dominion of Canada and such Province;

Second. Of controversies between such Province and any other Province or Provinces which have passed a like Act;

Third. Of suits, actions or proceedings in which the parties thereto, by their pleadings, have raised the question of the validity of an Act of the Parliament of Canada, when, in the opinion of a judge of the Court in which the same are pending, such question is material;

Fourth. Of suits, actions or proceedings in which the parties thereto, by their pleadings, have raised the question of the validity of an Act of the Legislature of such Province, when, in the opinion of a judge of the court in which the same are pending, such question is material ;

This section and the two sections of this Act next following shall be in force in the class or classes of cases in respect of which such Act so agreeing and providing has been passed. 38 V. c. 11, s. 54.

Proceedings in cases first and secondly mentioned—And in those thirdly and fourthly mentioned—Decision to be sent to court appealed from.

73. The proceedings in the cases firstly and secondly mentioned in the next preceding section shall be in the Exchequer Court, and an appeal shall lie in any such case to the Supreme Court; and in the cases thirdly and fourthly mentioned in such section, the judge who has decided that such question is material shall, at the request of the parties, and may, without such request, if he thinks fit, order the case to be removed to the Supreme Court for the decision of such question, and it shall be removed accordingly; and after the decision of the Supreme Court the said case shall be sent back, with a copy of the judgment on the question raised, to the court or judge whence it came, to be then and there dealt with as to justice appertains. 38 V. c. 11, ss. 55 & 56; 39 V. c. 26, s. 17.

To what cases preceding sections apply.

74. The two sections next preceding shall apply only to cases of a civil nature, and shall take effect in the cases therein provided for respectively, whatever is the value of the matter in dispute, and there shall be no further appeal to the Supreme Court on any point decided by it in any such case, nor on any other point in such case, unless the value of the matter in dispute exceeds five hundred dollars. 38 V. c. 11, s. 57.

The Legislature of Ontario passed an Act in 1877 consenting to the jurisdiction provided for by section 72 being exercised. This Act was chapter 37 of the R. S. O. 1877, and has been re-enacted as chapter 49 of the R. S. O. 1897. See Appendix III. The Legislature of Nova Scotia has passed a similar Act—Chapter III. of the Revised Statutes, 5th series and New Brunswick, 51 V. c. 9. The Legislature of British Columbia has also passed a similar Act. 44 V. c. 6.

75-90. [These sections, which applied to the Exchequer Court, have been repealed by 50-51 V. c. 16, sch. B.]

SUPREME AND EXCHEQUER COURTS.
EVIDENCE.

Affidavits.

91. All persons authorized to administer affidavits to be used in any of the superior courts of any Province, may administer oaths, affidavits and affirmations in such Province to be used in the Supreme Court or in the Exchequer Court. 38 V. c. 11, s. 74.

Commissioners for receiving affidavits may be appointed.

92. The Governor in Council may, by commission from time to time, empower such persons as he thinks necessary, within or out of Canada, to administer oaths, and to take and receive affidavits, declarations and affirmations in or concerning any proceeding had or to be had in the Supreme Court or in the Exchequer Court; and every such oath, affidavit, declaration or affirmation so taken or made shall be as valid and of the like effect, to all intents, as if it had been administered, taken, sworn, made or affirmed before that one of the said courts in which it is intended to be used, or before any judge or competent officer thereof in Canada:

Style of commissioner.

2. Every commissioner so empowered shall be styled "a commissioner for administering oaths in the Supreme Court and in the Exchequer Court of Canada." 39 V. c. 26, s. 10.

Before whom affidavits, etc., may be made out of Canada—Their effect.

93. Any oath, affidavit, affirmation or declaration administered, sworn, affirmed or made out of Canada, before any commissioner authorized to take affidavits to be used in Her Majesty's High Court of Justice in England, or before any notary public, and certified under his hand and official seal, or before the mayor or chief magistrate of any city, borough or town corporate in Great Britain or Ireland, or in any colony or possession of Her Majesty out of Canada, or in any foreign country, and certified under the common seal of such city, borough or town corporate, or before a judge of any court of supreme jurisdiction in any colony or possession of Her Majesty or dependency of the Crown out of Canada, or before any consul, vice-consul, acting consul, pro-consul or consular agent of Her Majesty exercising his functions in any foreign place, and certified under his official seal, concerning any proceeding had or to be had in the Supreme Court or Exchequer Court, shall be as valid, and of like effect, to all intents, as if it had been administered, sworn, affirmed or made before a commissioner appointed under this Act. 39 V. c. 26, s. 12.

No proof required of signature or seal of commissioner, etc.

94. Every document purporting to have affixed, imprinted or subscribed thereon or thereto, the signature of any commissioner appointed under this Act, or the signature of any person authorized to take affidavits to be used in any of the superior courts of any Province, or the signature of any such commissioner authorized to receive affidavits to be used in Her Majesty's High Court of Justice in England, or the signature and official seal of any such notary public, or the signature of any such mayor or chief magistrate, and the common seal of the corporation, or the signature of any such judge, and the seal of the court or the signature and official seal of any such consul, vice-consul, acting consul, pro-consul or consular agent, in testimony of any oath, affidavit, affirmation or declaration, having been administered, sworn, affirmed or made by or before him, shall be admitted in evidence without proof of any such signature or seal being the signature or signature and seal of the person whose signature or signature and seal the same purport to be, or of the official character of such person. 39 V. c. 26, s. 13.

Informality not to be an objection in the discretion of the judge—Not to be set up as defence in case of perjury.

95. No informality in the heading or other formal requisites of any affidavit, declaration or affirmation, made or taken before any person under any provision of this or any other Act, shall be an objection to its reception in evidence in the Supreme Court or the Exchequer Court, if the court or judge before whom it is tendered thinks proper to receive it; and if the same is actually sworn to, declared or affirmed by the person making the same before any person duly authorized thereto, and is received in evidence, no such informality shall be set up to defeat an indictment for perjury. 39 V. c. 26, s. 15.

Examination on interrogatories or by commission of persons who cannot conveniently attend.

96. If any party to any proceeding had or to be had in either the Supreme Court or the Exchequer Court, is desirous of having therein the evidence of any person, whether a party or not, or whether resident within or out of Canada, the court or any judge thereof, if in its or his opinion it is, owing to the absence, age or infirmity, or the distance of the residence of such person from the place of trial, or the expense of taking his evidence otherwise, or for any other reason convenient so to do, may, upon the application of such party, order the examination of any such person upon oath, by interrogatories or otherwise, before the Registrar of the court, or any commissioner for taking affidavits in the court, or any other person or persons to be named in such order, or may order the issue of a commission under the seal of the court for such examination; and may, by the same or any subsequent order, give all such directions touching the time, place and manner of such examination, the attendance of the witnesses and the production of papers thereat, and all matters connected therewith, as appears reasonable :

Interpretation—"Witness."

2. The person, whether a party or not, to be examined under the provisions of this Act, is hereinafter called a "Witness." 39 V. c. 26, s. 1.

Duty of persons taking such examination.

97. Every person authorized to take the examination of any witness, in pursuance of any of the provisions of this Act, shall take such examination upon the oath of the witness, or upon affirmation, in any case in which affirmation instead of oath is allowed by law. 39 V. c. 29, s. 2, *part;* 40 V. c. 22, s. 1.

Further examination may be ordered—Penalty for non-compliance.

98. The Supreme Court or Exchequer Court, or a judge thereof, may, if it is considered for the ends of justice expedient so to do, order the further examination, before either the court or a judge thereof, or other person, of any witness; and if the party on whose behalf the evidence is tendered neglects or refuses to obtain such further examination, the court or judge, in its or his discretion, may decline to act on the evidence. 39 V. c. 26, s. 3.

Notice to adverse party.

99. Such notice of the time and place of examination as is prescribed in the order, shall be given to the adverse party. 39 V. c. 26, s. 4.

Neglect or refusal to attend to be deemed contempt of court—As to production of papers, etc.

100. When any order is made for the examination of a witness, and a copy of the order, together with a notice of the time and place of attendance, signed by the person or one of the persons to take the examination, has been duly served on the witness within Canada, and he has been tendered his legal fees for attendance and travel, his refusal or neglect to attend for examination or to answer any proper question put to him on examination, or to produce any paper which he has been notified to produce, shall be deemed a contempt of court and may be punished by the same process as other contempts of court; but he shall not be compelled to produce any paper which he would not be compelled to produce, or to answer any question which he would not be bound to answer in court. 39 V. c. 26, s. 5; 40 V. c. 22, s. 2.

Effect of consent of parties.

101. If the parties in any case pending in either of the said courts consent, in writing, that a witness may be examined within or out of Canada by interrogatories or otherwise, such consent and the proceedings had thereunder shall be as valid in all respects as if an order had been made and the proceedings had thereunder. 39 V. c. 26, s. 6.

Return of examinations taken in Canada—Use thereof.

102. All examinations taken in Canada, in pursuance of any of the provisions of this Act, shall be returned to the court; and the depositions, certified under the hands of the person or one of the persons taking the same, may, without further proof, be used in evidence, saving all just exceptions. 39 V. c. 26, s. 7.

And of those taken out of Canada—Use thereof.

103. All examinations taken out of Canada, in pursuance of any of the provisions of this Act, shall be proved by affidavit of the due taking of such examinations, sworn before some commissioner or other person authorized under this or any other Act to take such affidavit, at the place where such examination has been taken, and shall be returned to the court; and the depositions so returned, together with such affidavit, and the order or commission, closed under the hand and seal of the person or one of the persons authorized to take the examination, may, without further proof, be used in evidence, saving all just exceptions. 39 V. c. 26, s. 8.

Reading examination.

104. When any examination has been returned, any party may give notice of such return, and no objection to the examination being read, shall have effect, unless taken within the time and in the manner prescribed by general order. 39 V. c. 26, s. 9.

GENERAL PROVISIONS.

Process and officers of the court.

105. The process of the Supreme Court shall run throughout Canada, and shall be tested in the name of the Chief Justice, or in case of a vacancy in the office of chief justice, in the name of the senior puisné judge of the court, and shall be directed to the sheriff of any county or other judicial division into which any Province is divided; and the sheriffs of the said respective counties or divisions shall be deemed and taken to be *ex officio* officers of the Supreme Court, and shall perform the duties and functions of sheriffs in connection with the said courts; and in any case where the sheriff is disqualified, such process shall be directed to any of the coroners of the county or district. 38 V. c. 11, ss. 66 and 75.

See section 107 and notes.

The section as it formerly stood referred also to the process of the Exchequer Court and made the sheriffs officers of that court. Now, with regard to the Exchequer Court, see sections 42 & 43 of chapter 16 of 50-51 V.

Further powers of commissioners.

106. Every Commissioner for administering oaths in the Supreme Court and in the Exchequer Court of Canada, who resides within Canada, may take and receive acknowledgments or recognizances of bail, and all other recognizances in the Supreme Court. 39 V. c. 26, s. 11.

This section formerly applied to the Exchequer Court as well as the Supreme Court.

Enforcement of orders for payment of money.

["**107.** An order in the Supreme Court for payment of money, whether for costs or otherwise, may be enforced by such writs of execution as the court prescribes."] 39 V. c. 26, s. 35.

Section substituted by 50-51 V. c. 16, sch. A, for the original section, which provided that an order in either the Supreme or Exchequer Court for the payment of money might be enforced by the same writs of execution as a judgment in the Exchequer Court.

General Order No. 85 prescribes the writs to be used. See section 105.

Rule 59 provided, that "The payment of costs, if so ordered, may be enforced by process of execution in the same manner and by means of the same writs and according to the same practice as might be in use from time to time in the Exchequer Court of Canada." See *post* Part IV. By General Order 85 Rules 59 and 60 have been repealed, the writs to be issued out of the Supreme Court prescribed and the practice relating thereto regulated.

Rules 166, *et seq.*, of the Exchequer Court provide for the issuing of writs in that court. See Audette's Manual, p. 281.

No attachment for non-payment only.

["**108**. No attachment as for contempt shall issue in the Supreme Court for the non-payment of money only."]

Substituted by 50-51 V. c. 16, sch. A, for the original section which applied also to the Exchequer Court. See General Order 85, *post*.

Judges may make rules of procedure and as to costs.

["**109**. The judges of the Supreme Court, or any five of them, may, from time to time, make general rules and orders for regulating the procedure of and in the Supreme Court, and the bringing of cases before it from courts appealed from or otherwise [for empowering the Registrar to do any such thing, and to transact any such business, and to exercise any such authority and jurisdiction in respect of the same as by virtue of any statute or custom or by the practice of the court is now or may be hereafter done, transacted or exercised by a judge of the court sitting in Chambers, and as may be specified in such rule or order], and for the effectual execution and working of this Act, and the attainment of the intention and objects thereof,—and for fixing the fees and costs to be taxed and allowed to, and received and taken by, and the rights and duties of the officers of the court,— and for awarding and regulating costs in such court in favour of and against the Crown, as well as the subject; and such rules [and orders] may extend to any matter of procedure or otherwise not provided for by this Act, but for which it is found necessary to provide, in order to insure the proper working of this Act and the better attainment of the objects thereof; and all such rules which are not inconsistent with the express provisions of this Act, shall have force and effect as if herein enacted; and copies of all such rules shall be laid before both Houses of Parliament at the session next after the making thereof."] 38 V. c. 11, s. 79; 39 V. c. 26, ss. 32 and 37.

Substituted section: see 50-51 V. c. 16, sch. A.

The portion of this section relating to the giving to the Registrar the jurisdiction of a Judge in Chambers is new. Rule 83, passed in pursuance of this section, confers upon the Registrar all the authority and jurisdiction of a Judge in Chambers, except in relation to matters of *habeas corpus* and *certiorari*.

By the Interpretation Act, section 7, sub-section 45, it is provided, that:

"Whenever power to make by-laws, regulations, rules or orders is conferred, it shall include the power, from time to time, to alter or revoke the same and make others."

How costs to and against the Crown shall be paid.

["**110.** Any moneys or costs awarded to the Crown shall be paid to the Minister of Finance and Receiver-General, and he shall pay out of any unappropriated moneys forming part of the Consolidated Revenue Fund of Canada, any moneys or costs awarded to any person against the Crown."]

Substituted section: see 50-51 V. c. 16, sch. A.

Fees to be paid by stamps.

111. All fees payable to the Registrar under the provisions of this Act shall be paid by means of stamps, which shall be issued for that purpose by the Minister of Inland Revenue, who shall regulate the sale thereof; and the proceeds of the sale of such stamps shall be paid into the Consolidated Revenue Fund of Canada. 38 V. c. 11, s. 72.

Publication of reports of decisions.

["**112.** The reports of the decisions of the Supreme Court may, if the Governor in Council so determines, be published by the Registrar of the Supreme Court."]

Substituted section: see 50-51 V. c. 16, sch. A.

PART III.

APPEALS UNDER SPECIAL ACTS.

PART III.

APPEALS UNDER SPECIAL ACTS.

I.—Criminal Appeals.

II.—Exchequer Appeals.

III.—Election Appeals.

IV.—Appeals under Winding-Up Act.

I. CRIMINAL APPEALS.

Appeals to the Supreme Court of Canada in criminal matters were originally provided for by sections 49 & 50 of the Supreme and Exchequer Courts Act of 1875.

By section 31 of the Supreme Court Amendment Act of 1876, all jurisdiction in *habeas corpus* matters, arising out of any claim for extradition made under any treaty, was taken away.

Secs. 49 & 50 of the Act of 1875 were consolidated in sections 68 & 69 R. S. C. c. 135.

These sections of chapter 135 were repealed by chapter 50 of 50 & 51 V., which in its turn was repealed by The Criminal Code, 1892. These appeals are now governed by sections 742, 750 and 751 of the Code, which are as follows:

742. An appeal from the verdict or judgment of any court or judge having jurisdiction in criminal cases, or of a magistrate proceeding under section seven hundred and eighty-five, on the trial of any person for an indictable offence, shall lie upon the application of such person if convicted, to the Court of Appeal in the cases hereinafter provided for, and in no others.

2. Whenever the judges of the Court of Appeal are unanimous in deciding an appeal brought before the said court, their decision shall be final. If any of the judges dissent from the opinion of the majority, an appeal shall lie from such decision to the Supreme Court of Canada as hereinafter provided.

750. Any person convicted of any indictable offence, whose conviction has been affirmed on an appeal taken under section seven hundred and forty-two, may appeal to the Supreme Court of Canada against the affirmance of such conviction; and the Supreme Court of Canada shall make such rule or order thereon, either in affirmance of the conviction or for granting a new trial, or otherwise, or for granting or refusing such application, as the justice of the case requires, and shall make all other necessary rules and orders for carrying such rule or order into effect; Provided, that no such appeal can be taken if the Court of Appeal is unanimous in affirming the conviction, nor unless notice of appeal in writing has been served on the Attorney-General within fifteen days after such affirmance or such further time as may be allowed by the Supreme Court of Canada, or a judge thereof.

2. Unless such appeal is brought on for hearing by the appellant at the session of the Supreme Court during which such affirmance takes place or the session next thereafter, if the said court is not then in session, the appeal shall be held to have been abandoned, unless otherwise ordered by the Supreme Court or a judge thereof.

3. The judgment of the Supreme Court shall, in all cases, be final and conclusive. 50 & 51 V. c. 50, s. 1.

751. Notwithstanding any royal prerogative, or any thing contained in the Interpretation Act or in the Supreme and Exchequer Courts Act, no appeal shall be brought in any criminal case from any judgment or order of any court in Canada to any court of appeal or authority by which, in the United Kingdom, appeals or petitions to Her Majesty in Council may be heard. 51 V. c. 43, s. 1.

Sub-sections (*b*) and (*e*) of section 3 (explanation of terms) are as follows :

(*b*) The expression "Attorney-General" means the Attorney-General or Solicitor-General of any province in Canada in which any proceedings are taken under this Act, and, with respect to the North-west Territories and the District of Keewatin, the Attorney-General of Canada: R. S. C. c. 150, s. 2 (*a*).

(*e*) The expression "Court of Appeal" includes the following courts : R. S. C. c. 174, s. 2 (*h*) ;

(i.) In the Province of Ontario, any division of the High Court of Justice;

(ii.) In the Province of Quebec, the Court of Queen's Bench, appeal side;

(iii.) In the Provinces of Nova Scotia, New Brunswick and British Columbia, and in the North-west Territories, the Supreme Court in banc;

(iv.) In the Province of Prince Edward Island, the Supreme Court of Judicature;

(v.) In the Province of Manitoba, the Court of Queen's Bench.

For the sake of convenience it has been thought better to deal with these appeals separately, but it must be borne in mind that all the general provisions of the Supreme and Exchequer Courts Act apply to such appeals, unless the special Act relating to any particular class of appeals otherwise provides, or the provisions of such special Act are inconsistent with such an application. See section 25, Supreme and Exchequer Courts Act.

No appeal is allowed " if the court affirming the conviction is unanimous, nor unless notice of appeal in writing has been served on the Attorney-General for the proper Province within fifteen days after such affirmance, or such further time as may be allowed." (Section 750.) Therefore, there is no appeal from a judgment ordering a new trial. *Viau* v. *The Queen*, Oct., 1898.

And the appeal must be brought on for hearing at the session of the Supreme Court, during which such affirmance takes place, or the session next thereafter if the said court is not then in session, unless otherwise ordered. (Section 750, sub-sec. 2.)

In *Amer* v. *The Queen*, 2 Can. S. C. R. 592, it was held that the affirmance of a conviction by two judges of the Court of Queen's Bench for Ontario, the third judge of said court being absent, was the affirmance by a unanimous court within the meaning of the Act.

Where a motion for a reserved case made on two grounds was refused, and the Court of Queen's Bench for Lower Canada was unanimous in sustaining the refusal as to one of such grounds but not as to the other, it was held that an appeal to the Supreme Court could only be based on the one as to which there was a dissent. *McIntosh* v. *The Queen*, 23 Can. S. C. R. 180.

Contempt of Court is a criminal proceeding and unless it comes within section 68 of The Supreme Court Act (sec. 750 of the Code) an appeal does not lie to the Supreme Court from a judgment in proceedings therefor. *Ellis* v. *The Queen*, 22 Can. S. C. R. 7.

By sec. 750, sub-section 3 and section 751, the judgment of the Supreme Court is final, and no appeal can be had to the Privy Council, notwithstanding the royal prerogative.

These appeals are therefore in this respect on a different footing from other appeals, in which Her Majesty's prerogative may still be exercised.

Section 71 of the Supreme and Exchequer Courts Act provides as follows: "The judgment of the Supreme Court shall in all cases be final and conclusive and no appeal shall be brought from any judgment or order of the Supreme Court to any court of Appeal established by the Parliament of Great Britain and Ireland by which appeals or petitions to Her Majesty in Council may be ordered to be heard; saving any right which Her Majesty may be graciously pleased to exercise by virtue of her royal prerogative."

Appeals from the appellate tribunals of the various provinces of Canada to Her Majesty's Privy Council are regulated by statutes giving an appeal direct from such tribunals, and the Supreme and Exchequer Courts Act has not interfered with any such right.

By section 91 of British North America Act the exclusive legislative authority of the Parliament of Canada is declared to extend to all matters coming within the classes of subjects therein enumerated and, among others, "No. 27, the criminal law, except the constitution of courts of criminal jurisdiction, but including the procedure in criminal cases."

By section 101 of the British North America Act it is provided, that "The Parliament of Canada may, notwithstanding anything in this Act, from time to time provide for the constitution, maintenance and organization of a general Court of Appeal for Canada and for the establishment of any additional courts for the better administration of the laws of Canada."

As the right of appeal now stands in Canada the Supreme Court of Canada, as we have seen, is not a final court, section 71 of the Supreme and Exchequer Courts Act expressly saying, "saving any right which Her Majesty may be graciously pleased to exercise by virtue of her royal prerogative," and it having been the continued practice of the Judicial Committee to entertain appeals from the Supreme Court where it has considered that any error of law has been made, and substantial interests have been involved.

See notes to section 71 of the Supreme and Exchequer Courts Act.

The Supreme Court can be considered a general Court of Appeal for the Dominion in only a limited sense, while in addition to this power of appealing from the Supreme Court itself to the Privy Council, there exists in every province the right of appeal to the same tribunal from the appellate court of such province.

It cannot at the present day be contended that the general Court of Appeal for Canada is limited to dealing with questions arising solely under the laws of Canada. The Parliament of Canada by its legislation has decided otherwise, and the Supreme Court of Canada, by an exercise of jurisdiction, extending now over twelve years, an exercise of jurisdiction recognized by the Judicial Committee of the Privy Council, has also decided otherwise.

It is submitted that it was intended by the Constitutional Act that the jurisdiction of the Supreme Court should be general and exclusive, and its judgments final, both as regards Civil and Criminal appeals.

The procedure in Criminal appeals in the Supreme Court is regulated by rules 46, 47, 48 & 49.

No printed case, or factum, is required, and no fees have to be paid to the Registrar, Dig. S. C. D. p. 684, No. 185. And no security has to be given. See section 46, sub-section 2, Supreme and Exchequer Courts Act.

II. EXCHEQUER APPEALS.

These appeals are now regulated by sections 51, 52 & 53, chapter 16 of 50-51 V., which are as follows, as amended by 53 V. c. 35, and 54-55 V. c. 26 :—

APPEALS FROM THE EXCHEQUER COURT.

Proceedings in appeals — Deposit — Notice — What notice may contain.

[**51.** Any party to any action, suit, cause, matter or other judicial proceeding, in which the actual amount in controversy exceeds five hundred dollars, who is dissatisfied with any final judgment given therein by the Exchequer Court, in virtue of any jurisdiction now or hereafter, in any manner, vested in such court, and who is desirous of appealing against such judgment, may, within thirty days from the day on which such judgment has been given, or within such further time as the judge of such court allows, deposit with the Registrar of the Supreme Court the sum of fifty dollars by way of security for costs; and thereupon the Registrar shall set the appeal down for hearing before the Supreme Court on the first day of the next session; and the party appealing shall thereupon, within ten days after the deposit, give to the parties affected by the appeal, or their respective attorneys or solicitors, by whom such parties were represented before the judge of the Exchequer Court, notice in writing that the case has been so set down to be heard in appeal as aforesaid; and in such notice the said party so appealing may, if he so desires, limit the subject of the appeal to any special defined question or questions; and the said appeal shall thereupon be heard and determined by the Supreme Court.]

Substituted for the original section by 53 V. c. 35.

The repealed section gave an appeal to " any party to a suit in the Exchequer Court " which has been enlarged to comprise an " action, suit, cause, matter or other judicial proceeding," which are the expressions used in R. S. C. c. 135, in relation to appeals in general.

A substantial change from the original section is that the appeal is now from "any final judgment" of the Exchequer Court, whereas it was formerly from "the decision" in a suit which, it has been considered, did not confine these appeals to final judgments. *Per* Strong, J., in *Danjou* v. *Marquis*, 3 Can. S. C. R. 257.

No appeal when amount does not exceed $500—Exceptions—Validity of Acts—Sums payable to H. M. and title to lands.

52. No appeal shall lie from any judgment of the Exchequer Court in any action, suit, cause, matter or other judicial proceeding, wherein the actual amount in controversy does not exceed the sum or value of five hundred dollars, unless such action, suit, cause, matter or other judicial proceeding,—

(*a*) Involves the question of the validity of an Act of the Parliament of Canada, or of the Legislature of any of the Provinces of Canada, or of any Ordinance or Act of any of the councils or legislative bodies of any of the territories or districts of Canada; or—

[(*b*) Relates to any fee of office, duty, rent, revenue or any sum of money payable to Her Majesty, or to any title to lands, tenements or annual rents, or to any question affecting any patent of invention, copyright, trade mark or industrial design, or to any matter or thing where rights in future might be bound.]

Leave to appeal in such cases.

2. Provided that an appeal shall not lie in any cases in this section mentioned unless the same is allowed by a judge of the Supreme Court of Canada.

Sub-section (*b*) was substituted for that in the Exchequer Court Act by 54-55 V. c. 26. It extends the excepted cases to those relating to patents of invention, etc., and makes the "rights in future" independent of the classes of subjects mentioned to which they have been held to relate in section 29 of the Supreme Court Act.

It is to be observed that while section 51 provides, as to appeals where the amount in controversy is over $500, that the appeal must be brought within a certain time after judgment, by a deposit as security for costs, and notice must be given of its having been set down for hearing, section 52 makes no such provision as to appeals where the amount is less than $500, nor are the said provisions extended to the latter class of appeals.

No deposit by the Crown.

53. If the appeal is by or on behalf of the Crown no deposit shall be necessary but the person acting for the Crown shall file with the Registrar a notice stating that the Crown is dissatisfied with such decision, and intends to appeal against the same, and thereupon the like proceedings shall be had as if such notice were a deposit by way of security for costs.

The words in section 51, " in which the actual amount in controversy exceeds five hundred dollars," were not in the original section providing for appeals to the Supreme Court, but appeals to the Exchequer Court from the official arbitrators were limited to cases in which the claim exceeded in value five hundred dollars, according to the *bona fide* belief of the party or parties complaining of the award as shown on affidavit. R. S. C. c. 40, repealed by 50-51 V. c. 16, sch. B.

And by section 51 of 50-51 V. c. 16, the time within which notice of setting down may be given was extended from three days to ten, as in the present section.

In other respects this section is identical with section 68 of 38 V. c. 11.

The amount of deposit required by way of security for costs has hitherto proved entirely inadequate. Most of the appeals have involved large interests. The framers of the original section may have intended to check frivolous appeals on interlocutory applications, rather than to provide for security in the event of an appeal from the final judgment.

Section 52 extends the jurisdiction in certain cases, although the actual amount in controversy may be under $500, provided the appeal be allowed by a judge of the Supreme Court. (Subsection 2.)

No deposit is required if the appeal is by or on behalf of the Crown. A notice stating that the Crown is dissatisfied with " a decision," takes the place of a deposit. (Section 53.)

The rules of the Supreme Court relating to proceedings in ordinary appeals regulate the proceedings also in Exchequer appeals. See Rule 45.

As to extending the time for appealing, see section 42, and notes p. 64, and Audette's Manual, p. 115-6.

With respect to section 52, see section 29, and notes, *ante*, relating to appeals from the Province of Quebec, for the construction of the various limitations of the right of appeal.

Where the Registrar has set down an appeal, and for any reason the parties fail to bring it on for hearing, the Registrar should not set it down a second time without an order. *Per* Fournier, J., in *McQueen* v. *The Queen*.

54-55 VICTORIA, CHAPTER 29.

An Act to provide for the exercise of Admiralty Jurisdiction within Canada, in accordance with "The Colonial Courts Admiralty Act, 1890."

[*Assented to 31st July, 1891.*

Whereas by the third section of the Act of the Parliament of the United Kingdom, passed in the session held in the fifty-third and fifty-fourth years of Her Majesty's reign, chapter twenty-seven, intituled "An Act to amend the Law respecting the exercise of Admiralty Jurisdiction in Her Majesty's Dominions and elsewhere out of the United Kingdom," it is amongst other things provided that the Legislature of a British possession may, by any colonial law, declare any court of unlimited civil jurisdiction, whether original or appellate, in that possession, to be a Colonial Court of Admiralty, and provide for the exercise by such court of its jurisdiction under the said Act; and whereas the authority given is exercisable by the Parliament of Canada by virtue of the powers vested in it by "The British North America Act, 1867," and "The Interpretation Act, 1889," of the United Kingdom; and whereas the expression "unlimited civil jurisdiction," as defined by the Act first herein referred to, which may be cited as "The Colonial Courts of Admiralty Act, 1890," means civil jurisdiction unlimited as to the value of the subject-matter at issue, or as to the amount that may be claimed or recovered; and whereas by the second section of the said "Colonial Courts of Admiralty Act, 1890," it is amongst other things enacted that every court of law in a British possession, which is, for the time being, declared in pursuance of the said Act to be a Court of Admiralty, or which, if no such declaration is in force in the possession, has therein original unlimited civil jurisdiction shall be a Court of Admiralty with the jurisdiction in the said Act mentioned; and whereas the Exchequer Court of Canada is a court of law which, within Canada, has original unlimited civil jurisdiction as defined by the said Act, and it is desirable, in pursuance of the said Act, to declare the said court to be a Court of Admiralty: Therefore, Her Majesty, by and with the advice and consent of the Senate and House of Commons of Canada, enacts as follows:—

1. This Act may be cited as "The Admiralty Act, 1891."

2. In this Act the expression "the Exchequer Court," or "the court," means the Exchequer Court of Canada.

3. In pursuance of the powers given by "The Colonial Courts of Admiralty Act, 1890," aforesaid, or otherwise in any manner vested in the Parliament of Canada, it is enacted and declared that the Exchequer Court of Canada is and shall be, within Canada, a Colonial Court of Admiralty, and as a Court of Admiralty shall, within Canada, have and exercise all the jurisdiction, powers and authority conferred by the said Act and by this Act.

* * * *

5. The Governor in Council may, from time to time, constitute any part of Canada an Admiralty district for the purposes of this Act, and fix the limits thereof, and provide for the establishment at some place therein of a registry of the Exchequer Court on its Admiralty side.

2. The Governor in Council may also, from time to time, change the limits of any Admiralty district, creating new districts, and assign to any district a name and place of registry.

6. The Governor in Council may, from time to time, appoint any judge of a superior or county court, or any barrister of not less than seven years' standing, to be a local judge in Admiralty of the Exchequer Court in and for any Admiralty district; and every such local judge of admiralty shall hold office during good behaviour, but shall be removable by the Governor-General on address of the Senate and House of Commons; and such judge shall be designated a local judge in Admiralty of the Exchequer Court.

* * * *

14. An appeal may be made to the Exchequer Court from any final judgment, decree or order of any local judge in Admiralty, and, with the permission of such local judge or of the judge of the Exchequer Court, from any interlocutory decree or order therein, on security for costs being first given, and subject to such other provisions as are prescribed by general rules or orders;

2. An appeal may, however, be made direct to the Supreme Court of Canada from any final judgment, decree or order of a local judge, subject to the provisions of "The Exchequer Court Act" regarding appeals.

*   *   *   *

23. On the coming into force of this Act, the Maritime Court of Ontario shall be abolished, but subject to the following provisions:—

(1) All judgments of such court shall be executed and may be appealed from in like manner as if this Act had not been passed, and all appeals from such court pending at the commencement of this Act shall be heard and determined and the judgment thereon executed as nearly as may be in like manner as if this Act had not been passed;

(2) All proceedings pending in such court at the commencement of this Act shall be continued in the district registry corresponding to that in which they were instituted or are now pending;

(3) The procedure and practice (including fees and costs) now in force in such court shall, until otherwise provided by general rule or order, be followed, as nearly as may be, in any proceeding now pending in such court, or hereafter instituted in the registry of any Admiralty district in the Province of Ontario;

(4) The provisions of the fifth and sixth sub-sections of the fourteenth section of "The Maritime Court Act" shall apply to any proceeding instituted in the registry of any Admiralty district in the Province of Ontario.

III. ELECTION APPEALS.

The Supreme and Exchequer Courts Act, section 25, paragraph (*d*) gives jurisdiction in appeals from the court or a judge, as provided in "The Dominion Elections Act," but this is clearly an error, for "The Dominion Controverted Elections Act."

The sections of "The Dominion Controverted Elections Act," relating to appeals, are as follows:—

Appeal to Supreme Court—From judgment on preliminary objection—Proviso—From judgment on question of law or fact.

50. An appeal shall lie to the Supreme Court of Canada under this Act by any party to an election petition who is dissatisfied with the decision of the court or a judge:—

(*a*) From the judgment, rule, order, or decision, of any court or judge on any preliminary objection to an election petition, the allowance of which objection has been final and conclusive and has put an end to such petition, or which objection, if it had been allowed, would have been final and conclusive and have put an end to such petition: Provided always that, unless the court or judge appealed from otherwise orders, an appeal in the last-mentioned case shall not operate as a stay of proceedings, nor shall it delay the trial of the petition;

(*b*) From the judgment or decision on any question of law or of fact of the judge who has tried such petition. 38 V. c. 11, s. 48, *part*; 42 V. c. 39, s. 10.

In the *Bellechasse Election Case*, 5 Can. S. C. R. 91, it was held by the Supreme Court, that an Appellate Court in election cases ought not to reverse, on mere matters of fact, the finding of the judge who has tried the petition, unless the court is convinced beyond doubt that his conclusions are erroneous.

In the *Berthier Election Case*, 9 Can. S. C. R. 102, the Supreme Court being of opinion that on the facts the judgment of the court below on certain charges was not clearly wrong, refused to reverse the judgment.

And in the *Montcalm Election Case*, 9 Can. S. C. R. 93, it was again held that the Supreme Court on appeal will not reverse on mere matters of fact, unless the evidence is of such a nature as to convey an irresistible conviction that the judgment is erroneous.

A judgment of the Supreme Court of New Brunswick, setting aside an order of a judge rescinding a previous order made, authorizing the withdrawal of the deposit money and removal of the petition off the files, is not a judgment on a preliminary objection within the meaning of the Act. *Gloucester Election Case*, 8 Can. S. C. R. 205.

Nor a judgment of the Supreme Court of Nova Scotia making absolute a rule to set aside an order extending the time for service of a petition, *Kings County (N. S.) Case*, 8 Can. S. C. R. 192.

Nor will an appeal lie from a judgment on a motion made to the court to dismiss an election petition because the trial has not been commenced within six months from the time when such petition has been presented, as required by section 32 of the Dominion Controverted Elections Act. *L'Assomption Case*, 14 Can. S. C. R. 429.

But when, at the trial, an objection was made on this ground to the jurisdiction which the trial judge overruled, it was held that an appeal lay from his decision. *The Glengarry Case*, 14 Can. S. C. R. 453.

An objection to the sufficiency of the notice of trial under section 31 of the Dominion Controverted Elections Act is not an objection which can be relied on in an appeal under section 50. *The Pontiac Case*, 20 Can. S. C. R. 626.

The ruling of the Election Court on an objection that the trial judges could not proceed with the petition, because it and another petition filed against the appellant had not been bracketed together by the prothonotary as directed by section 30 of the Act, is not an appealable judgment or decision under section 50. *The Vaudreuil Case*, 22 Can. S. C. R. 1.

There is no appeal from the decision of a judge in Chambers on a motion to have preliminary objections to an election petition struck out for not being filed in time which is not a decision on preliminary objections within section 50, and if it were no judgment on such motion could put an end to the petition. *The West Assiniboia Case*, 27 Can. S. C. R. 215.

The appeal given by section 50 can only be taken in respect to preliminary objections filed under section 12 of the Act. *The Marquette Case*, 27 Can. S. C. R. 219.

Deposit in case of appeal.

51. The party so desiring to appeal shall, within eight days from the day on which the court or judge has given such decision, deposit with the clerk of the court which gave such decision, or of which the judge who gave such decision is a member, or with the proper officer for receiving moneys paid into such court, at the place where the hearing of the preliminary objections, or where the trial of the petition took place, as the case may be, if in the Province of Quebec, and at the chief office of the said court, if in any other Province, the sum of one hundred dollars as security for costs, and also a further sum of ten dollars as a fee for making up and transmitting the record to the Supreme Court of Canada.

Transmission of record to Supreme Court.

2. Upon such deposit being so made the said clerk or other proper officer shall make up and transmit the record of the case to the Registrar of the Supreme Court of Canada, who shall set down the said appeal for hearing by the Supreme Court of Canada at the nearest convenient time and according to any rules of the Supreme Court of Canada in that behalf made under "The Supreme and Exchequer Courts Act":

In the case of other appeals the time for appealing may be extended under special circumstances. (Section 42 Supreme and Exchequer Courts Act.) But the provisions of this section (42) "shall not apply in the case of an election petition."

The rules specially regulating appeals in election cases are 50-55, both inclusive, as amended by General Order, No. 86, which refer to the printing of the record and the deposit and printing of the factums. Rule 12 provides for the convening of a special session of the court for the hearing of election appeals, among others. The usual sessions of the court are regulated by section 20, Supreme and Exchequer Courts Act.

Rules 56 and 57, providing for the payment of fees to the Registrar and taxation of costs, are also applicable. The Registrar will not enter the appeal for hearing without the preliminary fee of $10 being paid.

There are certain other rules which by the practice of the court have been followed as closely as possible with regard to election appeals; special mention may be made of Rule 16, providing for the entry of the name of an agent in the agents' book, and of the rules respecting interlocutory applications, Rules 39-43.

APPLICATIONS.

Preliminary proceedings in appeal—Appeal to be heard and determined by Supreme Court.

3. The party so appealing shall, within three days after the said appeal has been so set down as aforesaid or within

such further time as the court or judge by whom such decision appealed from was given or by whom the petition was tried allows, give to the other parties to the said petition affected by such appeal, or the respective attorneys, solicitors or agents by whom such parties were represented on the hearing of such preliminary objections or at the trial of the petition, as the case may be, notice in writing of such appeal having been so set down for hearing as aforesaid, and may in such notice, if he so desires, limit the subject of the said appeal to any special and defined question or questions; and the appeal shall thereupon be heard and determined by the Supreme Court of Canada, which shall pronounce such judgment upon questions of law or of fact, or both, as in the opinion of such court ought to have been given by the court or judge whose decision is appealed from; and the Supreme Court of Canada may make such order as to the money deposited as aforesaid, and as to the costs of the appeal as it thinks just; and in case it appears to the court that any evidence duly tendered at the trial was improperly rejected, the court may cause the witness to be examined before the court or a judge thereof, or upon commission:

In the *North Ontario Election Case*, 3 Can. S. C. R. 374, it was held, that the provision as to notice is imperative and the giving of such notice a condition precedent to the exercise of any jurisdiction by the Supreme Court to hear the appeal. But the judge who tried the petition may extend the time for giving the notice after the expiration of the three days, the power of the judge being a general and exclusive power to be exercised according to sound discretion.

In the *Bellechasse Election Case*, 5 Can. S. C. R. 91, in which the judge who tried the petition, subject to an objection to his jurisdiction, dismissed the petition on the ground that he had no jurisdiction, on appeal the Supreme Court reversed his decision and ordered the record to be transmitted to the proper officer of the lower court to have the cause proceeded with according to law and disposed of on the merits; and when the judgment on the merits was appealed from, the Supreme Court held that it had jurisdiction to entertain the appeal.

In addition to the costs of the appeal, provided for by this section, the Supreme Court has full power by section 54 of the Dominion Controverted Elections Act to deal with the costs of the court below. (See *infra*.)

Report to the Speaker—Decision to be final.

4. The Registrar shall certify to the Speaker of the House of Commons the judgment and decision of the court upon the several questions as well of fact as of law, upon which the court or judge appealed from might otherwise have determined and certified his decision in pursuance of this Act, in the same manner as the said court or judge should otherwise have done, and with the same effect; and the judgment and decision of the Supreme Court of Canada shall be final. 38 V. c. 11, s. 25, *part, and* s. 48, *part.*

Before an appeal from the judgment on trial of an election petition could be heard Parliament was dissolved which put an end to the proceedings on the petition. The respondent, in order to obtain payment of his costs out of the money deposited in court for security, moved before a Judge in Chambers to have the appeal dismissed for want of prosecution or the record remitted to the court below. The learned judge refused the motion, and being of opinion that the money deposited for security should be disposed of by the Election Court, he directed the Registrar to certify to that court that the appeal was not heard and that the petition dropped by reason of the dissolution of Parliament. *Halton Election Case,* 19 Can. S. C. R. 557.

With respect to the finality of the decision of the Supreme Court, it has been decided by the Judicial Committee that no appeal in a controverted election case will be entertained by the Privy Council. *Glengarry Case, Kennedy* v. *Purcell,* 59 L. T. 279.

The judgment of their Lordships of the Judicial Committee, after stating the facts of the case, proceeds as follows:

" It appears that the decision of the Supreme Court did not turn on the merits of the case, but entirely on questions of procedure, which were three in number. First, whether the time during which Parliament was sitting should be computed as part of the six months allowed for the commencement of the trial. Secondly, whether after the expiry of the six months the court had power to extend the time for trial. Thirdly, whether the appellant, not objecting to the enlargement when the order was made, was entitled to object afterwards. On all or some of these questions two out of the five judges who heard the appeal were in favour of the petitioner, but the other three judges decided in favour of Mr. Purcell on all of them.

"It is now urged by the petitioner that inasmuch as the questions decided are important questions of law affecting the construction of the election statutes, and there is good ground for doubts as to the soundness of the decisions, Her Majesty in Council should entertain an appeal. On the other side the importance of the questions is not denied, nor is it denied that the decisions on them are fairly open to argument. But it is contended, first, that the subject matter is not one with respect to which the prerogative of the Crown exists; and secondly, that if the prerogative does exist, it is not proper to exercise it.

"To support the first proposition, the case of *Theberge* v. *Landry*, 2 App. Cas. 102, is relied on. That case arose under the Quebec Elections Act of 1875, by which the jurisdiction to try election petitions was given to the Superior Court, whose decisions were declared "not susceptible of appeal." The petitioner sought to appeal on the merits of the election. The decision of the committee was, not that the prerogative of the Crown was taken away by the general prohibition of appeal, but that the whole scheme of handing over to courts of law disputes which the Legislative Assembly had previously decided for itself, showed no intention of creating tribunals with the ordinary incident of an appeal to the Crown.

"In the case of *Valin* v. *Langlois*, 5 App. Cas. 115, the petitioner asked for leave to appeal from a decision of the Supreme Court of Canada under the Controverted Elections Act of 1874, which is one of the statutes consolidated by the Act now in question. The ground of appeal was that the Act, being a Dominion Act, was *ultra vires* of the Dominion, in assuming to give the courts in Quebec jurisdiction over elections in Quebec to the Canadian House of Commons. This committee held that there was no ground for any such contention, and dismissed the petition. But it was said that if they had doubted the soundness of the decision below they would have advised Her Majesty to grant leave to appeal. That opinion is now relied on as limiting or contravening the effect of the decision in *Theberge* v. *Landry*.

"Their Lordships do not think that for the present purpose any useful or substantial distinction can be taken between the statute which was the subject of decision in *Theberge* v. *Landry*, that which was the subject of decision in *Valin* v. *Langlois*, and those which are now in question. In all three cases there is the broad consideration of the inconvenience of the Crown interfering in election matters, and the unlikelihood that the Colonial Legislature should have intended any such result. In all three there is the creation of a special tribunal for the trial of petitions, in the sense that the litigation is not left to follow the course of an ordinary lawsuit, but is subjected to a special procedure and limitations of its own. And in all three there is the same expression of the intention to make the Colonial decision final. But such variance as there is between the two cited cases is only to this extent, that the committee in the latter case must have thought that the question of the existence of the prerogative was still susceptible of argument, when the dispute went to the very root of the validity of a law passed by Parliament to take effect in a province. Their opinion on an *ex parte* hearing, and on the sole question whether or no there should be any further argument on the matter at all, cannot be put higher than that.

"Their Lordships do not find it necessary to give any decision on the abstract question of the existence of the prerogative in this case, because they are satisfied that if it exists it ought not to be exerted in the case before them.

"It is true that the questions are very debatable, and that they affect the administration of the whole law on this subject. But the range of cases affected by them must be very narrow. It is not suggested that in the present Parliament there is a single case except the one under appeal. There can be no other case till fresh elections take place; and if the decisions now given have really misinterpreted the mind of the Legislature, and are calculated to establish rules of procedure less convenient than those intended, the Legislature can at once set the matter right. This peculiarity of the subject matter largely diminishes the force of the consideration, usually a strong one, that the decision complained of affects general questions of law.

"The next observation is that the statutes show throughout a desire to have these matters decided quickly. There are the most obvious reasons for such a desire. The legal duration of a Parliament, is, as their Lordships understand, five years, and its usual duration four years. It is most important that no long time should elapse before the constitution of the body is known. And yet if the Crown were to entertain appeals in such cases, the necessary delays attending such appeals would greatly extend the time of uncertainty which the Legislature has striven to limit.

"Again, the intention to confine the decision locally within the colony itself is just as clear as the intention to get it passed speedily, because it is expressed that the decision of the Supreme Court shall be final. And it seems to their Lordships that there are strong reasons why such matters should be decided within the colony, and why the prerogative of the Crown should not, even if it legally can, be extended to matters over which it had no power, and with which it had no concern, until the Legislative bodies chose to hand over to judicial functionaries that which was formerly settled by themselves. Before advising such an extension of the prerogative, their Lordships would require to find indications of an intention that the new proceedings should so follow the course of ordinary law as to attract the prerogative. But the indications they do find are of the contrary tendency.

"The result is that their Lordships cannot advise Her Majesty to grant the leave asked, and that the petition must be dismissed with costs."

The following are the sections of the Dominion Controverted Elections Act relating to the certificate of the judge of the court below:

JUDGE'S REPORT.

"43. At the conclusion of the trial the judge shall determine whether the member whose election or return is complained of, or any and what other person, was duly returned or elected, or whether the election was void, and other matters arising out of the petition, and requiring his determination,—and shall, except only in the case of appeal hereinafter mentioned, within four days after the expiration of eight days from the day on which he shall so have given his decision, certify in writing such determination to the Speaker, appending thereto a copy of the notes of the evidence; and the determination thus certified shall be final to all intents and purposes. 37 V. c. 10, s. 29; 38 V. c. 10, s. 3."

"44. When any charge is made in an election petition of any corrupt practice having been committed at the election to which the petition relates, the judge shall, in addition to such certificate, and at the same time, report in writing to the Speaker, as follows :—

(*a*) Whether any corrupt practice has or has not been proved to have been committed by or with the knowledge and consent of any candidate at such election, stating the name of such candidate, and the nature of such corrupt practice;

(*b*) The names of any persons who have been proved at the trial to have been guilty of any corrupt practice;

(*c*) Whether corrupt practices have, or whether there is reason to believe that corrupt practices have, extensively prevailed at the election to which the petition relates;

(*d*) Whether he is of opinion that the inquiry into the circumstances of the election has been rendered incomplete by the action of any of the parties to the petition, and that further inquiry as to whether corrupt practices have extensively prevailed is desirable. 37 V. c. 10, s. 30; 39 V. c. 10, s. 1."

"45. The judge may, at the same time, make a special report to the Speaker as to any matters arising in the course of the trial, an account of which ought, in his judgment, to be submitted to the House of Commons. 37 V. c. 10, s. 31."

Supreme Court may adjudge that costs be paid fully or in part by either party—Recovery of such costs.

54. In appeals under this Act to the Supreme Court of Canada, the said court may adjudge the whole or any part of the costs in the court below to be paid by either of the parties; and any order directing the payment of such costs shall be certified by the Registrar of the Supreme Court of Canada to the court in which the petition was filed, and the same proceedings for the recovery of such costs may thereupon be taken in the last-mentioned court as if the order for payment of costs had been made by that court or by the judge before whom the petition was tried. 39 V. c. 26, s. 16.

The usual practice has been to certify the judgment of the Supreme Court to the court below, and to leave to the latter court the enforcement of the payment of the costs. But the court may issue writs to enforce payment of the costs of an election appeal. This was done in the North Ontario Election case (*Wheeler* v. *Gibbs*), but the execution was stayed by Taschereau, J., to permit an application to the court for an amendment of the judgment, to enable the respondent to set-off against the costs of appeal, costs allowed respondent in court below. The amendment was made, and execution stayed by the court, February, 1881. The payment of interlocutory costs will be enforced by writs of execution issued by the Supreme Court. This was done in the North Ontario Election case on the 23rd January, 1880.

A motion to dismiss an election appeal either by an appellant who wishes to discontinue, or by a respondent, should be made to the court. *Soulanges Election case*; *North York Election case*, Dig. S. C. D. p. 682, No. 70, and No. 71. See *ante* p. 77.

IV. APPEALS UNDER "THE WINDING-UP ACT."

See section 25, paragraph (c), Supreme and Exchequer Courts Act. The Winding-Up Act is c. 129, R. S. C., and the provisions relating to appeals are the following:

Appeals.

74. Any person dissatisfied with an order or decision of the court or a single judge in any proceeding under this Act may, by leave of a judge of the court, appeal therefrom, if the question to be raised on the appeal involves future rights, or if the order or decision is likely to affect other cases of a similar nature in the winding-up proceedings, or if the amount involved in the appeal exceeds five hundred dollars:

2. Such appeal shall lie—
In Ontario, to the Court of Appeal for Ontario;
In Quebec, to the Court of Queen's Bench;
In any of the other Provinces, and in the North-West Territories, to the full court:

In Keewatin.

3. In the District of Keewatin any person dissatisfied with an order or decision of the court or a single judge, in any proceeding under this Act, may, by leave of a judge of the Supreme Court of Canada, appeal therefrom to the Supreme Court of Canada:

Practice—Security on appeal and time for, limited.

4. All appeals shall be regulated, as far as possible, according to the practice in other cases of the court appealed to; but no such appeal shall be entertained unless the appellant has, within fourteen days from the rendering of the order or decision, or within such further time as the court appealed from allows, taken proceedings therein to perfect his appeal, nor unless, within the said time, he has made a deposit or given sufficient security, according to the practice

of the court, that he will duly prosecute the said appeal, and pay such damages and costs as may be awarded to the respondent. 45 V. c. 23, s. 78, *part, and* s. 79; 49 V. c. 25, s. 16.

If not proceeded with, appeal may be dismissed.

75. If the party appellant does not proceed with his appeal, according to the law or the rules of practice, as the case may be, the court appealed to, on the application of the respondent, may dismiss the appeal, with or without costs. 45 V. c. 23, s. 80.

Further appeal to Supreme Court.

76. An appeal shall lie to the Supreme Court of Canada, by leave of a judge of the said Supreme Court, from the judgment of the Court of Appeal for Ontario, the Court of Queen's Bench in Quebec, or the full court in any of the other Provinces or in the North-West Territories, as the case may be, if the amount involved in the appeal exceeds two thousand dollars. 45 V. c. 23, s. 78, *part.*

Besides the appellate jurisdiction, the Supreme Court may act under the section following:

Various provincial courts to be auxiliary to one another.

84. The courts of the various Provinces, and the judges of the said courts respectively, shall be auxiliary to one another for the purposes of this Act; and the winding up of the business of the company, or any matter or proceeding relating thereto may be transferred from one court to another with the concurrence, or by the order or orders, of the two courts, or by an order of the Supreme Court of Canada. 45 V. c. 23, s. 86.

In the Act 45 V. c. 23, from which the foregoing sections 74, 75 & 76 are chiefly taken, the arrangements of the sections was different. The provisions relating to security, time for appealing and dismissal of appeals (now found in sub-section 4, of section 74 and in section 75) were inserted after the section providing for an appeal to the Supreme Court of Canada. By the present arrangement the provisions of the Supreme and Exchequer Courts Act, relating to procedure in appeals generally are applicable to these appeals. But for all such appeals the leave of the Supreme Court or a judge thereof, must be obtained, and in appeals under sub-section 3 of section 74, security must be given according to the practice of the court below, while in other appeals the security may be given in either court. (See section 46 Supreme and Exchequer Courts Act.) And a motion to dismiss for not proceeding with an appeal, may be made either to the court or a judge in Chambers. (See section 53, Supreme and Exchequer Courts Act).

An appeal shall lie * * * "If the amount involved in the appeal exceeds $2,000." Nothing is said about an appeal where future rights are involved, or the decision is likely to affect other cases of a similar nature in the winding-up proceedings. Under 45 V. c. 23, an appeal would seem to have been allowed in all these cases to the Supreme Court of Canada.

Attention might be called to the different wording used in what may be called the subject-matter limitation imposed in various classes of appeals to the Supreme Court, in section 24, paragraph (*h*), Supreme and Exchequer Courts Act; section 29, Supreme and Exchequer Courts Act; sections 51 & 52 of chapter 16 of 50-51 V., and in the above section 76.

In June, 1898, the Acting Registrar in Chambers held that an appeal to the Supreme Court of Canada under the Winding-up Act does not lie from an interlocutory judgment: *McCaskill* v. *Common*. Nor from the judgment of the Court of Queen's Bench for Lower Canada quashing an appeal to that Court for want of jurisdiction. *Ibid*, affirmed by King, J., Oct., 1898, who held that the proposed appeal had no merits, and leave should also be refused on that ground.

PART IV.

SUPREME COURT RULES.

PART IV.

SUPREME COURT RULES.

TABLE OF RULES.

Rule 1. Filing case.
    2. Case to contain reasons for judgment.
    3. Case to contain copy of any order enlarging time.
    4. Case may be remitted to court below.
    5. Motion to dismiss for delay.
    6. Certificate of security given.
    7. Case to be printed and twenty-five copies to be deposited with Registrar.
    8. Form of case.
    9. Case not to be filed unless rules complied with.
    10. Certified copies of original documents and exhibits to be deposited with Registrar.
    11. Notice of hearing of appeal.
    12. Special notice convening court, form of.
    13. Form of notice of hearing.
    14. When to be served.
    15. How notice of hearing to be served.
    16. "The Agent's Book."
    17. Suggestion by respondent who appears in person.
    18. If no suggestion filed.
    19. Suggestion by respondent who elects to appear by attorney.
    20. Election of domicil by respondent who appears in person.
    21. Service when respondent appears in person without electing domicil.
    22. Changing attorney or solicitor.

RULE 23. Factums to be deposited with Registrar.
24. What to contain.
25. How to be printed.
26. Motion by respondent to dismiss appeal on ground of delay in filing factum.
27. Appellant may inscribe *ex parte* if factum not filed.
28. Setting aside inscription *ex parte*.
29. Registrar to seal up factums first deposited.
30. Interchange of factums.
31. Registrar to inscribe appeals for hearing.
32. Counsel at hearing.
33. Postponement of hearing.
34. Default by parties in attending hearing.
35. How orders to be signed and dated.
36. Adding parties by suggestion.
37. Suggestion may be set aside.
38. Determining questions of fact arising on motion.
39. Motions.
40. Notice of motion, how served.
41. Affidavits in support of motion.
42. Giving further time.
43. Setting down motions.
44. Appeal abandoned by delay.
45. Rules applicable to exchequer appeals.
46. Rules not applicable to criminal appeals, nor *habeas corpus*.
47. Case in criminal appeals and *habeas corpus*.
48. When case to be filed.
49. Notice of hearing in criminal appeals and in appeals in matters of *habeas corpus*.
50. Preceding rules not applicable in election cases.
51. Printing record in election appeals. (Repealed.)
52. Copies of record. (Repealed.)
53. Factum in election appeals.
54. When to be deposited.
55. Order dispensing with printing of record or factum in election appeals.
56. Fees to be paid Registrar.
57. Costs.

SUPREME COURT RULES. 129

RULE 58. Court or judge may order payment of fixed sum for costs.
59. How payment of costs may be enforced. (Repealed.)
60. Contempts, how punished. (Repealed.)
61. Cross appeals.
62. Notice to be given.
63. Factum in cross appeals.
64. Translation of factum.
65. Translation of judgments and opinions of the judges of court below.
66. Payment of money into court.
67. Payment of money out of court.
68. How made.
69. Formal objections.
70. Extending or abridging time.
71. Registrar to keep necessary books.
72. Computation of time.
73. Adjournment if no quorum.
74. Christmas vacation.
75. Long vacation.
76. Interpretation.
77. Interpretation.
78. Rule amending Rule 52. (Repealed.)
79. Provision for Acting Registrar in absence of Registrar. (Lapsed.)
80. Amending rules 11, 14, 15, 23, 31, 62 and 63.
81. Amending schedule D (Tariff of Fees).
82. Provision for allowance to agents.
83. Jurisdiction of Registrar in Chambers.
84. Substituting new schedule of fees payable to Registrar.
85. Writs, and practice regulating.
86. Repealing rules 51 and 52 and substituting other provisions in election appeals.
87. Provision for Acting Registrar in absence or illness of Registrar. (Lapsed.)

In pursuance of the provisions contained in the 79th section of the 38th Victoria, chapter 11, intituled " An Act to establish a Supreme Court and a Court of Exchequer for the Dominion of Canada," it is ordered that the following rules in respect of the matters hereafter mentioned shall be in force in the Supreme Court of Canada:—

By the Revised Statutes of Canada, 38th Victoria, chapter 11, has been repealed. But by the Interpretation Act, section 7, subsection 50, it is provided that:

"Whenever any Act is repealed, wholly or in part, and other provisions are substituted, all by-laws, orders, regulations, rules and ordinances made under the repealed Act shall continue good and valid in so far as they are not inconsistent with the substituted Act, enactment or provision, until they are annulled or others made in their stead."

RULE 1.

Filing case.

The first proceeding in appeal in this court shall be the filing in the office of the Registrar of a case pursuant to section 29 of the Act, [s. 44, c. 135, R. S. C.] certified under the seal of the court appealed from.

This rule must be read subject to any provisions giving power to the Supreme Court or a judge thereof to approve of the security, or allow an appeal, or to dismiss an appeal for want of prosecution, or to extend the time for printing and filing case.

For form of certificate, see Appendix, Forms.

RULE 2.

Case to contain reasons for judgment.

The case in addition to the proceedings mentioned in the said section 29, [s. 44 of c. 135, R. S. C.] shall invariably contain a transcript of all the opinions or reasons for their judgment delivered by the judges of the court or courts below, or an affidavit that such reasons cannot be procured, with a statement of the efforts made to procure the same.

When the opinions of the judges of the courts below have been already issued in the regular reports, the Court of Appeal for Ontario has dispensed with the re-printing of such opinions in the appeal book, which merely contains a reference to the report and page at which such opinions may be found. See Rule 18 of that court. Cases have sometimes been sent to the Supreme Court thus prepared, but this practice is irregular under Rule 2. When it is thought desirable to dispense with printing of the opinions in the case the more regular practice would be to apply in Supreme Court Chambers for an order. The affidavit referred to in this rule should be filed and a copy of it printed in the case. In cases from the Province of Quebec the clerk of appeals frequently certifies that he has applied to the judges for their reasons and has not been furnished with them. Such certificate has always been accepted in lieu of the affidavit mentioned in this rule.

Attention has been called by the court to the fact that Quebec cases frequently contain a certificate as to the opinions in the Court of Queen's Bench, and as to those in the Superior Court the rule is not complied with.

RULE 3.

Case to contain copy of any order enlarging time.

The case shall also contain a copy of any order which may have been made by the court below or any judge thereof enlarging the time for appealing.

See section 42 of the Act. Orders extending the time for *filing the case* should be obtained from the Supreme Court or judge thereof.

RULE 4.

Case may be remitted to court below.

The court, or a judge thereof, may order the case to be remitted to the court below, in order that it may be made more complete by the addition thereto of further matter.

Under the statute, section 44, Supreme and Exchequer Courts Act, the case is to be stated by the parties, or in the event of difference to be settled by the court appealed from or a judge thereof. A party feeling aggrieved by the omission of what he may consider necessary or proper material may apply to a Judge of the Supreme Court in Chambers, on notice, to have the case remitted for correction. The application should not be made in the first instance to the court; *Aetna Ins. Co.* v. *Brodie*, Dig. S. C. D. p. 673, No. 18. Where material has been unnecessarily added, no application to remit is required. The unnecessary matter will be disregarded by the court, and, as a general rule, will not be allowed on taxation when its insertion has been objected to at the proper time.

The judge of the court below when settling the case should not abstain from exercising his judgment as to whether certain material should or should not form part of the case. Where a judge of the court below certified that the examination of one D. was made part of the case *quantum valeat*, the case was remitted to the court below to have it made clear whether the examination did or did not form part of the case; *McCall* v. *Wolff*, Dig. S. C. D. p. 673, No. 19.

The printed case certified to the Registrar of the Supreme Court will be remitted to the court below for correction, if not a correct print of the case settled by the judge. In *Parker* v. *Montreal City Passenger Railway Company*, Dig. S. C. D. p. 674, No. 24, where it appeared that certain papers which a judge of the court below had directed should form part of the case had been incorrectly printed, especially the factum of the respondent in said court, which had been translated, and in which interpolations had been made, the Registrar, on application of the respondent, was directed to remit the case to the court below to be corrected.

RULE 5.

Motion to dismiss for delay.

If the appellant does not file his case in appeal with the Registrar within one month after the security required by the Act shall be allowed, he shall be considered as not duly prosecuting his appeal, and the respondent may move to dismiss the appeal pursuant to section 41 of the Act, [s. 53, c. 135, R. S. C.]

Section 53 of the Revised Act, chapter 135, which provides for the dismissal of an appeal for delay, is as follows:

" If an appellant unduly delays to prosecute his appeal, or fails to bring the appeal on to be heard at the first session of the Supreme Court, after the appeal is ripe for hearing, the respondent may, on notice to the appellant, move the Supreme Court, or a judge thereof in Chambers, for the dismissal of the appeal; and such order shall thereupon be made as the said court or judge deems just." 38 V. c. 11, s. 41.

See notes to this section at pp. 75, *et seq.*

The immediate consequence of failing to file the case with the Registrar of the Supreme Court within the month after security has been allowed, is that the appellant lays himself open to a motion to dismiss for want of prosecution. If, therefore, the appellant sees that it will be impossible to print his case within the time given by the rule, and has been unable to obtain or unwilling to ask the consent of the respondent to any extension of time, he must apply before the expiry of the month, if possible, to the Registrar of the Supreme Court in Chambers, for further delay. The application should be on the usual four clear days' notice and be supported by affidavit, setting forth the reasons for making it. See Rules 39, 40, 41 & 42.

Rules 42 and 70 give full power to the court or a judge to enlarge or abridge the time for doing any act, the former rule expressly providing, among other things, for giving further reasonable time for filing the printed case.

A motion to dismiss for want of prosecution should not be made to the court, but in Chambers. *Martin* v. *Roy*, Dig. S. C. D.

p. 682, No. 69; *The steam propeller St. Magnus*—before the full court, 1887.

And the court has refused to interfere with the discretion exercised by a Judge in Chambers. See *Whitfield* v. *The Merchants Bank*, Dig. S. C. D. p. 681, No. 66; *Winnipeg* v. *Wright*, 13 Can. S. C. R. 441.

It was formerly held that in an election appeal, the motion should be made to the court. *North York Election Case*, Dig. S. C. D. p. 682, No. 71; *Charlevoix Election Case*, Ibid. p. 695, No. 124. But since *The Halton Case*, 19 Can. S. C. R. 557, such motions have been made in Chambers. See notes to sec. 53, p. 75, *ante.*

It is not a sufficient excuse for not inscribing an appeal for hearing that the respondent has not filed his factum. *Whitfield* v. *The Merchants Bank*, Dig. S. C. D. p. 681, No. 66.

It is the duty of the appellant's solicitor to prosecute his appeal with all reasonable despatch, and to inscribe it for hearing *ex parte* if the respondent be in default in depositing his factum; and any carelessness or neglect in acquainting himself and complying with the requirements of the rules, may lay him open to the serious penalty of the dismissal of the appeal, or at least to the payment of a considerable amount of costs, that great "instrument of correction in the hands of the court." See *Cote* v. *Stadacona Ass. Co.*, Dig. S. C. D. p. 682, No. 68.

Under exceptional circumstances an order directing an appeal to stand dismissed if the case is not filed at a certain date may be vacated and further time to file it allowed. See notes to sec. 53.

Rule 44, provides that unless an appeal is brought on for hearing by the appellant within one year next after the security shall have been allowed, it shall be held to have been abandoned without any order to dismiss being required, unless the Supreme Court or a judge thereof shall otherwise order.

RULE 6.

Certificate of security given.

The case shall be accompanied by a certificate under the seal of the court below, stating that the appellant has given proper security to the satisfaction of the court whose judgment is appealed from, or of a judge thereof, and setting forth the nature of the security to the amount of five hundred dollars, as required by the thirty-first section of the said Act, and a copy of any bond or other instrument by which security may have been given shall be annexed to the certificate.

In practice a copy of the bond by which security may have been given, is generally printed in the case, but this is unnecessary. A copy certified under the seal of the court below may be forwarded with the case.

The section of the Act relating to the giving of security is number 46. See notes to said section *ante* p. 67.

RULE 7.

Case to be printed and twenty-five copies deposited with Registrar.

The case shall be printed by the party appellant, and twenty-five printed copies thereof shall be deposited with the Registrar for the use of the judges and officers of the court.

The case as settled between the parties, or by the judge of the court below, is to be printed, but there have been many appeals in which a portion of the printing has been dispensed with, such as pamphlets or other printed documents, books of account, statements, etc.; sometimes evidence which has been printed for use in the court below, although not in the form required by the rules of the Supreme Court, and only a few copies can be procured. The judges have invariably relaxed the requirements as to printing, when doing so would save large expense, and not cause any serious inconvenience.

But no application should be made to dispense with any part of the printing until the case has been settled; *Carrier* v. *Bender*, Dig. S. C. D. p. 674, No. 22; and such an application should be made to a judge of the Supreme Court and not to a judge of the court below.

In some cases an order has been made by a Judge of the Supreme Court allowing less than twenty-five copies of the case to be deposited, but this will only be done when the circumstances are exceptional.

No provision has been made for the delivery of a printed copy of the case to the respondent, as in the case of factums. In practice this can give very little inconvenience, for the respondent will have in his possession, or can easily procure, a copy of all the material embodied in the case.

In Ontario the Court of Appeal by General Order 68, provides that in addition to the number of copies required for the use of that court, thirty copies are to be deposited with the Registrar for the purpose of being delivered, in the event of an appeal to the Supreme Court of Canada, to the party appealing to that court, for use upon such appeal. This does not apply to appeals from the County Courts of Ontario, for in such cases no appeal lies to the Supreme Court.

. As to what the case should contain, see section 44 of the Act, *ante* p. 64, and also Rule 2 and notes therein.

RULE 8.
Form of case.

The case shall be in demy quarto form. It shall be printed on paper of good quality, and on one side of the paper only, and the type shall be small pica leaded, and the size of the case shall be eleven inches by eight and one-half inches, and every tenth line shall be numbered in the margin. An index to the pleadings, depositions, and other principal matters shall be added.

Directions as to form of case will be found inside the front cover of each number of the Supreme Court Reports.

RULE 9.
Case not to be filed unless rules complied with.

The Registrar shall not file the case without the leave of the court or a judge, if the foregoing order has not been complied with, nor if it shall appear that the press has not been properly corrected, and no costs shall be taxed for any case not prepared in accordance with this order.

The case is to be printed so as to procure a certain degree of uniformity, and all that is required is a substantial compliance with Rule 8, *May* v. *McArthur*, Dig. S. C. D. p. 674, No. 23.

The numbering may be from the top of each page.

For the purpose of making notes it is more convenient to have the book with the printed pages to the left.

By the tariff, Schedule D, the Registrar is authorized to tax reasonable charges for disbursements necessarily incurred in proceedings in appeal; and by Rule 81, amending the tariff, he may tax "for engrossing for printer copy of case as settled, when such engrossed copy is necessarily and properly required, per folio of 100 words, 10 cents; for correcting and superintending printing per 100 words, 5 cents."

It is the duty of the appellant to avoid unnecessary expense, and the costs of any printed material not properly required, or of printing done in an unnecessarily expensive style, will be disallowed on taxation.

The printing should average from forty to forty-seven lines to the page, and not be uselessly leaded or paragraphed. The price paid should be a reasonable price, and the affidavit of disbursements, in addition to stating that the printing charges have been paid, should state that such charges are usual and reasonable in the locality in which the work has been done.

The index should be sufficient to enable any document to be easily found. It is objectionable to refer to an exhibit under its letter merely, without identifying it more fully. As a rule it is more convenient to have the index at the beginning of the case.

RULE 10.

Certified copies of original documents and exhibits to be deposited with Registrar.

Together with the case, certified copies of all original documents and exhibits used in evidence in the court of first instance, are to be deposited with the Registrar, unless their production shall be dispensed with by order of a judge of this court; but the court or a judge may order that all or any of the originals shall be transmitted by the officer having the custody thereof to the Registrar of this court, in which case the appellant shall pay the postage for such transmission.

Exhibits which have a bearing upon the question at issue in the appeal should form part of the case, and be printed. When this has been done, there is no necessity to send certified copies. Sometimes it is sufficient to print extracts from the exhibits. Whenever it is desirable that the original exhibits should be inspected by the judges of the Supreme Court, an order for the transmission of such exhibits should be obtained from a judge or the Registrar of that court in Chambers.

RULE 11.

[As amended by Rule 80.]

Notice of hearing of appeal.

After the filing of the case, a notice of the hearing of the appeal shall be given by the appellant for the next following session of the court as fixed by the Act, or as specially convened for hearing appeals according to the provisions thereof, if sufficient time shall intervene for that purpose, and if between the filing of the case and the first day of the next ensuing session there shall not be sufficient time to enable the appellant to serve the notice as hereinafter prescribed, then such notice of hearing shall be given for the session following the then next ensuing session.

Rule 13 regulates the form of the notice of hearing.

By Rule 14, as amended by Rule 80, the notice of hearing shall be served at least fifteen days before the first day of the session at which the appeal is to be heard. Rule 15, as amended by Rule 80, provides for the manner of service.

By Rule 49 special provision is made for notice of hearing in criminal appeals and appeals in matters of *habeas corpus*, the time varying in the different Provinces.

RULE 12.

Special notice convening court, form of.

The notice convening the court under section 14 of the Act, [ss. 21 and 22, c. 135, R. S. C.] for the purpose of hearing election or criminal appeals, or appeals in matters of *habeas corpus*, or for other purposes, shall, pursuant to the directions of the chief justice or senior puisné judge, as the case may be, be published by the Registrar in the *Canada Gazette*, and shall be inserted therein for such time before the day appointed for such special session as the said chief justice or senior puisné judge may direct, and may be in the form given in Schedule A, to these rules appended.

RULE 13.

Form of notice of hearing.

The notice of hearing may be in the form given in Schedule B to these Rules appended.

When an appeal is heard *ex parte*, the court requires an affidavit proving service of notice of hearing. Dig. S. C. D. p. 684, No. 87.

RULE 14.

[As amended by Rule 80.]

When to be served.

The notice of hearing shall be served at least 15 days before the first day of the session at which the appeal is to be heard.

This does not apply to election appeals; Rule 50; nor to criminal or *habeas corpus* appeals Rule 49.

RULE 15.

[As amended by rule 80.]

How notice of hearing to be served.

Such notice shall be served on the attorney or solicitor who shall have represented the respondent in the court below, at his usual place of business, or on the booked agent, or at the elected domicil of such attorney or solicitor at the City of Ottawa, and if such attorney or solicitor shall have no booked agent or elected domicil at the City of Ottawa, the notice may be served by affixing the same in some conspicuous place in the office of the Registrar, and mailing on the same day a copy thereof prepaid to the address of such attorney or solicitor.

See next Rule respecting "The Agent's Book."

See Rule 40 as to service of notices of motion.

And see Rules 20 and 21 as to service of notice of hearing on respondent who appears in person.

RULE 16.

"The Agent's Book."

There shall be kept in the office of the Registrar of this court a book to be called "The Agent's Book," in which all advocates, solicitors, attorneys and proctors practising in the said Supreme Court may enter the name of an agent (such agent being himself a person entitled to practice in the said court), at the said City of Ottawa, or elect a domicil at the said city.

It is provided by the Supreme and Exchequer Courts Act, R. S. C. c. 135, as amended by 50-51 V. c. 16, as follows:

"16. All persons who are barristers or advocates in any of the Provinces, may practise as barristers, advocates and counsel in the Supreme Court."

"17. All persons who are attorneys or solicitors of the superior courts in any of the Provinces, may practise as attorneys, solicitors and proctors in the Supreme Court."

"18. All persons who may practise as barristers, advocates, counsel, attorneys, solicitors or proctors in the Supreme Court, shall be officers of such court."

In *Wallace* v. *Burkner*, the Supreme Court intimated that conducting business with the Registrar's office by correspondence is a highly irregular practice. Practitioners should understand the importance of appointing an agent early in the course of an appeal. As soon as a case is transmitted to the Supreme Court the appellant's solicitor should authorize some practitioner in Ottawa, to act as agent and enter his name as such in the "agent's book." The authority may be a general one to act in all appeals, or may be limited to any particular appeal.

The authority must be in writing and filed in the Registrar's office. No special form is required. The following is sufficient:

"I hereby authorize you to enter your name as my agent in the 'agent's book' of the Supreme Court of Canada, and to act as such agent in all appeals to that court in which I may be concerned [or in the following appeal, viz.   ] Dated, etc."

The authority may be revoked by a subsequent one and a new entry in the book.

By Rule 82, it is ordered that an allowance shall be taxed by the Registrar to the duly entered agent in any appeal, in the discretion of the Registrar to $20.

Any neglect to appoint an agent, or any neglect by an agent when appointed, may seriously prejudice the rights of the parties. An agent should keep a general supervision over the procedure in an appeal, see that the appeal is duly entered and the fee paid on entering it, attend to the depositing of the factum and the inscribing of the appeal, keep his principal advised with reference to all interlocutory applications, be present in court to hear judgment and notify his principal of the result, take out and serve on the agent of the other party an appointment to tax costs and settle the minutes of the judgment, and attend the taxation and settlement. Sometimes questions arise on the settlement of the minutes requiring a thorough acquaintance on the part of the agent with the nature of the appeal and the judgment. It is not very satisfactory to find after a judgment has been entered that an important provision has been omitted necessitating an application to the full court at a considerable expense.

RULE 17.

Suggestion by respondent who appears in person.

In case any respondent who may have been represented by attorney or solicitor in the court below, shall desire to appear in person in the appeal, he shall immediately after the allowance by the court appealed from, or a judge thereof, of the security required by the Act, file with the Registrar a suggestion in the form following:

"A v. B.

"I, A. B., intend to appear in person in this appeal.

(Signed),   A. B."

When a respondent conducts an appeal in person he should be careful to comply with Rule 20 and elect some domicil or place at the city of Ottawa at which all notices and papers may be served upon him, otherwise by Rule 21 the notice of hearing may be served upon him by being affixed in some conspicuous place in the office of the Registrar, and by Rule 40 service of all notices of motion may be made on him in the same way.

When a party to an appeal appears in person he will be entitled to tax, if successful, and granted costs, the usual costs between party and party other than counsel fees. A respondent who is an advocate and who has argued the appeal in person cannot tax counsel fees. *Charlevoix Election Case (Valin v. Langlois)*, Dig. S. C. D. p. 677, No. 43.

RULE 18.

If no suggestion filed.

If no such suggestion shall be filed, and until an order shall have been obtained as hereinafter provided for a change of solicitor or attorney, the solicitor or attorney who appeared for any party respondent in the court below shall be deemed to be his solicitor or attorney in the appeal to this court.

RULE 19.

Suggestion by respondent who elects to appear by attorney.

When a respondent has appeared in person in the court below he may elect to appear by attorney or solicitor in the appeal, in which case the attorney or solicitor shall file a suggestion to that effect in the office of the Registrar, and thereafter the notice of hearing and all other papers are to be served on such attorney or solicitor as hereinbefore provided.

RULE 20.

Election of domicil by respondent who appears in person.

A respondent who appears in person may, by a suggestion filed in the Registrar's office, elect some domicil or place at the city of Ottawa, at which all notices and papers may be served upon him, in which case service at such place of the notice of hearing and all other notices and papers shall be deemed good service on the respondent.

RULE 21.

Service when respondent appears in person without electing domicil.

In case the respondent, who shall have appeared in person in the court appealed from, or who shall have filed a suggestion to Rule 17, shall not, before service, have elected a domicil at the city of Ottawa, the notice of hearing may be served by affixing the same in some conspicuous place in the office of the Registrar.

Rules 17, 18, 19, 20 & 21, all refer only to a respondent, and provide for the manner in which he may appear in an appeal. No provision has been made for the filing of a suggestion by an appellant who wishes to appear in person, nor for his electing to appear by solicitor in the Supreme Court when he has appeared in person in the court below, nor for election of domicil by an appellant who wishes to appear in person. But an appellant can prosecute an appeal in person, or by the solicitor who appeared for him in the cause below, or he may instruct some other solicitor to prosecute the appeal—and the rule as to entering an agent would of course apply to any solicitor so acting for the appellant. Besides, Rule 40 which regulates the mode of serving notices of motion is applicable as well to an appellant as a respondent, and from this rule it may be inferred that an appellant appearing in person may elect a domicil in the city of Ottawa.

RULE 22.

Changing attorney or solicitor.

Any party to an appeal may on an *ex parte* application to a judge obtain an order to change his attorney or solicitor, and after service of such order on the opposite party, all services of notices and other papers are to be made on the new attorney or solicitor.

One attorney's name only should appear on record. In an application to change the name of solicitor, it was shown that Messrs. A. and B. appeared on the case as solicitors, and that A. had died. It was desired to have the name of B. alone inserted as solicitor. Application refused by the Chief Justice of the Supreme Court as unnecessary: *Gilmour & Rankin* v. *Bull*, 1 Kerr, N. B., referred to. *The Exchange Bank* v. *Springer*, 24th February, 1887.

FACTUMS.

RULE 23.

[As amended by Rule 80.]

Factums to be deposited with Registrar.

At least fifteen days before the first day of the session at which the appeal is to be heard, the parties appellant and respondent shall each deposit with the Registrar, for the use of the court and its officers, twenty-five copies of his factum or points for argument in appeal.

RULE 24.

What to contain.

The factum or points for argument in appeal shall contain a concise statement of the facts, and of the points of law intended to be relied on, and of the arguments and authorities to be urged and cited at the hearing, arranged under the appropriate heads.

RULE 25.

How to be printed.

The factum or points for argument in appeal shall be printed in the same form and manner as hereinbefore provided for with regard to the case in appeal, and shall not be received by the Registrar unless the requirements hereinbefore contained, as regards the case, are all complied with.

RULE 26.

Motion by respondent to dismiss appeal on ground of delay in filing factum.

If the appellant does not deposit his factum or points for argument in appeal within the time limited by Order 23, the respondent shall be at liberty to move to dismiss the appeal on the ground of undue delay, as provided for by section 41 of the Act, [s. 53, c. 135, R. S. C.]

RULE 27.

Appellant may inscribe ex parte if factum not filed.

If the respondent fails to deposit his factum or points for argument in appeal within the said prescribed period, the appellant may set down or inscribe the cause for hearing *ex parte*.

See Rule 31.

RULE 28.

Setting aside inscription ex parte.

Such setting down or inscription *ex parte* may be set aside or discharged upon an application to a judge in Chambers sufficiently supported by affidavits.

RULE 29.

Registrar to seal up factums first deposited.

The factum or points for argument in appeal first deposited with the Registrar shall be kept by him under seal, and shall in no case be communicated to the opposite party until the latter shall himself bring in and deposit his own factum or points.

RULE 30.

Interchange of factums.

So soon as both parties shall have deposited their said factum or points for argument in appeal, each party shall, at the request of the other, deliver to him three copies of his said factum or points.

Rule 23, as originally passed, required that the factums should be deposited at least one month before the first day of the session at which the appeal was to be heard. By Rule 80 the time was altered and fixed at fifteen days.

Parties should bear in mind that these rules respecting factums have been passed for the convenience of the court. They must be strictly complied with: *Lord* v. *Davidson*, Dig. S. C. D. p. 683, No. 80; and cannot be waived by consent of parties: *Cote* v. *Stadacona Assur. Co.*, Dig. S. C. D. p. 683, No. 77. The factum should be as complete as possible, but the court has never refused leave to counsel to hand in for the use of the judges a printed list of authorities cited at the hearing not already mentioned in the factum. An additional argumentative factum is never, or very rarely, received, and would not be accepted by the Registrar for distribution among the judges without special leave of the court. The additional list of authorities should be printed and copies sent to the Registrar as soon as possible after the argument of the appeal. The factum should not contain irrelevant matter, or reproduce documents already printed in the case, when a reference to them will answer the purpose.

In *Fuller* v. *Ames*, Dig. S. C. R. p. 140, No. 10, Taschereau, J., held that an objection to the admission of evidence on which a claim for prescription was founded should not be entertained when taken for the first time in the Supreme Court. But in *Dorion* v. *Crowley*, Ibid, p. 709, No. 12, the Court gave effect to a claim for prescription, though not raised before, and in *Breakey* v. *Carter*, Ibid. p. 463, though raised for the first time in the Court of Queen's Bench.

The facts of the case and points for argument should be concisely and yet completely set out. In one case when a point was raised at the hearing which was not in the factum, and the respondent objected that he was not prepared to argue it, the court adjourned the hearing for a week: *Western Counties Ry. Co.* v. *Windsor & Annapolis Ry. Co.*, Dig. S. C. D. p. 683, No. 75. Any improper reflections upon the conduct of the judges of the courts below will be ordered to be struck out and subject the solicitor to the censure of the court and the loss of his costs: *Wallace* v. *Souther*, Dig. S. C. D. p. 682, No. 73; *Vernon* v. *Oliver*, 11 Can. S. C. R. 156.

Objections to a factum as containing unnecessary matter may be urged at the hearing: *Coleman* v. *Miller*, Dig. S. C. D. p. 683, No. 78; or may be urged before the Registrar on taxation.

The form and manner of printing must be the same as those for the case, see Rule 8; and the Registrar, by Rule 25, is directed not to receive the factum unless these requirements have been complied with.

Default on the part of the respondent in depositing a factum does not justify the appellant in neglecting to deposit his, or relieve him from the risk of a motion to dismiss under Rule 26; *Whitfield* v. *The Merchants Bank*, Dig. S. C. D. p. 681, No. 66. It is the duty of the appellant to prosecute his appeal with all reasonable despatch and in strict conformity with the requirements of the statute and rules. If the respondent is in default the appeal is inscribed *ex parte*, and the Registrar is not at liberty to inscribe in any other way. The word "may" in Rule 27, therefore, means "must," if the appellant inscribes the appeal. Rule 28 provides a mode of relief in a proper case against this inscription *ex parte*.

In certain circumstances the court has dispensed with an oral argument of the appeal, and allowed the case to be submitted on the factums. See Dig. S. C. D. p. 684, Nos. 81-84.

No factums are required in criminal appeals, nor in *habeas corpus* appeals—Rule 47. In election appeals a factum must be printed as in ordinary appeals—Rule 53; but need be deposited only three days before the session—Rule 54. In a proper case an order may be obtained dispensing with the factum in these appeals—Rule 55.

Rule 63, as amended by Rule 80, provides for the depositing of factums in a cross appeal, the time within which such factums must be deposited, and the interchange of such factums between the parties.

Rule 64 provides for the translation of a factum, if required by a judge. There has been no case in which this has been required.

INSCRIPTION OF APPEAL.

RULE 31.
[As amended by Rule 80.]

Registrar to inscribe appeals for hearing.

Appeals shall be set down or inscribed for hearing in a book to be kept for that purpose by the registrar at least fourteen days before the first day of the session of the court fixed for the hearing of the appeal. But no appeal shall be so inscribed which shall not have been filed twenty clear days before said first day of said session, without the leave of the court or a judge.

It is the duty of the appellant to inscribe the appeal. He cannot inscribe if the "case" has not been filed twenty clear days before the first day of the session, as provided by the latter part of this rule, nor unless his own factum has been deposited within the time fixed by Rule 23, nor until the time allowed by that rule has passed, leaving the respondent in default.

By the statute, Supreme and Exchequer Courts Act, section 20, the regular sessions always begin on a Tuesday. The case, therefore, should be filed not later than the third Tuesday preceding the opening of the session (20 clear days). The factums, under Rule 23, should be deposited not later than the third Saturday preceding the opening of the session, and the appeal should be inscribed on the third Monday preceding—that is the Monday following the last day for depositing the factums. If the respondent has failed to deposit his factum the appeal must be inscribed for hearing *ex parte*. This inscription *ex parte* can only be vacated on application supported by affidavit accounting for the delay. A mere consent on the part of the appellant or his solicitor would not be sufficient. See Rules 27 and 28.

c.s.e.c.—10

On the third Monday preceding the first day of the session, assuming the session to be a regular one beginning on a Tuesday, the agent for the appellant should attend the registrar's office, write out a *præcipe* for a search, to satisfy himself that the "case" has been filed twenty days before the first day of the session, and to ascertain whether the respondent's factum has been deposited or not. If the case has been regularly filed, the agent can then file with the registrar a *præcipe* requesting him to inscribe the appeal.

The appeal may be inscribed at any time, provided the factums of both parties have been deposited and the case filed within the proper time. If the appellant wishes to inscribe before the time has expired for depositing the factums, he should not neglect to make a search before filing with the registrar a request to inscribe, for if the case has not been regularly filed, or if the factum of respondent has not been deposited, the request will not be complied with, and unless another request be made when the appeal is ready for inscription, the appellant may find himself open to a motion to dismiss for not having duly inscribed his appeal.

The respondent cannot inscribe the appeal, even though the appellant make default in inscribing. His remedy is by motion to dismiss for want of prosecution. See section 53 of the Supreme and Exchequer Courts Act, and notes thereon, and Rule 26.

There are special rules relating to the inscription of election appeals, Exchequer appeals, criminal appeals, and appeals in matters of *habeas corpus.*

1. As to election appeals. See section 51, sub-section 2 of the Dominion Controverted Elections Act and notes thereon, *ante,* p. 114. This section provides that an election appeal, after the transmission of the record by the clerk or other proper officer of the court below, shall be set down by the registrar of the Supreme Court for hearing at the nearest convenient time, and according to any rules of the Supreme Court of Canada in that behalf. The only rules of the Supreme Court directly affecting the inscription are the one requiring a fee of $10 to be paid on entering every appeal, and the rules relating to the printing of the record and the depositing of factums (53, 54 and 86). If the fee be paid in time to enable the registrar to have the record printed and to enable the factums to be deposited within the time specified, the appeal will be immediately inscribed by the registrar for the ensuing session.

2. As to Exchequer appeals. By section 51 of chapter 16 of 50-51 V., it is provided that after the deposit of $50 by way of security for costs, or filing of notice of intention to appeal on behalf of the Crown, section 53, the registrar shall set the appeal down for hearing before the Supreme Court on the first day of the next session.

3. As to criminal appeals and appeals in matters of *habeas corpus*. These may be set down for hearing as soon as the certified written case, mentioned in Rule 47, has been received by the registrar, provided the time limit specified in Rule 48 does not interfere. In that event an application may be made to a judge, or to the court if in session, for special leave to inscribe.

Election appeals take precedence on the inscription list. On special application criminal and *habeas corpus* appeals have been given an early hearing during the session. Exchequer appeals are placed in the several lists according to the respective Provinces in which the cases were tried.

HEARING.

RULE 32.

Counsel at hearing.

No more than two counsel on each side shall be heard on any appeal, and but one counsel shall be heard in reply.

In some cases the court has relaxed this rule and heard more than two counsel :—*e.g.*, where intricate questions requiring a consideration of the law of both the Provinces of Ontario and Quebec have been raised. Dig. S. C. D. p. 678, Nos. 52, 53 and 54. And where in an appeal between private suitors, the validity of an Act of the Provincial Legislature has been questioned, the Attorney-General of the Province has been heard. Dig. S. C. D. p. 678, No. 51. The fact of there being a cross appeal is not in itself sufficient ground to cause the court to depart from its rule. Dig. S. C. D. p. 678, No. 52.

The counsel for the appellant are first heard, then the counsel for respondent, and one of the counsel for the appellant replies.

No rule has been laid down as to whether senior or junior counsel should first address the court. In cases from the Province of Quebec, it is not unusual for the junior counsel to speak first and then the senior counsel. In cases from the other provinces the senior counsel first addresses the court and is followed by his junior.

Any one attacking the validity of a statute should begin, as all statutes should *prima facie* be considered within the jurisdiction of the Legislature passing them. Dig. S. C. D. p. 679, Nos. 55 and 56.

When the question before the court was whether the Canada Temperance Act, 1878, section 6, had been complied with, and whether a proclamation should issue under section 7, the court directed the parties to begin who sought to sustain the affirmative. Dig. S. C. D. p. 679, No. 57.

The court refused to hear counsel residing in the State of New York. Dig. S. C. D. p. 679, No. 59.

As a rule only one counsel on each side is heard on the argument of a motion.

RULE 33.

Postponement of hearing.

The court may in its discretion postpone the hearing until any future day during the same session, or at any following session.

The power of altering the order of hearing appeals is reserved to the court by section 58 of the Supreme and Exchequer Courts Act. This applies only to changing the order of the list for the session at the time being held. The above rule goes further and provides for the postponement of an appeal to any following session. If both parties consent to the postponement of the hearing of an appeal on the list, counsel can either notify the court when the appeal is called, or inform the registrar in writing of their wish to withdraw the appeal, and the registrar will inform the court when the appeal is called. As a rule when an appeal is merely withdrawn it should be re-inscribed for hearing by the appellant on the usual *præcipe* filed with the registrar. When the court directs an appeal to stand for hearing at a subsequent session, no re-inscription is required, as the registrar will place the appeal on the list, in accordance with the direction of the court.

If the case does not contain the formal judgment of the court below, or the reasons of the judges of the court below, or affidavit required by Rule 2, that such reasons could not be procured, or a proper index, or is in any other respect imperfect, the court may direct the postponement of the hearing. Dig. S. C. D. p. 672, No. 14: *Lewin* v. *Howe*, February session, 1888; or place it at the foot of the list to permit missing matter to be added. Dig. S. C. D. p. 672, No. 15.

If it appears that the respondent has taken an appeal to the Privy Council from the same judgment, the court will postpone the hearing until such appeal is decided. *McGreevy* v. *McDougall*, Mar., 1888; *Bessey* v. *Eddy*, Oct., 1898.

RULE 34.

Default by parties in attending hearing.

Appeals shall be heard in the order in which they have been set down, and if either party neglect to appear at the proper day to support or resist the appeal, the court may hear the other party, and may give judgment without the intervention of the party so neglecting to appear, or may postpone the hearing upon such terms as to payment of costs or otherwise as the court shall direct.

If neither party be represented when the appeal is called for hearing, it will be struck out of the list. If the appellant be not represented and counsel for respondent asks for the dismissal of the appeal, it will be dismissed with costs. Dig. S. C. D. p. 681, No..65. If respondent's counsel, instead of asking for dismissal of the appeal, asks for the postponement of the hearing to the following session, the request will usually be granted.

In *Titus* v. *Colville*, May term, 1890, the court reinstated an appeal dismissed for non-appearance of counsel for appellant, but refused to do so in *Foran* v. *Handley*, in 1892, and *Hall Mines* v. *Moore*, May, 1898.

If respondent be not represented, counsel for appellant may be heard *ex parte*, or may ask for the postponement of the hearing.

RULE 35.

How orders to be signed and dated.

All orders of this court in cases of appeal shall bear date on the day of the judgment or decision being pronounced, and shall be signed by the registrar.

This rule refers to orders of the court. An order made by a Judge in Chambers is signed by the judge. And orders made by the registrar sitting as a Judge in Chambers are signed by the registrar—Rule 83.

When one of the parties has died between the hearing and pronouncing of judgment, the court, on application, may direct its order to be dated and entered *nunc pro tunc*, as of the day of hearing. Dig. S. C. D. p. 688, Nos. 102-104.

Even after the final judgment has been signed and entered and transmitted to the court below, the Supreme Court has power to amend such judgment, and will do so if it is clear that by oversight or mistake an error has occurred. *Rattray* v. *Young*, Dig. S. C. D. p. 692, No. 110.

When a judgment is amended it will be amended to read *nunc pro tunc*. Dig. S. C. D. p. 689, Nos. 105 and 109.

ADDING PARTIES TO THE APPEAL.

RULE 36.

Adding parties by suggestion.

In any case not already provided for by the Act, in which it becomes essential to make an additional party to the appeal, either as appellant or respondent, and whether such proceeding becomes necessary in consequence of the death or insolvency of any original party, or from any other cause, such additional party may be added to the appeal by filing a suggestion as nearly as may be in the form provided for by section 43 of the Act [s. 55, c. 135, R. S. C.].

RULE 37.

Suggestion may be set aside.

The suggestion referred to in the next preceding rule may be set aside, on motion, by the court or a judge thereof.

These rules supplement the provisions of sections 54 to 57 of the Supreme and Exchequer Courts Act; see *ante*, pp. 76, 77 and 78.

In *Guest* v. *Diack*, Oct. 1897, the executrix of a respondent who had died pending the appeal, was substituted for him, and a suggestion allowed to be filed by appellant.

And where the appellant had made an assignment in insolvency after the appeal had been taken, his assignee was added as an appellant, the sureties to the bond for security for costs filing a consent and an undertaking to be bound by the bond, notwithstanding the change of parties. *Ostrom* v. *Sills*, March, 1898.

RULE 38.

Determining questions of fact arising on motion.

Upon any such motion, the court or a judge thereof may, in their or his discretion, direct evidence to be taken before a proper officer for that purpose, or may direct that the parties shall proceed in the proper court for that purpose to have any question tried and determined, and in such case all proceedings in appeal may be stayed until after the trial and determination of the said question.

MOTIONS.

RULE 39.

Motions.

All interlocutory applications in appeals shall be made by motion, supported by affidavit to be filed in the office of the registrar before the notice of motion is served. The notice of motion shall be served at least four clear days before the time of hearing.

RULE 40.

Notice of motion, how served.

Such notice of motion may be served upon the solicitor or attorney of the opposite party by delivering a copy thereof to the booked agent, or at the elected domicile of such solicitor or attorney, to whom it is addressed, at the City of Ottawa. If the solicitor or attorney has no booked agent, or has elected no domicile at the City of Ottawa, or if a party to be served with notice of motion has not elected a domicile at the City of Ottawa, such notice may be served by affixing a copy thereof in some conspicuous place in the office of the registrar of this court.

RULE 41.

Affidavits in support of motion.

Service of a notice of motion shall be accompanied by copies of affidavits filed in support of the motion.

Rule 43 provides that "motions to be made before the court are to be set down in a list or paper, and are to be called on each morning of the session before the hearing of appeals is proceeded with."

Although, under Rule 46, these rules as to motions do not apply to criminal appeals, nor to appeals in matters of *habeas corpus*, and under Rule 50 do not apply to election appeals, yet the practice of the court has been the same with respect to motions in all classes of appeals, so far at least as Rules 39, 41 and 43, lay down the procedure.

Rule 40 shows the importance of appointing an agent or electing a domicil. See Rule 16 and notes. *Ex abundanti cautela*, in addition to effecting service in the mode pointed out by Rule 40, a copy of the papers should be mailed to, or otherwise served on the solicitor of the opposite party. This should invariably be done in election, criminal or *habeas corpus* appeals.

Affidavits used in reply are filed in the **registrar's office after being read.**

RULE 42.

Giving further time.

Upon application supported by affidavit, and after notice to the opposite party, the court or a judge thereof may give further reasonable time for filing the printed case, depositing the printed factum or points of either party, and setting down or inscribing the appeal for hearing, as required by the foregoing rules.

This is a special rule governing the extension of time for doing certain specified acts therein mentioned. A more general power for extending or abridging the time for " doing any act or taking any proceeding " is given by Rule 70.

An application under Rule 42, should not be made merely on consent. Some good and substantial reason should be shown by affidavit for asking the indulgence desired. The time limit laid down by the rules for doing any of the acts referred to in Rule 42, has been fixed after full consideration, as the most reasonable and convenient for both the judges and the parties, and will not be readily extended without very strong grounds being shown. As to the time within which the case should be filed, see Rules 5 and 31. As to depositing factums, see Rule 23; and as to inscribing, see Rule 31.

RULE 43.

Setting down motions.

Motions to be made before the court are to be set down in a list or paper, and are to be called on each morning of the session before the hearing of appeals is proceeded with.

The solicitor or agent for the party on whose behalf a motion is to be made before the court should attend at the registrar's office on the morning of the day when the motion is to be brought on for hearing and put it on the list. This list is placed before the Chief Justice, who calls the motions in the order in which they are set down. See Rules 39, 40 and 41 as to motions generally.

RULE 44.

Appeal abandoned by delay.

Unless the appeal is brought on for hearing by the appellant within one year next after the security shall have been allowed, it shall be held to have been abandoned without any order to dismiss being required, unless the court or a judge thereof shall otherwise order.

RULE 45.

Rules applicable to Exchequer appeals.

The foregoing rules shall be applicable to appeals from the Exchequer Court of Canada, except in so far as the Act has otherwise provided.

See chapter 16 of 50-51 V. ss. 51, 52 and 53, *ante*, pp. 106-108.

These sections effect a few changes in the procedure relating to Exchequer appeals:

1. The security is different both in amount and manner of giving it. The amount is $50, instead of $500, as in ordinary appeals, although no good reason can be given why there should be this difference, Exchequer appeals, as a rule, being rather more costly than others. The security is given by depositing the amount with the Registrar of the Supreme Court. If the appeal be on behalf of the Crown no deposit is required, a notice filed with the registrar taking its place.

2. The time within which security must be given is different. In ordinary appeals sixty days are allowed within which to give the security; section 40 of chapter 135, Revised Statutes, Canada, as amended by schedule (A) of chapter 16 of 50-51 V. In Exchequer appeals security must be given within thirty days.

3. The appeal has to be inscribed by the Registrar of the Supreme Court for the next session as soon as the security is given. Therefore Rule 31 is not applicable to such an appeal.

4. Notice of hearing must be given within ten days after the deposit; and the notice may limit the appeal to any defined question or questions. Rule 11 provides for notice of hearing in ordinary appeals.

In other respects the procedure in Exchequer appeals is the same as that in ordinary appeals.

RULES APPLICABLE TO CRIMINAL APPEALS AND APPEALS IN MATTERS OF HABEAS CORPUS.

RULE 46.

Rules not applicable to criminal appeals, nor habeas corpus.

The foregoing rules shall not, except as hereinbefore provided, apply to criminal appeals nor to appeals in matters of *habeas corpus*.

RULE 47.

Case in criminal appeals and habeas corpus.

In the cases mentioned in the next preceding rule, no printed case shall be required, and no factum or points for argument in appeal need be deposited with the registrar, but such appeals may be heard on a written case, certified under the seal of the court appealed from, and which case shall contain all judgments and opinions pronounced in the court below.

RULE 48.

When case to be filed.

In criminal appeals, and in appeals in cases of *habeas corpus*, and unless the court or a judge shall otherwise order, the case must be filed as follows:

(1) In appeals from any of the Provinces other than British Columbia, at least one month before the first day of the session at which it is set down to be heard.

(2) In appeals from British Columbia, at least two months before the said day.

RULE 49.

Notice of hearing in criminal appeals and in appeals in matters of habeas corpus.

In cases of criminal appeals and appeals in matters of *habeas corpus*, notice of hearing shall be served the respective times hereinafter fixed before the first day of the general or special session at which the same is appointed to be heard, that is to say:

(1) In appeals from Ontario and Quebec, two weeks.
(2) In appeals from Nova Scotia, New Brunswick and Prince Edward Island, three weeks.
(3) In appeals from Manitoba, one month.
(4) In appeals from British Columbia, six weeks.

The sections of the Supreme and Exchequer Courts Act specially applicable to *habeas corpus* appeals are 32, 33, 34 and 35. Criminal appeals are governed by sections 742, 750 and 751 of the Criminal Code, 1892.

Both with regard to appeals in matters of *habeas corpus* and criminal appeals the intention of the Legislature appears to have been that these appeals should be heard promptly. Section 35 of the Supreme and Exchequer Courts Act says: "An appeal to the Supreme **Court** in any *habeas corpus* matter shall be heard at an **early** day, whether in or out of the prescribed sessions of the court."

And with respect to criminal appeals sub-section 2, of section 750 of the Criminal Code provides: "Unless such appeal is brought on for hearing by the appellant at the session of the Supreme Court, during which such affirmance [of the conviction] takes place or the session next thereafter, if the said court is not then in session, the appeal shall be held to have been abandoned, unless otherwise ordered by the Supreme Court."

The delays specified in Rules 48 and 49, not only do not seem to accord with the spirit of these sections, but in the majority of cases could not be complied with, so far as criminal appeals are concerned. But in practice the court has invariably shown itself ready to expedite such appeals, by shortening the delays to the utmost reasonable extent and giving such appeals precedence on the list for hearing, upon application made.

ELECTION APPEALS.

RULE 50.

Preceding rules not applicable in election cases.

The foregoing rules are not to apply to appeals in controverted election cases.

Notwithstanding this rule, the practice adopted by the court in election appeals has been similar in many respects to that laid down for ordinary appeals. The same procedure has been followed as regards agents and their appointment, the election of domicil, motions in chambers and before the court, the signing and dating of orders, the number of counsel to be heard. Rule 12 is by its terms applicable to election as well as other appeals; and by Rules 53 and 54, the rules regulating the printing and interchange of factums (25 and 30), are made applicable to election appeals.

RULES 51 & 52.

These rules were repealed by General Order No. 86, which substituted the following provisions therefor.

In controverted election appeals the party appellant shall obtain from the registrar, upon payment of the usual charges therefor, a certified copy of the record, or of so much thereof as a judge may direct to be printed, and shall have forty (40) copies of the said certified copy printed in the same form as hereinafter provided for the Cas in ordinary appeals, and immediately after the completion of the printing shall deliver to the registrar thirty (30) of such printed copies, twenty-five (25) thereof for the use of the court and its officers and five (5) thereof for the use of the respondent, and to be handed by the registrar to the respondent or his solicitor or booked agent upon application made therefor.

For printing in election appeals the same fees shall be allowed on taxation as for printing the Case in ordinary appeals.

RULE 53.

Factum in election appeals.

The *factum* or points for argument in appeal in controverted election appeals shall be printed as hereinbefore provided in the case of ordinary appeals.

See Rules 24 and 25, *ante*, p. 142.

RULE 54.

When to be deposited.

The points for argument in appeal or *factum* in controverted election cases shall be deposited with the registrar at least three days before the first day of the session fixed for the hearing of the appeal, and are to be interchanged by the parties in manner hereinbefore provided with regard to the *factum* or points in ordinary appeals.

See Rules 25 and 30.

Rule 55 provides for dispensing with a *factum* in certain cases.

RULE 55.

Order dispensing with printing of record or factum in election appeals.

In election appeals a Judge in Chambers may, upon the application of the appellant, make an order dispensing with the printing of the whole or any part of the record, and may also dispense with the delivery of any *factum* or points for argument in appeal. Such order may be obtained *ex parte*, and the party obtaining it shall forthwith cause it to be served upon the adverse party.

In practice such an order is seldom or never made *ex parte*. Four clear days' notice should be given of the intention to apply for it. The order is usually obtained when the appeal has been limited by the notice provided for by the statute, sub-section 3, section 51, Dominion Controverted Elections Act, to any defined question or questions, of fact or of law. And it is the duty of the appellant to apply for such an order whenever it will save useless expense, otherwise he may have to pay the costs of printing the unnecessary matter in any event. See judgment of Taschereau, J., in *Brassard* v. *Langevin*, 1 Can. S. C. R. 201. See also judgment of Henry, J., at page 231.

RULE 56.

Fees to be paid Registrar.

The fees mentioned in Schedule (C) to these orders shall be paid to the registrar by stamps to be prepared for that purpose.

The Schedule C originally appended to the Orders has been repealed, and a new schedule substituted by General Order 84, which see. With a few exceptions, fees are not payable in criminal and *habeas corpus* appeals.

The Supreme Court has no power to allow an appeal in *forma pauperis*. The payment of the fees fixed by the schedule will not, therefore, be dispensed with any more than the giving of the security required by the Act. Dig S. C. D. p. 695, No. 125. *Dominion Cartridge Co.* v. *Cairns*, per Sedgewick, J., in Chambers, May, 1898.

RULE 57.

Costs.

Costs in appeal between party and party shall be taxed pursuant to the tariff of fees contained in Schedule (D) to these orders.

By section 109 of the Supreme and Exchequer Courts Act it is provided, that the judges of the Supreme Court, or any five of them may, from time to time, make general rules and orders, among other things, "for fixing the fees and costs to be taxed and allowed to, and received and taken by, and the rights and duties of, the officers of the court, and for awarding and regulating costs in such court in favour of and against the Crown, as well as the subject."

By section 62 of the Act, "The Supreme Court may, in its discretion, order the payment of the costs of the court appealed from, and also of the appeal, or any part thereof, as well when the judgment appealed from is varied or reversed, as where it is affirmed."

Section 51 provides for the costs of a respondent when the appellant discontinues his appeal. By section 52 an appellant may consent to the judgment appealed from being reversed, but it will not be reversed with costs unless the consent includes them.

In controverted election appeals by sub-section 3 of section 51, of the Dominion Controverted Elections Act, the Supreme Court of Canada may make such order as to the money deposited as security for costs, and as to the costs of the appeal, as it thinks just. Section 53 of the said Act provides for the recovery of costs awarded by the court below against a petitioner out of the deposit made by the petitioner, or if deposit insufficient, by execution.

And by section 54 of the Act it is provided, that:

"In appeals under this Act, to the Supreme Court of Canada, the said court may adjudge the whole or any part of the costs in the court below to be paid by either of the parties; and any order directing the payment of such costs shall be certified by the Registrar of the Supreme Court of Canada to the court in which the petition was filed, and the same proceedings for the recovery of such costs may thereupon be taken in the last mentioned court as if the order for payment of costs had been made by that court or by the judge before whom the petition was tried." 39 V. c. 26, s. 16.

In appeals under the Winding-up Act, chapter 129, Revised Statutes of Canada, costs are regulated by the provisions of the Supreme and Exchequer Courts Act. So far as appeals to the Supreme Court of Canada from the District of Keewatin are concerned, section 75 of the Winding-up Act is also applicable, which provides, that if the appellant does not proceed with his appeal according to the law or the rules of practice, as the case may be, the court appealed to on the application of the respondent, may dismiss the appeal with or without costs.

With regard to criminal appeals, no special provision has been made by the Criminal Code as to costs, which in such appeals are therefore entirely regulated by the provisions of the Supreme and Exchequer Courts Act and the practice of the court.

As a rule no costs are given in criminal appeals, or in *habeas corpus* appeals. See Dig. S. C. D. p. 677, No. 41. But where an appeal in a *habeas corpus* matter had been proceeded with after the discharge of the prisoner and for the mere purpose of deciding the question of costs, the appeal was dismissed with costs. *Ibid*, p. 421, No. 24.

Where the judgment appealed from is affirmed by reason of the court being equally divided, the uniform practice has been to dismiss the appeal without costs. See Dig. S. C. R. p. 676, No. 39.

And see notes to section 59 as to the costs when an appeal is quashed.

Costs in Exchequer appeals also are regulated entirely by the provisions of the Supreme and Exchequer Courts Act and the rules of the court.

SECURITY FOR COSTS.

Security for costs must be given in all appeals, except :

1. Appeals by or on behalf of the Crown. See sub-section 2 of section 46, Supreme and Exchequer Courts Act.

When an appeal by or on behalf of the Crown comes from the Exchequer Court, section 53 of chapter 16 of 50-51 V. (the Exchequer Court Act) provides that no deposit by way of security shall be required, a notice of intention to appeal filed with the registrar of the Supreme Court taking its place.

2. Criminal appeals. Sub-section 2 of section 46, Supreme and Exchequer Courts Act.

3. Proceedings for or upon a writ of *habeas corpus*. Ibid.

4. Election appeals in which the security for costs is regulated by section 51 of the Dominion Controverted Elections Act, and by that section fixed at $100, by deposit.

5. In Exchequer Court appeals, in which, by section 51 of chapter 16 of 50-51 V., the security is fixed at $50, by deposit.

There would at first sight be some difficulty in finding good reasons for fixing the security at $100 and $50 respectively in election and Exchequer appeals, instead of $500, as in ordinary appeals. In practice, owing to the fact that the records in such cases have usually been very voluminous, the deposit has been altogether inadequate to serve as security for the costs. It may be that in these cases it was thought desirable not to place difficulties in the way of appealing, and of having them, if possible, inexpensively and promptly disposed of.

In Exchequer appeals, especially, it may be said the Crown should be willing to facilitate an appeal by a subject seeking redress from it. Where the appeal is by the subject he needs no security from the Crown, and therefore none is required by the statute.

In all other appeals the security, mode of giving and amount, are regulated by section 46 of the Supreme and Exchequer Courts Act (see said section and notes thereon).

And as to when costs will or will not be given, see notes to section 62 of the Act.

PRACTICE ON TAXATION.

It will be observed that Rule 57 relates only to costs " between party and party." The registrar is not authorized to tax costs between solicitor and client. *Boak* v. *Merchants Marine Ins. Co.,* Dig. S. C. D. p. 677, No. 45.

The agent of the successful party attends the registrar's office for an appointment. It is usual to take one appointment for the settlement of the minutes of judgment and taxation of the costs. The agent has this appointment served with a copy of the minutes of judgment and of the bill. The bill is always prepared by the agent or solicitor, and never by the registrar, and the agent or solicitor prepares also the minutes of judgment. At the time appointed the agents or solicitors for the respective parties attend before the registrar, who settles the minutes and taxes the costs. If either party is dissatisfied with the taxation he should apply to the registrar sitting as a Judge in Chambers for a revival of the taxation, giving due notice to the other side, and setting out his objections in writing. If the registrar refuses to alter his taxation, an appeal can be taken to a judge, under Rule 83. It is not usual to interfere with the taxation of the registrar on a mere question of amount. He must have exercised his discretion on a wrong principle.

An application for a fiat for an increased counsel fee should also be made to the registrar in Chambers, after the taxation, and upon notice. An appeal must be one of exceptional importance and difficulty to justify such an application.

RULE 58.

Court or judge may order payment of fixed sum for costs.

The court or a judge may direct a fixed sum for costs to be paid in lieu of directing the payment of costs to be taxed.

This rule is followed frequently in interlocutory applications. In these applications it has been the practice to specify in the orders the amount to be paid as costs, instead of directing such costs to be taxed. But an order or judgment dealing with the general costs of an appeal always leaves the amount to be taxed.

By the tariff of fees (schedule D) a sum of $25, subject to be increased by order of the court or a judge, may be taxed on a motion to quash an appeal under section 59 of the Act.

RULE 59.

This rule, which provided for the manner in which payment of costs might be enforced, has been repealed by General Order 85. The rule read as follows : " The payment of costs, if so ordered, may be enforced by process of execution in the same manner and by means of the same writs, and according to the same practice as may be in use from time to time in the Exchequer Court of Canada."

It is provided by the Supreme and Exchequer Courts Act, as follows :

"105. The process of the Supreme Court shall run throughout Canada, and shall be tested in the name of the Chief Justice, or in case of a vacancy in the office of Chief Justice, in the name of the senior puisné judge of the court, and shall be directed to the sheriff of any county or other judicial division into which any province is divided; and the sheriffs of the said respective counties or divisions shall be deemed and taken to be *ex officio* officers of the Supreme Court, and shall perform the duties and functions of sheriffs in connection with the court; and in any case where the sheriff is disqualified, such process shall be directed to any of the coroners of the county or district." 38 V. c. 11, ss. 66 and 75.

"107. An order in the Supreme Court for payment of money, whether for costs or otherwise, may be enforced by such writs of execution as the court prescribes." 39 V. c. 26, s. 35.

"108. No attachment as for contempt shall issue in the Supreme Court for the non-payment of money only." 39 V. c. 26, s. 36.

These sections, 107 and 108, have been substituted by chapter 16 of 50-51 V., sched. A, for original sections.

In pursuance of section 107, General Order 85, before mentioned, has been passed to prescribe the writs which shall be issued out of the Supreme Court, and to regulate the practice in relation thereto, including the fees to be paid to sheriffs.

Hitherto the court has always refused to issue a writ of execution to enforce payment of costs ordered by any final judgment, but has left parties to their remedies in the court below.

Section 67 of the Supreme and Exchequer Courts Act, provides as follows :

"67. The judgment of the Supreme Court in appeal shall be certified by the registrar of the court to the proper officer of the court of original jurisdiction, who shall thereupon make all proper and necessary entries thereof; and all subsequent proceedings may be taken thereupon, as if the judgment had been given or pronounced in the said last-mentioned court." 38 V. c. 11, s. 46.

But the court will direct the issue of the necessary writs to enforce payment of interlocutory costs.

RULE 60.

This Rule has also been repealed by General Order 85, which deals with the subject matter of the rule, the punishment of contempts. The rule read as follows: "Contempts incurred by reason of non-compliance with any order of the court other than an order for payment of money, may be punished in the same manner and by means of the same process and writs, and according to the same practice as may be in use from time to time in the Exchequer Court of Canada."

As we have seen, by section 108 of the Supreme and Exchequer Courts Act, it is provided that "no attachment as for contempt shall issue in the Supreme Court for the non-payment of money only." General Order 85 provides for other cases.

CROSS-APPEALS.

RULE 61.

Cross-appeals.

It shall not under any circumstances be necessary for a respondent to give notice of motion by way of cross-appeal, but if a respondent intends upon the hearing of an appeal to contend that the decision of the court below should be varied, he shall, within the time specified in the next rule, or such time as may be prescribed by the special order of a judge, give notice of such intention to any parties who may be affected by such contention. The omission to give such notice shall not in any way interfere with the power of the court on the hearing of an appeal to treat the whole case as open, but may, in the discretion of the court, be ground for an adjournment of the appeal, or for special order as to costs.

The wording of this rule is substantially the same as that of order 58, rule 6, of the Supreme Court, 1883 (English). See Annual Practice, 1897, page 1064, and notes.

The giving "notice of motion by way of cross appeal," would not be a procedure applicable in the Supreme Court of Canada, where an appeal is not initiated by a notice of motion, as it is to the Court of Appeal in England. Order 58, rule 1, of the Supreme Court (English) says, "All appeals to the Court of Appeal shall be by way of rehearing, and shall be brought by notice of motion in a summary way, and no petition, case or other formal proceeding other than such notice of motion shall be necessary."

Rule 16 of the Court of Appeal for Ontario, the procedure in which court is substantially the same as in the Supreme Court of Canada, says: "A cross-appeal shall not under any circumstances be necessary, but if a respondent intends upon the hearing to contend that the decision should be varied, he shall, with his reasons against the appeal, give notice of such contention to any parties who may be affected by such contention, and such notice shall concisely state the grounds of such contention in the same manner as reasons of appeal are stated. The omission to give such notice shall not diminish the powers conferred by the Act upon the Court of Appeal, but may, in the discretion of the court, be ground for the adjournment of the appeal or for a special order as to costs."

The practice under Rule 61 would seem, to some extent at least, to differ from the practice of the Judicial Committee as to cross-appeals, and resemble rather the practice of the Court of Appeal in England. But where the rule may not be applicable, reference will still have to be made to the procedure of the Judicial Committee (see section 39 of the Supreme and Exchequer Courts Act), which is concisely stated in Lattey's Handy Book on Privy Council Practice as follows, page 58:

"Each party who feels aggrieved by a decree, should appeal from that portion he complains of. It often happens that both plaintiff and defendant in the court below appeal from the same decree, in which case there are cross-appeals. When there are cross-appeals an order is usually made to consolidate them. The application for an order to consolidate two appeals can be made by either party at any time, and must be on petition to Her Majesty, and has to be moved by counsel. This order is only made when the same parties who are appellants in one case are respondents in the other, and *vice versa*." See also Macpherson's Privy Council Practice, pages 91-93. See also *Hiddingh* v. *Denyssen*, 12 App. Cas. 107.

The Judicial Committee by the order of consolidation, will, if necessary, protect a cross-appellant against being prejudiced by the withdrawal of the appeal by the appellant, or by the dismissal of the appeal of the latter for want of prosecution, by giving liberty to prosecute the cross-appeal in such an event as a separate cause. See Macpherson, page 93.

Under the English Court of Appeal Practice, where an appellant withdraws his appeal, a respondent who has given notice under the rule is entitled to elect whether he will continue or withdraw from it. *The Beeswing*, 10 P. D. 18, and *Mason* v. *Cattley*, Law Notes, 1885, page 15.

The rule does not apply to a respondent who seeks to have an order varied on a point in which the appellant has no interest, but he must give a notice of appeal. *In re Cavender's Trusts*, 16 Ch. D. 270.

Where both an appeal and a cross-appeal were dismissed, the appellants were ordered to pay the costs after deducting such as had been occasioned by the notice given by the respondent.

The Lauretta, 4 P. D. 25. And where one of the respondents gave a cross-notice, affecting his co-respondent, the costs were apportioned. *Harrison* v. *Cornwall Minerals Railway Co.*, 18 Ch. D. 346. But where the costs cannot have been materially increased by the notice, they ought not to be apportioned. *Robinson* v. *Drakes*, 23 Ch. D. 98.

In the Supreme Court of Canada it was held where a respondent who had given notice of cross-appeal moved for leave to proceed with the cross-appeal notwithstanding that the original case had not been filed in time to be proceeded with at the then session, that if the cross-appellant desired to proceed with his cross-appeal he should have himself filed the original case; Dig. S. C. D. p. 680, No. 60. But if an appellant chooses to avail himself of his right to discontinue his appeal under section 51 of the Supreme and Exchequer Courts Act, what would be the position of a respondent who, intending to rely on the mode of procedure provided by rule 61, has failed to take a substantive appeal? He may not have even given the notice, for that, by rule 62, may be only a fifteen days' notice. It would seem safer where the respondent is greatly interested in having a variation of the judgment of the court below and not certain that the appellant will prosecute his appeal, to give notice of appeal and security, and then apply to consolidate the two appeals, following the practice of the Judicial Committee.

In *Pilon* v. *Brunet*, 5 Can. S. C. R. 319, a motion to quash an appeal on the ground that it should not have been brought as a substantive appeal, but as a cross-appeal, was dismissed. But the respondent, although successful in getting the judgment varied, was allowed only the costs of a cross-appeal taken under rule 61.

In the Court of Appeal for Ontario, where one of two defendants, both of whom had given notice of appeal and who joined in the appeal bond, gave notice of discontinuance, an objection on the part of the plaintiff who had given notice of cross-appeal to the prosecution of the appeal by the other defendant was overruled. See *Arscott* v. *Lilley*, 14 Ont. App. R. 283.

In *Stephens* v. *Chaussee*, 15 Can. S. C. R. 379, an action brought to recover damages for death caused by negligence, the Court of Queen's Bench for Lower Canada (appeal side) reduced the amount of the verdict. On the hearing in appeal before the Supreme Court counsel for respondent contended that the original verdict should be restored. But it was held that this could not be done, there being no cross-appeal.

In *City of Montreal* v. *Labelle*, 14 Can. S. C. R. 741, also an action brought to recover damages for death caused by negligence, a sum was awarded by the court below to plaintiffs by way of *solatium*. Counsel for respondent urged upon the Supreme Court at the hearing, that even if this were illegal, as the court intimated it was, being contrary to the law as laid down by the court in *C. P. R.* v. *Robinson*, 14 Can. S. C. R. 105, yet it was competent to the court to give the judgment which the court below ought to have given, and to award substantial damages other than for a *solatium*. But *held*, that if the respondent wished to urge such a contention he should have given notice by way of cross-appeal.

But in *Toronto Junction* v. *Christie*, 25 Can. S. C. R. 551, it was held that under the Ontario Judicature Act, R. S. O. [1887] c. 44, ss. 47 and 48, the Court of Appeal for Ontario has power to increase damages awarded to a respondent without a cross-appeal, and the Supreme Court has the like power under its Rule No. 61.

RULE 62.

[As amended by Rule 80.]

Notice to be given.

Subject to any special order which may be made, notice by a respondent under the last preceding rule shall be [15 days'] notice.

By Rule 61, the notice may be given within the time specified in this rule, " or such time as may be prescribed by the special order of a judge."

RULE 63.

[As amended by Rule 80.]

Factum in cross-appeals.

A respondent who gives a notice, pursuant to the two last preceding rules shall, before or within two days after he has served such notice, deposit a printed *factum* or points for argument in appeal with the registrar as hereinbefore provided as regards the principal appeal, and the parties upon whom such notice has been served shall within [one week] after service thereof upon them, deposit their printed *factum* or points with the registrar, and such *factum* or points shall be interchanged between the parties as hereinbefore provided as to principal appeal.

See Rules 23, 24, 25, 29 & 30.

TRANSLATIONS.

RULE 64.

Translation of factum.

Any judge may require that the *factum* or points for argument in appeal of any party shall be translated into the language with which such judge is most familiar, and in that case the judge shall direct the registrar to cause the same to be translated, and shall fix the number of copies of the translation to be printed, and the time within which the same shall be deposited with the registrar, and the party depositing such *factum* shall thereupon cause the same forthwith to be printed at his own expense and such party shall not be deemed to have deposited his *factum* until the required number of the printed copies of the translation shall have been deposited with the registrar.

RULE 65.

Translation of judgments and opinions of judges of court below.

Any judge may also require the registrar to cause the judgments and opinions of the judges in the court below to be translated, and in that case the judge shall fix the number of copies of the translation to be printed and the time within which they shall be deposited with the registrar, and such translation shall thereupon be printed at the expense of the appellant.

RULE 66.

Payment of money into court.

Any party directed by an order of the court or a judge to pay money into court must apply at the office of the registrar for a direction so to do, which direction must be taken to the Ottawa branch or agency of the Bank of Montreal, and the money there paid to the credit of the cause or matter, and after payment the receipt obtained from the bank must be filed at the registrar's office.

RULE 67.

Payment of money out of court.

If money is to be paid out of court, an order of the court or a judge must be obtained for that purpose, upon notice to the opposite party.

RULE 68.

How made.

Money ordered to be paid out of court is to be so paid upon the cheque of the registrar, counter-signed by a judge.

RULE 69.

Formal objections.

No proceeding in the said court shall be defeated by any formal objection.

Section 95 of the Supreme and Exchequer Courts Act, provides that:

"No informality in the heading or other formal requisites of any affidavit, declaration or affirmation, made or taken before any person under any provision of this or any other Act, shall be an objection to its reception in evidence in the Supreme Court or the Exchequer Court, if the court or judge before whom it is tendered thinks proper to receive it; and if the same is actually sworn to, declared or affirmed by the person making the same before any person duly authorized thereto, and is received in evidence, no such informality shall be set up to defeat an indictment for perjury."

RULE 70.

Extending or abridging time.

In any appeal or other proceeding the court or a judge may enlarge or abridge the time for doing any act, or taking any proceeding, upon such (if any) terms as the justice of the case may require. *Canadian Mutual v. Lee 34*

Substantially the same as the first part of English Order 64, Rule 7, which, however, says further, "and any such enlargement may be ordered although the application for the same is not made until after the expiration of the time appointed or allowed." Rule 70 has been frequently acted upon and applications entertained after the expiration of the time appointed or allowed.

The time for doing certain acts cannot be extended or abridged by consent, such as the time within which the case must be filed or case inscribed, under Rule 31, or the time within which the factums must be deposited under Rule 23. See Rule 42 and notes.

The rule only applies where a limited time is fixed for something to be done, and not where it is ordered that some one act must be done before another. *Pilcher* v. *Hinds,* 11 Ch. D. 905.

For cases showing grounds on which applications for enlargement of time may be granted or refused, see Annual Practice, 1897, pages 1115-6, and Wilson's Judicature Acts, 6th Ed., page 469. See also notes to similar rule in McLellan's Judicature Acts, pages 554 & 555; also *Ibid.* notes to Rule 317, c., p. 432; also *Lanydon* v. *Robinson*, 12 Ont. Pr. R. 139; *Re Gabourie*, 12 Ont. Pr. R. 252; *Platt* v. *G. T. R.*, 12 Ont. Pr. R. 380; see also notes to section 42, Supreme and Exchequer Courts Act, *ante*, p. 62.

RULE 71.

Registrar to keep necessary books.

The registrar is to keep in his office all appropriate books for recording the proceedings in all suits and matters in the said Supreme Court.

RULE 72.

Computation of time.

In all cases in which any particular number of days not expressed to be clear days, is prescribed by the foregoing rules, the same shall be reckoned exclusively of the first day and inclusively of the last day, unless such last day shall happen to fall on a Sunday, or a day appointed by the Governor-General for a public fast or thanksgiving, or any other legal holiday or non-juridical day, as provided by the statutes of the Dominion of Canada.

Days are clear days when expressed to be "at least" a certain number of days; *Reg.* v. *Shropshire Justices*, 8 A. & E. 173; Fisher's Digest, 8323; *Webster* v. *Lees*, 3 C. L. T. 504; *Rumohr* v. *Marx*, 18 C. L. J. 444, 19 C. L. J. 10, 3 C. L. T. 31.

In all cases expressed to be clear days, or where the term "at least" is added, both days are to be excluded.

The word "forthwith" in statutes and rules of court must be construed with reference to the objects of the provisions and the circumstances of the case. *Ex parte Lamb*, 19 Ch. D. 169.

The word "month" it is submitted, when used in the rules, means a calendar month, although there is no interpretation of the word in the rules themselves. By section 109 of the Supreme and Exchequer Courts Act, the rules, when not inconsistent with the express provisions of the Act, are to have force and effect as if enacted therein; and by section 7 of the Interpretation Act, paragraph 25, the expression "month" means a calendar month in every Act of the Parliament of Canada, unless the context otherwise requires.

A calendar month when not exactly coterminous with a given calendar month is from the day of the commencement, reckoning that day, to and inclusive of the day in the succeeding month immediately preceding the day corresponding to the day of the commencement. *Migotti* v. *Colvill*, 4 C. P. D. 233; *Freeman* v. *Read*, 11 W. R. 802; *Wright* v. *Leys*, 10 Ont. Pr. R. 354.

By the Interpretation Act, paragraph 26, the expression "holiday" includes Sundays, New Year's Day, the Epiphany, the Annunciation, Good Friday, the Ascension, *Corpus Christi*, St. Peter and St. Paul's Day, All Saints' Day, Conception Day, Easter Monday, Ash Wednesday, Christmas Day, the birthday or the day fixed by proclamation for the celebration of the birthday of the reigning sovereign, Dominion Day, and any day appointed by proclamation for a general fast or thanksgiving.

By 56 V. c. 30, the Annunciation, *Corpus Christi* and the Festival of St. Peter and St. Paul are no longer holidays.

And by paragraph 27 of The Interpretation Act: "If the time limited by any Act for any proceeding, or the doing of any thing under its provisions, expires or falls upon a holiday, the time so limited shall be extended to, and such thing may be done on, the day next following which is not a holiday."

RULE 73.

Adjournment if no quorum.

If it happens at any time that the number of judges necessary to constitute a quorum for the transaction of the business to be brought before the court is not present, the judge or judges then present may adjourn the sittings of the court to the next or some other day, and so on from day to day until a quorum shall be present.

See section 19 of the Supreme and Exchequer Courts Act, *ante* p. 17.

VACATIONS.

RULE 74.

Christmas vacation.

There shall be a vacation at Christmas, commencing on the 15th of December and ending on the 10th of January.

RULE 75.

Long vacation.

The long vacation shall comprise the months of July and August.

Chambers are not held in vacation: see Rule 83; and only applications of urgency should be made; Dig. S. C. D. p. 697, No. 131, *Ibid.* p. 706, No. 148. Where judgment was pronounced on the 30th June and security given on the 3rd July, and no steps taken to further prosecute the appeal till the 17th September following, the appellant's solicitor being under the impression that the time of vacation did not count, a motion to dismiss for want of prosecution was refused without costs, and further time given to appellant, up to the 10th October then next. *Herbert* v. *Donovan*, Dig. S. C. D. p. 706, No. 149.

The delay of 60 days for bringing an appeal prescribed by sec. 40 is not suspended during the vacation. *News Printing Co.* v. *Macrae*, 26 Can. S. C. R. 695.

In vacation, the registrar's office is open from 11 o'clock in the forenoon to 12 o'clock noon every juridical day.

RULE 76.
Interpretation.

In the preceding rules the term "a judge" means any judge of the said Supreme Court transacting business out of court.

By virtue of Rule 83, the term would include the registrar sitting in chambers for the transaction of business under that rule.

RULE 77.
Interpretation.

In the preceding rules the following words have the several meanings hereby assigned to them over and above their several ordinary meanings, unless there be something in the subject or context repugnant to such construction, that is to say:

(1) Words importing the singular number include the plural number, and words importing the plural number include the singular number.

(2) Words importing the masculine gender include females.

(3) The word "party" or "parties" includes a body politic or corporate, and also Her Majesty the Queen and Her Majesty's Attorney-General.

(4) The word "affidavit" includes affirmation.

(5) The words "the Act" mean "*The Supreme and Exchequer Courts Act.*"

SCHEDULE A.

NOTICE CALLING SPECIAL SESSION.

Dominion of }
  Canada.

The Supreme Court will hold a special session at the city of Ottawa on the day of , 18 for the purpose of hearing causes and disposing of such other business as may be brought before the court (or for the purpose of hearing election appeals, criminal appeals, or appeals in cases of *habeas corpus,* or for the purpose of giving judgments only, as the case may be).

By order of the Chief Justice, or by order of Mr. Justice

          (Signed)   R. C.
                                   Registrar.

Dated this   day of   , 18

SCHEDULE B.

FORM OF NOTICE OF HEARING APPEAL.

In the Supreme Court }
  of Canada.

J. A., appellant, *v.* A. B., respondent. Take notice that this appeal will be heard at the next session of the Court, to be held at the city of Ottawa on the day of , 18

    To   , appellant's solicitor or attorney, or appellant in person.

Dated this   day of   , 18

SCHEDULE C.

TARIFF OF FEES TO BE PAID TO THE REGISTRAR OF THE SUPREME COURT OF CANADA.

[As substituted by General Order 84 for the original schedule.]

On entering every appeal	$ 10 00
On entering every judgment, decree or order in the nature of a final judgment	10 00
On entering every other judgment, decree or order.	2 00
On filing every document or paper	10
Every search	25
Every appointment	50
Every enlargement of any appointment, or on application in Chambers	50

The foregoing items are not to apply to criminal appeals or appeals in matters of *habeas corpus* arising out of a criminal charge.

On sealing every writ (besides filing)	2 00
Amending every document, writ or other paper	50
Taxing every bill of costs (besides filing)	1 00
Every allocatur	1 00
Every fiat	50
Every reference, inquiry, examination or other special matter referred to the registrar, for every meeting not exceeding one hour	1 00
Every additional hour or less	1 00.
For every report made by the registrar upon such reference, etc.	1 00
Upon payment of money into court, or deposited with the registrar, every sum under $200.00	1 00
A percentage on money over $200.00 paid in at the rate of one per cent.	
Receipt for money	25
Comparing, examining and certifying transcript record on appeal to the Privy Council	10 00
Comparing any other document, paper or proceeding with the original on file or deposit in the registrar's office, per folio	2½
Every other certificate required from registrar	1 00

Copy of any document, paper or proceeding or any
    extract therefrom, per folio .... $ 10
Every affidavit, affirmation or oath administered by
    registrar   25
Every commission or order for examination of
    witnesses 1 50

All fees payable to the registrar are to be paid in stamps. See section 111, Supreme and Exchequer Courts Act, and Rule 56.
See Rule 57 and notes.

SCHEDULE D.

Referred to in Rule 57 of the Supreme Court of Canada.
See Rule 57 and notes.

TARIFF OF FEES.

To be taxed between party and party in the Supreme Court of Canada:

On special case required by section 29 [now section 44] of the Act when prepared and agreed upon by the parties to the cause, including attendance on the judge to settle the same, if necessary, to each party $25 00

By rule Easter Term, 1891, the Clerk of the Supreme Court of New Brunswick is entitled to a fee of 10 cents per fol., not to exceed $25 in all, on every paper in a case settled for appeal.

Notice of appeal 4 00
On consent to appeal directly to the Supreme Court from the court of original jurisdiction 3 00

See section 26, sub-section 2, *ante* p. 34.

Notice of giving security 2 00
Attendance on giving security 3 00
On motion to quash proceedings under section 37 [now section 59] according to the discretion of the registrar to 25 00
Subject to be increased by order of the court or of a judge ....
On *factums* in the discretion of the registrar to ... 50 00
Subject to be increased by order of the court or a judge ....

For engrossing for printer copy of case as settled, when such engrossed copy is necessarily and properly required, per folio of 100 words ... $ 10

For correcting and superintending printing, per 100 words 05

Amendment to the tariff by Rule 81.

On dismissal of appeal if case be not proceeded with, in the discretion of the registrar to 25 00

Subject to be increased by order of the court or a judge ....

Suggestions under sections 42, 43 & 44 [now 54, 55 & 56] including copy and service 2 50

Notice of intention to continue proceedings under section 45 [now section 57]................ 4 00

On depositing money under section 48 [now section 51 of the Dominion Controverted Elections Act] in controverted election cases 2 50

Notice of appeal in election cases limiting the appeal to special and defined questions under section 48 [now section 51 of the Dominion Controverted Elections Act] 6 00

Allowance to cover all fees to attorney and counsel for the hearing of the appeal, in the discretion of the registrar to 200 00

Subject to be increased by order of the court or a judge ....

On printing *factums,* the same fees as in printing the case.

Besides the registrar's fees, reasonable charges for postages and disbursements necessarily incurred in proceedings in appeal will be taxed by the taxing officer.

[Allowance to the duly entered agent in any appeal, in the discretion of the registrar, to......... 20 00]

Addition to tariff by Rule 82.
For forms of bills of costs, see *post*, Appendix, Nos. 11 and 12.

RULE 78.

Amendment to Rule 52.

Rule 52 was repealed by General Order No. 86, and this rule was necessarily repealed with it although not mentioned in the General Order.

RULE 79.

This rule provided for the late Mr. Duval, *precis* writer of the court, acting as registrar in the absence of Mr. Cassels, the registrar.

RULE 80.

Amendments to certain rules.

It is ordered:

1. That rule *eleven* be and the same is hereby amended by striking out the word "*immediately*" at the beginning of such rule.

2. That rule *fourteen* be and the same is hereby amended by striking out the words "*one month*" therein contained, and by inserting in lieu thereof the words "*fifteen days.*"

3. That rule *fifteen* be and the same is hereby amended by inserting after the words "*and mailing,*" where they occur in such rule, the words "*on the same day,*" and by striking out the words "*in sufficient time to reach him in due course of mail before the time required for service.*"

4. That rule *twenty-three* be and the same is hereby amended by striking out the words "*one month*" at the beginning of said rule, and by inserting in lieu thereof the words "*fifteen days.*"

5. That rule *thirty-one* be and the same is hereby amended by striking out the words "*one month,*" where they occur in said rule, and by inserting in lieu thereof the words "*fourteen days*"; and by adding at the end of said rule the words "*but no appeal shall be so inscribed which shall not have been filed twenty clear days before said first day of said session, without the leave of the court or a judge.*"

6. That rule *sixty-two* be and the same is hereby amended by striking out the words "*one month's*" and by inserting in lieu thereof the words "*fifteen days'.*"

7. That rule *sixty-three* be and the same is hereby amended by striking out the words "*two weeks*" where they occur in said rule, and by inserting in lieu thereof the words "*one week.*"

RULE 81.

Amendments to tariff of fees.

It is hereby ordered that Schedule D. annexed to the rules of the Supreme Court of Canada be amended as follows :—

Instead of the item: " Printed case, per folio of 100 words, including correcting, superintending printing and all necessary attendances, 30 cts.," the following allowances shall be taxed by the registrar :—

"For engrossing for printer, copy of cases as settled, when such engrossed copy is necessarily and properly required, per folio of 100 words, 10 cts.

"For correcting and superintending printing, per 100 words, 5 cts."

RULE 82.

Allowance to agents.

It is hereby ordered, that an allowance shall be taxed by the registrar to the duly entered agent in any appeal, in the discretion of the registrar, to $20.

See Rule 16 and notes for the duties of an agent.

GENERAL ORDER No. 83.

Jurisdiction of Registrar in Chambers.

Whereas by "The Supreme and Exchequer Courts Act," section 109, as amended by chapter 16 of the Act passed in the 51st year of Her Majesty's reign intituled "An Act to amend 'The Supreme and Exchequer Courts Act,' and to make better provision for the trial of claims against the Crown," it is provided that the judges of the Supreme Court, or any five of them, may, from time to time, make general rules and orders for certain purposes therein mentioned, and among others for empowering the registrar to do any such thing, and to transact any such business, and to exercise any such authority and jurisdiction in respect of the same, as by virtue of any statute or custom, or by the practice of the court, was at the time of the last mentioned Act, or might be thereafter, done, transacted, or exercised by a judge of the court sitting in chambers, and as might be specified in such rule or order. It is therefore ordered :—

1. That the Registrar of the Supreme Court of Canada be and is hereby empowered and required to do any such

thing, and to transact any such business, and to exercise any such authority and jurisdiction in respect of the same, as by virtue of any statute or custom, or by the practice of the court, was at the time of the passing of the said last mentioned Act, and is now, or may be hereafter, done, transacted, or exercised by a judge of the said court sitting in chambers, except in matters relating to:—

  (a) Granting writs of *habeas corpus* and adjudicating upon the return thereof.

  (b) Granting writs of *certiorari*.

2. In case any matter shall appear to the said registrar to be proper for the decision of a judge, the registrar may refer the same to a judge, and the judge may either dispose of the matter, or refer the same back to the registrar with such directions as he may think fit.

3. Every order or decision made or given by the said registrar sitting in chambers shall be as valid and binding on all parties concerned, as if the same had been made or given by a judge sitting in chambers.

4. All orders made by the registrar sitting in chambers are to be signed by the registrar.

5. Any person affected by any order or decision of the registrar may appeal therefrom to a judge of the Supreme Court in Chambers.

(a) Such appeal shall be by motion on notice setting forth the grounds of objection and served within four days after the decision complained of, and two clear days before the day fixed for hearing the same, or served within such other time as may be allowed by a judge of the said court or the registrar.

(b) The motion shall be made on the Monday appointed by the notice of motion, which shall be the first Monday after the expiry of the delays provided for by the foregoing sub-section, or so soon thereafter as the same can be heard by a judge, and shall be set down not later than the preceding Saturday in a book kept for that purpose in the registrar's office.

6. For the transaction of business under these rules, the registrar, unless absent from the city, or prevented by illness or other necessary cause, shall sit every juridical day, except during the vacations of the court, at 11 a.m., or such other hour as he may specify from time to time by notice posted in his office.

October 17th, 1887.

GENERAL ORDER No. 84.

Tariff of fees to be paid registrar.

It is hereby ordered that Schedule C, referred to in Rule 56, being the Tariff of Fees to be paid to the registrar by stamps, be and the same is repealed, and the following substituted therefor:—

Here follows Schedule C, as found on page 172.

GENERAL ORDER No. 85.

Writs to be issued out of Supreme Court—Practice relating thereto—Tariff of fees to sheriffs.

Whereas by section 107 of the Supreme and Exchequer Courts Act, as substituted for the original section of such Act by Schedule A of chapter 16 of the Act passed in the fifty-first year of Her Majesty's reign, intituled: "An Act to amend 'The Supreme and Exchequer Courts Act' and to make better provision for the trial of claims against the Crown," it is provided that "an order in the Supreme Court for payment of money, whether for costs or otherwise, may be enforced by such writs of execution as the court prescribes."

And whereas it is desirable to make rules prescribing the writs which shall be issued out of the said court from time to time and regulating the practice in relation thereto:

It is therefore ordered :—

1. A judgment or order for the payment of money against any party to an appeal other than the Crown may be enforced by writs of *fieri facias* against goods and *fieri facias* against land.

2. A judgment or order requiring any person to do any act other than the payment of money or to abstain from

doing anything may be enforced by writ of attachment or by committal.

3. Writs of *fieri facias* against goods and lands shall be executed according to the exigency thereof, and may be in the following form :—

CANADA,
Province of   } In the Supreme Court of Canada.
Between
    A. B., (Plaintiff, *or as the case may be*) Appellant.
AND
    C. D., (Defendant, *or as the case may be*) Respondent.

Victoria, by the grace of God of the United Kingdom of Great Britain and Ireland Queen, Defender of the Faith :

To the Sheriff of   , Greeting :

We command you that of the goods and chattels of C. D., in your bailiwick, you cause to be made the sum of
and also interest thereon at the rate of six per centum per annum, from the   day of   [*day of judgment or order, or day on which money directed to be paid, or day from which interest is directed by the order to run, as the case may be*], which said sum of money and interest were lately before us in our Supreme Court of Canada, in a certain action [or certain actions, *as the case may be*], wherein A. B. is plaintiff and appellant, and C. D. and others are defendants and respondents [or in a certain matter there depending, intituled, "In the matter of E. F.," *as the case may be*], by a judgment [or order, *as the case may be*], of our said court, bearing date the   day of   , adjudged [or ordered, *as the case may be*], to be paid by the said C. D. to A. B., together with certain costs in the said judgment [or order, *as the case may be*] mentioned, and which costs have been taxed and allowed, by the taxing officer of our court, at the sum of   , as appears by the certificate of the said taxing officer, dated the   day of   . And that of the goods and chattels of the said C. D. in your bailiwick, you further cause to be made the said sum of   [costs], together with interest thereon at the rate of   per centum per annum, from the

day of   [*the date of the certificate of taxation. The writ must be so moulded as to follow the substance of the judgment or order*], and that you have that money and interest before us in our said court immediately after the execution hereof, to be paid to the said A. B., in pursuance of the said judgment [or order, *as the case may be*], and in what manner you shall have executed this our writ, make appear to us in our said court immediately after the execution thereof, and have there then this writ.

Witness the Right Honourable Sir Samuel Henry Strong, Knight, Chief Justice of our Supreme Court of Canada, at Ottawa, this   day of   in the year of our Lord, one thousand eight hundred and   , and in the year of our reign.

4. Upon the return of the sheriff or other officer, as the case may be, of "lands or goods on hand for want of buyers" a writ of *venditioni exponas* may issue to compel the sale of the property seized. Such writ may be in the form following:—

CANADA,
   Province of   } In the Supreme Court of Canada.

Between

   A. B., (Plaintiff, *or as the case may be*) Appellant.

AND

   C. D., (Defendant, *or as the case may be*) Respondent.

Victoria, etc. (*as in the writ of fieri facias.*)

To the Sheriff of   , *Greeting:*

Whereas by our writ we lately commanded you that the goods and chattels of C. D. [*here recite the fieri facias to the end*], and on the   day of   you returned to us, at our Supreme Court of Canada aforesaid, that by virtue of the said writ to you directed, you had taken goods and chattels of the said C. D., to the value of the money and interest aforesaid, which said goods and chattels remained on your hands unsold for the want of buyers. Therefore we being desirous that the said A. B. should be satisfied his money and interest aforesaid, command you that you expose for sale and sell, or cause to be sold, the goods and chattels of the said C. D., by you, in form aforesaid, taken, and every part thereof for the best price that can be gotten for the same, and have the money arising from such sale before us in our said Supreme Court of Canada immediately after the execution hereof, to be paid to the said A. B. and have there then this writ.

Witness, etc. (conclude as in writ of *fieri facias*).

5. In the mode of selling lands and goods and of advertising the same for sale, the sheriff or other officer is, except in so far as the exigency of the writ otherwise requires, or as is otherwise provided by these orders, to follow the laws of his province applicable to the execution of similar writs issuing from the highest court or courts of original jurisdiction therein.

6. A writ of attachment shall be executed according to the exigency thereof.

7. No writ of attachment shall be issued without the order of the court or a judge. It may be in the form following:

Victoria, etc. (*as in the writ of fieri facias*).

To the Sheriff of   , Greeting:

We command you to attach   so as to have him before us in our Supreme Court of Canada, there to answer to us, as well touching a contempt which he it is alleged hath committed against us, as also such other matters as shall be then and there laid to his charge, and further to perform and abide such order as our said Court shall make in this behalf, and hereof fail not, and bring this writ with you.

Witness, etc. (*as in the writ of fieri facias*).

8. In these rules the term "writ of execution" shall include writs of *fieri facias* against goods and against lands, attachment and all subsequent writs that may issue for giving effect thereto. And the term "issuing execution against any party" shall mean the issuing of any such process against his person or property as shall be applicable to the case.

9. All writs shall be prepared in the office of the Attorney-General, or by the attorney or solicitor suing out the same, and the name and the address of the attorney or solicitor

suing out the same, and if issued through an agent the name and residence of the agent also, shall be endorsed on such writ, and every such writ shall before the issuing thereof be sealed at the office of the registrar and a *præcipe* therefor shall be left at the said office, and thereupon an entry of issuing such writ, together with the date of sealing and the name of the attorney or solicitor suing out the same, shall be made in a book to be kept in the registrar's office for that purpose, and all writs shall be tested of the day, month and year when issued. A *præcipe* for a writ may be in the following form:

CANADA,
    Province of   } In the Supreme Court of Canada.

    Between
    A. B., (Plaintiff, *or as the case may be*) Appellant.
              AND
    C. D., (Defendant, *or as the case may be*) Respondent.

Seal a writ of *fieri facias* directed to the sheriff of   to levy of the goods and chattels of C. D.   the sum of $ and interest thereon at the rate of   per centum per annum, from the   day of   [and $ costs, *or as the case may be, according to* the writ required].

    Judgment [or order] dated   day of
    [Taxing Master's certificate, dated   ].
    [X. Y., Solicitor for *party on whose behalf writ is to issue.*]

10. No writ of execution shall be issued without the production to the officer by whom the same shall be issued of the judgment or order upon which the execution is to issue, or an office copy thereof showing the date of entry. And the officer shall be satisfied that the proper time has elapsed to entitle the judgment creditor to execution.

11. In every case of execution the party entitled to execution may levy the interest, poundage fees and expenses of execution over and above the sum recovered.

12. Every writ of execution for the recovery of money shall be endorsed with a direction to the sheriff, or other officer to whom the writ is directed, to levy the money really

due and payable and sought to be recovered under the judgment or order, stating the amount, and also to levy interest thereon if sought to be recovered, at the rate of six per cent. per annum, from the time when the judgment or order was entered up.

13. A writ of execution, if unexecuted, shall remain in force for one year only from its issue, unless renewed in the manner hereinafter provided; but such writ may, at any time before its expiration, by leave of the court or a judge, be renewed by the party issuing it for one year from the date of such renewal, and so on from time to time during the continuance of the renewed writ, either by being marked in the margin with a memorandum signed by the registrar or acting registrar of the court, stating the date of the day, month, and year of such renewal, or by such party giving a written notice of renewal to the sheriff, signed by the party or his attorney, and having the like memorandum; and a writ of execution so renewed shall have effect, and be entitled to priority according to the time of the original delivery thereof.

14. The production of a writ of execution, or of the notice renewing the same, purporting to be marked with the memorandum in the last preceding rule mentioned, showing the same to have been renewed, shall be *prima facie* evidence of its having been so renewed.

15. As between the original parties to a judgment or order, execution may issue at any time within six years from the recovery of the judgment or making of the order.

16. Where six years have elapsed since the judgment or order, or any change has taken place by death or otherwise in the parties entitled or liable to execution, the party alleging himself to be entitled to execution may apply to the court or a judge for leave to issue execution accordingly. And the court or judge may, if satisfied that the party so applying is entitled to issue execution, make an order to that effect. And the court or judge may impose such terms as to costs or otherwise as shall seem just.

17. Any party against whom judgment has been given, or an order made, may apply to the court or a judge for a

stay of execution or other relief against such a judgment or order, and the court or judge may give such relief and upon such terms as may be just.

18. Any writ may at any time be amended by order of the court or judge upon such conditions and terms as to costs and otherwise as may be thought just, and any amendment of a writ may be declared by the order authorizing the same to have relation back to the date of its issue, or to any other date or time.

19. Sheriffs and coroners shall be entitled to the fees and poundage prescribed by the schedule following:

SCHEDULE.

Every warrant to execute any process directed to the sheriff, when given to a bailiff	$ 75
Service of process, each defendant (no fee for affidavit of services in such cases to be allowed unless service made or recognized by the sheriff)	1 50
Serving other papers beside mileage	75
For each *additional* party served	50
Receiving, filing, entering and endorsing all writs, notices or other papers, each	25
Return of all process and writs (except subpœna) notices or other papers	50
Every search, not being a party to a cause or his attorney	30
Certificate of result of such search, when required (a search for a writ against lands of a party, shall include sales under writ against same party and for the then last six months)	1 00

Poundage on executions and on writs in the nature of executions where the sum made shall not exceed $1,000, six per cent.

When the sum is over $1,000 and under $4,000, three per cent., when the sum is $4,000 and over, one and a half per cent., in addition to the poundage allowed up to $1,000, exclusive of mileage, for going to seize and sell; and except all disbursements necessarily incurred in the care and removal of the property.

Schedule taken on execution or other process, including copy to defendant, not exceeding five folios	$1 00
Each folio above five	10
Drawing advertisements when required by law to be published in the *Official Gazette* or other newspaper, or to be posted up in a court house or other place, and transmitting same in each suit	1 50
Every necessary notice of sale of goods, in each suit	75
Every notice of postponement of sale, in each suit	25
The sum actually disbursed for advertisements required by law to be inserted in the *Official Gazette* or other newspaper.	
Bringing up prisoner on attachment or *habeas corpus*, besides travelling expenses actually disbursed, per diem	6 00
Actual and necessary mileage from the court house to the place where service of any process, paper or proceeding is made, per mile	13
Removing or retaining property, reasonable and necessary disbursements and allowances to be made by the registrar.	
Drawing bond to secure goods seized, if prepared by sheriff	1 50
Every letter written (including copy) required by party or his attorney respecting writs or process, when postage prepaid	50
Drawing every affidavit when necessary and prepared by sheriff	25
For services not hereinbefore provided for, the registrar may tax and allow such fees as in his discretion may be reasonable.	

CORONERS.

The same fees shall be taxed and allowed to coroners for services rendered by them in the service, execution and return of process, as allowed to sheriffs for the same services as above specified.

20. Every order of a judge may be enforced in the same manner as an order of the court to the same effect, and it

shall in no case be necessary to make a judge's order a rule or order of the court before enforcing the same.

21. No execution can issue on a judgment or order against the Crown for the payment of money. Where in any appeal there may be a judgment or order against the Crown directing the payment of money for costs, or otherwise, the registrar may, on the application of the party entitled to the money, certify to the Minister of Finance, the tenor and purport of the judgment or order, and such certificate shall be by the registrar sent to or left at the office of the Minister of Finance.

22. Rules 59 and 60 of the Supreme Court of Canada are hereby repealed.

Ottawa, October 18th, 1888.

GENERAL ORDER No. 86.

Rules 51 and 52 are hereby repealed and the following substituted therefor:

In Controverted Election Appeals the party appellant shall obtain from the Registrar, upon payment of the usual charges therefor, a certified copy of the record, or of so much thereof as a Judge may direct to be printed, and shall have forty (40) copies of the said certified copy printed in the same form as hereinbefore provided for the *Case* in ordinary appeals, and immediately after the completion of the printing shall deliver to the Registrar thirty (30) of such printed copies, twenty-five (25) thereof for the use of the Court and its officers and five (5) thereof for the use of the respondent and to be handed by the Registrar to the respondent or his solicitor or booked agent upon application made therefor.

For printing in election appeals the same fees shall be allowed on taxation as for printing the *Case* in ordinary appeals.

GENERAL ORDER No. 87.

This order provided for the duties of the late Registrar being performed, in his absence or incapacity through illness, by C. H. Masters, Reporter of the Court, and became of no effect on the Registrar's death.

PART V.

APPENDIX.

PART V.

APPENDIX.

CONTENTS OF APPENDIX.

1. Extracts from the various statutes relating to the Jurisdiction of the County Courts of Nova Scotia, New Brunswick, British Columbia and Prince Edward Island.
2. 50-51 Victoria, Chapter 16, amending "The Supreme and Exchequer Courts Act."
3. 51 Victoria, Chapter 37, An Act further to amend "The Supreme and Exchequer Courts Act."
4. 52 Victoria, Chapter 37, An Act further to amend "The Supreme and Exchequer Courts Act."
5. 53 Victoria, Chapter 35, An Act to amend "The Exchequer Court Act."
6. 54-55 Victoria, Chapter 35, An Act respecting "The Supreme and Exchequer Courts."
7. 54-55 Victoria, Chapter 26, An Act further to amend "The Exchequer Court Act."
8. 56 Victoria, Chapter 29, An Act further to amend "The Supreme and Exchequer Courts Act."
9. 59 Victoria, Chapter 14, An Act further to amend "The Supreme and Exchequer Courts Act."
10. Revised Statutes of Ontario, Chapter 42, respecting the Supreme Court of Canada and the Exchequer Court of Canada.
11. Extracts from Imperial Statutes and Orders in Council, relating to the Practice in Appeals to the Judicial Committee of the Privy Council.
12. Forms.

I.

Extracts From the Various Statutes

RELATING TO THE

Jurisdiction of the County Courts

OF

Nova Scotia, New Brunswick, British Columbia and Prince Edward Island.

NOVA SCOTIA.

The jurisdiction of the County Courts of Nova Scotia is regulated by sections 16, 17 and 27, of the Revised Statutes of Nova Scotia, 5th Series, chapter 105.

16. The Court shall not have cognizance of any action—

1. Where the title to land is brought in question;
2. In which the validity of any devise, bequest or limitation is disputed, except as hereinafter provided;
3. For criminal conversation or seduction;
4. For breach of promise of marriage.

17. Subject to the exceptions in the last preceding section, the county court shall have original jurisdiction and hold pleas in all actions *ex contractu* where the debt or damage does not exceed four hundred dollars, and in case of debt where it is not less than twenty dollars; and in all other actions where the damages claimed do not exceed two hundred dollars; and in all actions on bail bonds to the sheriff in any case in the county courts, whatever may be the penalty or amount sought to be recovered; and in all actions against a sheriff, or any officer of the county court, for any nonfeasance or malfeasance in connection with any matter transacted in the county courts; but the jurisdiction hereby conferred is declared to be concurrent with that of the Supreme Court, except as to actions of debt or assumpsit, in which the cause of action is less than eighty dollars, which shall only be brought to the Supreme Court by way of appeal from the county court.

27. In all cases where the property or effects distrained or sought to be recovered, or the plaintiff's claim or demand, does not exceed four hundred dollars, and in case the title to land is not *bona fide* brought into question, an order for replevin may issue from the county court of any county wherein such property, goods or other effects have been distrained, taken or detained.

And section 91 of chapter 105 provides for appeals from the County Courts to the Supreme Court of Nova Scotia sitting *en banc*:

91. An appeal from every judgment, rule, order or decision of a judge of the county court, made during the trial of a cause in court or at chambers, except orders made in the exercise of such discretion as by law belongs to him, and also from his charge to the jury, and their verdict or findings, shall be to the Supreme Court sitting *in banco*.

NEW BRUNSWICK.

In New Brunswick the jurisdiction of the County Courts is now regulated by chapter 9 of 45 Victoria (1882), "An Act in amendment of chapter 51 of the Consolidated Statutes of County Courts," brought into force by proclamation on 1st June, 1882. (See *N. B. Royal Gazette*, 25th May, 1882.)

2 The courts shall not have cognizance of any action—

1. Where the title to land is brought in question; or,

2. In which the validity of any devise, bequest, or limitation is disputed.

3. Subject to the exceptions in the last preceding section the county courts shall have jurisdiction and hold plea in all personal actions of debt, covenant, and assumpsit, when the debt or damages do not exceed the sum of four hundred dollars and in all actions of tort when the damage claimed does not exceed two hundred dollars, and in actions on bonds given to the sheriffs or otherwise in any case in a county court, whatever may be the penalty or amount sought to be recovered; provided always, that the said court for the city and county of St. John shall not have or exercise any jurisdiction in any cause in which the city court of St. John or the town of Portland civil court have jurisdiction.

Section 7 provides that an action brought in the Supreme Court that might have been brought in the County Court shall carry only County Court costs.

An appeal is given from the County Courts to the Supreme Court of New Brunswick, by section 51 of the Consolidated Statutes of New Brunswick, chapter 51:

51. In case any party in a cause in any of the said courts is dissatisfied with the decision of the judge upon any point of law, or with the charge to the jury, or with the decision upon motion for a non-suit or new trial, or in arrest of judgment, or for judgment *non obstante veredicto*, he may appeal to the Supreme Court.

By section 38 of the Consolidated Statutes of New Brunswick, chapter 51, the jurisdiction of the County Courts in replevin is limited to where the value of the goods or other property or effects distrained, taken or detained, does not exceed the sum of $200.

BRITISH COLUMBIA.

In British Columbia the jurisdiction of the County Courts is regulated by 48 V. c. 7.

21. Except as is otherwise hereinafter provided, the county courts shall not have cognizance of any action—

1. For any malicious prosecution or any libel or slander.

2. For criminal conversation, or seduction, or breach of promise of marriage; or,

3. Against a justice of the peace, or for anything done by him in the execution of his office.

22. Subject to the exceptions contained in the last preceding section, the county courts shall have jurisdiction and hold plea—

1. In all personal actions where the debt or damages claimed consists of a balance not exceeding $1,000 after an admitted set-off of any debt or demand claimed or recoverable by the defendant from the plaintiff.

EJECTMENT.

23. In actions of ejectment where the yearly value of the premises or the rent payable in respect thereof does not exceed $300; Provided that such actions of ejectment shall be brought and proceeded with in the county court holden in the district where the lands, tenements or hereditaments are situate.

WHERE TITLE COMES IN QUESTION.

24. The county courts shall have jurisdiction to try any action in which the title to any corporeal or incorporeal hereditaments shall come in question where the value of the lands, tenements, or hereditaments in dispute do not exceed $1,000, or the rent payable in respect thereof shall not exceed the sum of $300 by the year.

REPLEVIN.

26. Notwithstanding anything to the contrary contained in any statute or law in force in the Province, the county courts shall have jurisdiction in all actions of replevin where the value of the goods or other property or effects distrained, taken or detained does not exceed $1,000, and the title to the land be not brought in question.

Section 28 provides for interpleader by the sheriff.

Sections 31 to 39 provide for the recovery of tenements by landlord when term has expired, or been determined by notice, or for non-payment of rent, when neither the value of the premises, nor the rent payable in respect thereof, shall have exceeded $500 by the year.

JURISDICTION IN PROBATE.

40. Each county court shall have jurisdiction concurrently with the Supreme Court in all questions relating to testacy or intestacy, and to the validity of wills of persons dying within the territorial limits of its district where the personal estate of the deceased shall not exceed $2,500; and shall have power to grant probate of wills and letters of administration of the personal estates and effects of persons dying within the territorial limits of its district, and to take order for the due passing of the accounts of the executors and administrators of such deceased persons, and for the proper custody of the personal estate and effects of such deceased persons, and for the delivery of the same to the person entitled thereto.

EQUITABLE JURISDICTION.

42. The said county courts shall also respectively have and exercise, concurrently with the Supreme Court of British Columbia, all the power and authority of the Supreme Court of British Columbia in the suits or matters hereinafter mentioned, that is to say:—

1. In all suits by creditors, legatees (whether specific, pecuniary, or residuary) devisees (whether in trust or otherwise), heirs at law or next of kin, in which the personal, or real, or personal and real estate against, or for an account or administration of which the demand may be made shall not exceed in amount or value the sum of two thousand five hundred dollars;

2. In all suits for the execution of trusts, in which the trust estate or fund shall not exceed in amount or value the sum of two thousand five hundred dollars;

3. In all suits for foreclosure or redemption, or for enforcing any charge or lien, where the mortgage, charge, or lien shall not exceed in amount the sum of two thousand five hundred dollars;

4. In all suits for specific performance of, or for the reforming, or delivering up, or cancelling of any agreement for the sale, purchase or lease of any property, where, in the case of a sale or purchase the purchase money, or in case of a lease the value of the property shall not exceed two thousand five hundred dollars;

5. In all proceedings under the Trustees' Relief Acts or under the Trustee Acts, or under any of such Acts in which the trust estate or fund to which the proceeding relates shall not exceed in amount or value the sum of two thousand five hundred dollars;

6. In all proceedings relating to the maintenance or advancement of infants, in which the property of the infant shall not exceed in amount or value the sum of two thousand five hundred dollars;

7. In all suits for the dissolution or winding up of any partnership, in which the whole property, stock and credits of such partnership shall not exceed in amount or value the sum of two thousand five hundred dollars;

8. In all suits relative to water rights claimed under any Act, Statute, or Ordinance of the Province, in which the value of the right in dispute shall not exceed two thousand five hundred dollars;

9. In all proceedings for orders in the nature of injunctions, where the same are requisite for granting relief in any matter in which jurisdiction is given by this Act to the county court;

10. In applications for the sale of real estate under the "Intestate Estate Ordinance, 1868," where the total value of the real estate of such intestate shall not exceed in amount two thousand five hundred dollars;

11. In applications under the "Destitute Orphans Act, 1877."

172. If any party in a suit or matter relating to equitable jurisdiction, conferred by section 42 of this Act, shall be dissatisfied with the determination or direction of a judge of a county court on any matter of law or equity, or on the admission or rejection of any evidence, such party may appeal from the same to the Supreme Court of British Columbia, two or more of the judges whereof, other than a judge whose decision is appealed from, shall sit as a court of appeal for that purpose.   *   *   *   *   *

173. If either party in any other cause or matter where the amount claimed exceeds $50, shall be dissatisfied with the determination or direction of a judge of a county court in point of law, or upon the admission or rejection of any evidence, such party may appeal from the same to the Supreme Court of British Columbia, two or more of the judges whereof, other than the judge whose decision is appealed from, shall sit as a court of appeal for that purpose.

PRINCE EDWARD ISLAND.

In Prince Edward Island the jurisdiction of the County Courts is regulated by 41 V. c. 12. The court has jurisdiction in all actions *ex contractu* and *ex delicto* where the debt or damages claimed do not exceed $150 (being below the amount required to give jurisdiction to the Supreme Court) and in actions on bail bonds given to a sheriff in any case in a County Court, or on any other bond given under this Act, whatever may be the penalty or amount sought to be recovered. (Section 17.)

II.

50-51, Victoria, Chapter 16

AMENDING

THE SUPREME AND EXCHEQUER COURTS ACT.

50-51 VICTORIA, CHAPTER 16.

An Act to amend "The Supreme and Exchequer Courts Act," and to make better provision for the trial of Claims against the Crown.

[Assented to 23rd June, 1887.]

See Audette's Manual of Exchequer Court Practice, p. 67, where this Act is set out in full. The schedules are at pp. 120 *et seq.*

III.

SUPREME COURT ACT, 1888.

51 VICTORIA, CHAPTER 37.

An Act further to amend " The Supreme and Exchequer Courts Act," Chapter one hundred and thirty-five of the Revised Statutes of Canada.

[Assented to 22nd May, 1888.]

HER Majesty, by and with the advice and consent of the Senate and House of Commons of Canada, enacts as follows :—

1. Section nineteen of " *The Supreme and Exchequer Courts Act,*" as amended by the Act passed in the session held in the fiftieth and fifty-first years of Her Majesty's reign, and chaptered sixteen, is hereby repealed and the following substituted therefor :

" **19.** Any five of the judges of the Supreme Court shall constitute a quorum, and may lawfully hold the court: Provided always, that it shall not be necessary for all the judges who have heard the argument in any case to be present in order to constitute the court for delivery of judgment in such case, but in the absence of any judge, from illness or any other cause, judgment may be delivered by a majority of the judges who were present at the hearing; and in such case it shall not be necessary for five judges to be present at the delivery of such judgment; and any judge who has heard the case and is absent at the delivery of judgment may hand his opinion in writing to any judge present at the delivery of judgment, to be read or announced in open court, and then to be left with the registrar or reporter of the court."

2. The paragraph lettered (*h*) added to section twenty-four of the Act first above cited by section fifty-seven and Schedule A of the Act secondly above cited, is hereby amended by inserting the words "British Columbia" after the words "New Brunswick" in the first line of the said paragraph.

3. The said section twenty-four is hereby further amended by adding the following at the end thereof :—

"(*i*) And also by leave of the court or a judge thereof from the decision of the Supreme Court of the North-west Territories, although the matter may not have originated in a superior court."

4. The registrar shall, under the supervision of the Minister of Justice, have the management and control of the library of the court, and the purchase of all the books therefor.

IV.

52 VICTORIA, CHAPTER 37.

An Act further to amend "The Supreme and Exchequer Courts Act."

[*Assented to 16th April, 1889.*]

HER Majesty, by and with the advice and consent of the Senate and House of Commons of Canada, enacts as follows:—

1. Section nineteen of "The Supreme and Exchequer Courts Act," as amended by the Act passed in the session held in the fifty-first year of Her Majesty's reign, and chaptered thirty-seven, is hereby amended by adding thereto the following sub-section, that is to say:—

"**2.** No judge against whose judgment an appeal is brought, or who took part in the trial of the cause or matter, or in the hearing in a court below, shall sit or take part in the hearing of or adjudication upon the proceedings in the Supreme Court; and in any cause or matter in which a judge is unable to sit or take part in consequence of the provisions of this sub-section, any four of the other judges of the Supreme Court shall constitute a quorum and may lawfully hold the court."

2. Section twenty-four of "The Supreme and Exchequer Courts Act," as amended by the Act passed in the session held in the fiftieth and fifty-first years of Her Majesty's reign, and chaptered sixteen, and by the Act passed in the fifty-first year of Her Majesty's reign and chaptered thirty-seven, is hereby further amended by adding thereto the following paragraphs, that is to say:—

"(j) From the judgment of any court of last resort, created under provincial legislation to adjudicate concerning the assessment of property for provincial or municipal purposes, in cases where the person or persons presiding over such court is or are appointed by provincial or municipal authority, and the judgment appealed from involves the assessment of property at a value of not less than ten thousand dollars.

"(k) From any judgment on appeal from a case or proceeding instituted in any Court of Probate in any of the Provinces of Canada, other than the Province of Quebec, save and except where the matter in controversy does not exceed five hundred dollars."

3. In the event of the death of a sole plaintiff or defendant before the judgment of the court in which an action or an appeal is pending is delivered, and if such judgment is against the deceased party, his legal representatives, on entering a suggestion of the death, shall be entitled to proceed with and prosecute an appeal in the Supreme Court of Canada, in the same manner as if they were the original parties to the suit.

4. In the event of the death of a sole plaintiff or sole defendant, before the judgment of the court in which an action or an appeal is pending is delivered, and if such judgment is

in favour of such deceased party, the other party, upon entering a suggestion of the death shall be entitled to prosecute an appeal to the Supreme Court of Canada against the legal representatives of such deceased party, provided that the time limited for appealing shall not run until such legal representatives are appointed.

5. In the list "Number one, Maritime Provinces cases," and "Number three, Ontario cases," mentioned in the fifty-eighth section of "The Supreme and Exchequer Courts Act," the court may, by order, direct in what order the cases from the different provinces shall be entered.

V.

53 VICTORIA, CHAPTER 35.

An Act to amend "The Exchequer Court Act."

[*Assented to 16th May, 1890.*]

See Exchequer Appeals, part III.

VI.

54-55 VICTORIA, CHAPTER 25.

An Act to amend Chapter one hundred and thirty-five of the Revised Statutes, intituled "An Act respecting the Supreme and Exchequer Courts."

[*Assented to 30th September, 1891.*]

HER Majesty, by and with the advice and consent of the Senate and House of Commons of Canada, enacts as follows :—

1. Section twenty of chapter one hundred and thirty-five of the Revised Statutes, intituled "*An Act respecting the*

Supreme and Exchequer Courts," is hereby amended by substituting for the word " fourth " in the fifth line thereof the word " first " : Provided that this amendment shall not apply to the October session of the present year.

2. Section twenty-four of the said Act is hereby further amended by striking out from the paragraph thereof lettered (*d*) the words " upon the ground that the judge has not ruled according to law," and by inserting in the paragraph thereof lettered (*g*), after the words "*habeas corpus,*" the words "*certiorari* or prohibition."

3. Sub-section two of section twenty-nine of the said Act is hereby repealed, and the following sub-sections are substituted therefor :—

" 2. Where the matter in controversy involves any such question, or relates to any such fee of office, duty, rent, revenue or sum of money payable to Her Majesty, or to any such title to lands or tenements, annual rents or such like matters or things where rights in the future might be bound, or amounts to or exceeds the sum or value of two thousand dollars, there shall be an appeal from judgments rendered in the said Province, although such action, suit, cause, matter or judicial proceeding may not have been originally instituted in the superior court :

" 3. Provided that such appeals shall lie only from the Court of Queen's Bench, or from the Superior Court in Review in cases where, and so long as, no appeal lies from the judgment of that court when it confirms the judgment rendered in the court appealed from, which by the law of the Province of Quebec are appealable to the Judicial Committee of the Privy Council:

" 4. Whenever the right to appeal is dependent upon the amount in dispute, such amount shall be understood to be that demanded and not that recovered, if they are different."

4. Section thirty-seven of the said Act is hereby repealed, and the following is substituted therefor :—

" 37. Important questions of law or fact touching provincial legislation, or the appellate jurisdiction as to educational matters vested in the Governor in Council by "*The British North America Act, 1867*," or by any other Act or law, or touching the constitutionality of any legislation of the Parliament of Canada, or touching any other matter with reference to which he sees fit to exercise this power, may be referred, by the Governor in Council, to the Supreme Court for hearing or consideration; and the court shall thereupon hear and consider the same:

"2. The court shall certify to the Governor in Council, for his information, its opinion on questions so referred, with the reasons therefor, which shall be given in like manner as in the case of a judgment upon an appeal to the said court; and any judge who differs from the opinion of the majority shall, in like manner, certify his opinion and his reasons:

"3. In case any such question relates to the constitutional validity of any Act which has heretofore been or shall hereafter be passed by the Legislature of any Province, or of any provision in any such Act, or in case, for any reason, the Government of any Province has any special interest in any such question, the Attorney-General of such Province, or, in the case of the North-west Territories, the Lieutenant-Governor thereof, shall be notified of the hearing, in order that he may be heard if he thinks fit:

"4. The court shall have power to direct that any person interested, or, where there is a class of persons interested, any one or more persons as representatives of such class, shall be notified of the hearing upon any reference under this section, and such persons shall be entitled to be heard thereon:

"5. The court may, in its discretion, request any counsel to argue the case as to any interest which is affected and as to which counsel does not appear, and the reasonable expenses thereby occasioned may be paid by the Minister of Finance and Receiver-General out of any moneys appropriated by Parliament for expenses of litigation:

"6. The opinion of the court upon any such reference, although advisory only, shall, for all purposes of appeal to

Her Majesty in Council, be treated as a final judgment of the said court between parties:

"7. General rules and orders with respect to matters coming within the jurisdiction of the court under this section may be made in the same manner and to the same extent as is provided by this Act, with respect to other matters within its jurisdiction, and, in particular, such rules and orders as to the judges making them seem best for the investigation of questions of fact involved in any reference thereunder."

5. Section fifty-eight of the said Act is further amended by adding thereto the following words: "Provided that, at the October sittings of the court, the appeals entered on part numbered two shall be first heard, then those entered on part numbered three and finally those entered on part numbered one."

VII.

54-55 VICTORIA, CHAPTER 26.

An Act further to amend "The Exchequer Court Act."

[Assented to 30th September, 1891.]

HER Majesty, by and with the advice and consent of the Senate and House of Commons of Canada, enacts as follows:—

1. This Act may be cited as *"The Exchequer Court Amendment Act, 1891."*

* * * * * *

8. The paragraph lettered (b) of sub-section one of section fifty-two of the said Act is hereby repealed, and the following substituted therefor:—

"(b) Relates to any fee of office, duty, rent, revenue or any sum of money payable to Her Majesty, or to any title to lands, tenements or annual rents, or to any question affecting any patent of invention, copyright, trade mark or industrial design, or to any matter or thing where rights in future might be bound."

9. Every appeal from the Exchequer Court set down for hearing before the Supreme Court of Canada shall be entered by the registrar on the list for the Province in which the action, matter or proceeding, the subject of the appeal, was tried or heard by the Exchequer Court,—or if such action, matter or proceeding was partly heard or tried in one Province and partly in another, then on such list as the registrar thinks most convenient for the parties to the appeal.

VIII.

56 VICTORIA, CHAPTER 29.

An Act further to amend "The Supreme and Exchequer Courts Act."

[*Assented to 1st April, 1893.*]

HER Majesty, by and with the advice and consent of the Senate and House of Commons of Canada, enacts as follows :—

1. Paragraph (*b*) of section twenty-nine of *The Supreme and Exchequer Courts Act*, chapter one hundred and thirty-five of the Revised Statutes, is hereby amended by substituting for the words "or such like," in the third line thereof, the words "and other."

2. The sub-section substituted for sub-section two of section twenty-nine of the said Act by section three of chapter twenty-five of the Statutes of 1891, is hereby amended by substituting for the words "such like," in the fourth line thereof, the word "other."

IX.

59 VICTORIA, CHAPTER 14.

An Act further to amend "The Supreme and Exchequer Courts Act."

[Assented to 23rd April, 1896.]

HER Majesty, by and with the advice and consent of the Senate and House of Commons of Canada, enacts as follows:—

1. Sub-section one of section four of *The Supreme and Exchequer Courts Act,* chapter one hundred and thirty-five of the Revised Statutes of Canada, is hereby repealed and the following substituted therefor:—

"**4.** 1. The Supreme Court shall consist of a Chief Justice, to be called the Chief Justice of Canada, and five puisné judges, who shall be appointed by the Governor in Council by letters patent under the Great Seal."

2. The following proviso is hereby added at the end of section nineteen of the said Act as amended by section one of chapter thirty-seven of the Acts of 1888, and by section one of chapter thirty-seven of the Acts of 1889:—

"Provided further that any four judges shall constitute a quorum and may lawfully hold the court in cases where the parties consent to be heard before a court so composed."

X.

SPECIAL JURISDICTION ACT, ONTARIO.

An Act respecting the Supreme Court of Canada and the Exchequer Court of Canada.

R. S. O. 1897, cap. 49.

HER Majesty, by and with the advice and consent of the Legislative Assembly of the Province of Ontario, enacts as follows:—

Supreme Court and Exchequer Court of Canada to have jurisdiction.

1. The Supreme Court of Canada and the Exchequer Court of Canada, or the Supreme Court of Canada alone, according to the provisions of the Act of the Parliament of Canada, known as "The Supreme and Exchequer Courts Act," shall have jurisdiction in the following cases:—

In controversies between Canada and Ontario.

1. Of controversies between the Dominion of Canada and this Province.

In controversies between Ontario and certain other Provinces.

2. Of controversies between any other Province of the Dominion, which may have passed an Act similar to this present Act, and this Province.

In certain cases involving the validity of Acts of Canada or Ontario.

3. Of suits, actions or proceedings in which the parties thereto, by their pleadings, shall have raised the question of the validity of an Act of the Parliament of Canada, or of an Act of the Legislature of this Province, when in the opinion of a judge of the court in which the same are pending such question is material; and in such case the said judge shall, at the request of the parties, and may without such request, if he thinks fit, order the case to be removed to the Supreme Court in order to the decision of such question. R. S. O. 1887, c. 42, s. 1.

Limitation of appeal to Supreme Court of Canada.

2. In any action respecting property or civil rights, whether for damages or for specific relief, no appeal shall lie to the Supreme Court of Canada without the special leave of such court, or of the Court of Appeal, unless the title to real estate or some interest therein, or the validity of a patent is affected; or unless the matter in controversy on the appeal exceeds the sum or value of $1,000 exclusive of costs, or unless the matter in question relates to the taking of an annual or other rent, customary or other duty, or fee, or a like demand of a general or public nature affecting future rights. 60 V. c. 14, s. 7.

Authority of Judges of the Court of Exchequer as to use of Court House, etc.

3. In case sittings of the court of Exchequer of Canada are appointed to be held in any city, town or place in which a court house is situated, the judge presiding at any such sittings shall have, in all respects, the same authority as a judge of the high court in regard to the use of the court house and other buildings or apartments set apart in the county for the administration of justice. R. S. O. 1887, c. 42, s. 3.

Provisions similar to these, except those in sec. 2, have been enacted in Nova Scotia, R. S. N. S. 5 Ser. c. 111; in New Brunswick, 51 V. c. 9; and in British Columbia, 44 V. c. 6.

XI.
PRIVY COUNCIL APPEALS.

Extracts From

IMPERIAL STATUTES AND ORDERS IN COUNCIL

RELATING TO

PRACTICE IN APPEALS TO THE JUDICIAL COMMITTEE OF THE PRIVY COUNCIL.

---

7 & 8 V. c. 69.

11. And be it enacted, that it shall and may be lawful for the said judicial committee to make any general rule or regulation, to be binding upon all courts in the colonies and other foreign settlements of the Crown, requiring the judges' notes of the evidence taken before such court on any cause appealed, and of the reasons given by the judges of such court or by any of them, for or against the judgment pronounced by such court; which notes of evidence and reasons shall by such court be transmitted to the clerk of the Privy Council within one calendar month next after the leave given by such court to prosecute any appeal to Her Majesty in Council, and such order of the said committee shall be binding upon all judges of such courts in the colonies or foreign settlements of the Crown.

Rule issued by the Judicial Committee, directing the judges of the Courts in the colonies and foreign settlements of the Crown to give their reasons in writing for the judgment appealed from, and to transmit the same with the record.

At the Council Chamber, Whitehall, the 12th Feb., 1845. By the Judicial Committee of the Privy Council.

Whereas, by an Act passed in the eighth year of Her Majesty's reign, intituled, etc., (here follows a recital of 7 & 8 V. c. 69, s. 11).

Now, therefore, the lords of the said Judicial Committee of the Privy Council are pleased to order, as it is hereby ordered, that when any appeal shall be prosecuted from any judgment of any court in the colonies or foreign settlements of the Crown, the reasons given by the judges of such court, or by any of such judges, for or against such judgment shall be, by the judge or judges of such court communicated in writing to the registrar of such court, or other officer whose duty it is to prepare and certify the transcript record of the proceedings in the cause, and that the same be by him transmitted in original to the clerk of Her Majesty's Privy Council, at the same time when the documents and proceedings proper to be laid before Her Majesty in Council upon the hearing of the appeal are transmitted.

Whereof the judges of all such courts in the colonies or foreign settlements of the Crown are to take notice, and govern themselves accordingly.

C. C. Greville.

AT THE COURT AT BUCKINGHAM PALACE.

The 13th day of June, 1853.

PRESENT:

THE QUEEN'S MOST EXCELLENT MAJESTY

HIS ROYAL HIGHNESS PRINCE ALBERT.

LORD PRESIDENT.	EARL OF ABERDEEN.
LORD STEWARD.	EARL OF CLARENDON.
DUKE OF NEWCASTLE.	VISCOUNT PALMERSTON.
DUKE OF WELLINGTON.	MR. HERBERT.
LORD CHAMBERLAIN.	SIR JAMES GRAHAM, BART.

WHEREAS there was this day read at the Board a Report from the Right Honourable the Lords of the Judicial Committee of the Privy Council, dated the 30th May last past, humbly setting forth that the Lords of the Judicial Committee have taken into consideration the practice of the Committee with a view to greater economy, despatch, and efficiency in the appellate jurisdiction of Her Majesty in Council, and that their Lordships have agreed humbly to report to Her Majesty that it is expedient that certain changes should be made in the existing practice in Appeals, and recommending that certain Rules and Regulations therein set forth should henceforth be observed, obeyed, and carried into execution, provided Her Majesty is pleased to approve the same:

Her Majesty, having taken the said Report into consideration, was pleased, by and with the advice of Her Privy Council, to approve thereof, and of the Rules and Regulations set forth therein, in the words following, videlicet:—

I. That, any former usage or practice of Her Majesty's Privy Council notwithstanding, an Appellant who shall succeed in obtaining a reversal or material alteration of any judgment, decree, or order appealed from, shall be entitled to recover the costs of the Appeal from the Respondent, except in cases in which the Lords of the Judicial Committee may think fit otherwise to direct.

II. That the Registrar or other proper officer having the custody of records in any Court or special jurisdiction from which an Appeal is brought to Her Majesty in Council be directed to send by post, with all possible despatch,

One certified copy of the transcript record in each cause to the Registrar of Her Majesty's Privy Council, Whitehall;

And that all such transcripts be registered in the Privy Council Office, with the date of their arrival, the names of the parties, and the date of the sentence appealed from;

And that such transcript be accompanied by a correct and complete index of all the papers, documents, and exhibits in the cause;

And that the Registrar of the Court appealed from, or other proper officer of such Court, be directed to omit from such transcript all merely formal documents, provided such omission be stated and certified in the said index of papers;

And that especial care be taken not to allow any document to be set forth more than once in such transcript;

And that no other certified copies of the record be transmitted to agents in England by or on behalf of the parties in the suit;

And that the fees and expenses incurred and paid for the preparation of such transcript be stated and certified upon it by the Registrar or other officer preparing the same.

III. That when the record of proceedings or evidence in the cause appealed has been printed or partly printed abroad, the Registrar or other proper officer of the Court from which the Appeal is brought

Shall be bound to send home the same in a printed form, either wholly or so far as the same may have been printed,

And that he do certify the same to be correct, on two copies, by signing his name on every printed sheet,

And by affixing the seal, if any, of the Court appealed from to these copies, with the sanction of the Court.

And that in all cases in which the parties in Appeals shall think fit to have the proceedings printed abroad, they shall be at liberty to do so, provided they cause fifty copies of the same to be printed in folio,*

And transmitted, at their expense, to the Registrar of the Privy Council,

Two of which printed copies shall be certified as above by the officers of the Court appealed from;

And in this case no further expense for copying or printing the record will be incurred or allowed in England.

IV. That on the arrival of a written transcript of appeal at the Privy Council Office, Whitehall, the Appellant or the agent of the Appellant prosecuting the same shall be at liberty

To call on the Registrar of the Privy Council to cause it, or such part thereof as may be necessary for the hearing of the case,

And likewise all such parts thereof as the Respondent or his agent may require, to be printed by Her Majesty's Printer,

Or by any other printer on the same terms,

The Appellant or his agent engaging to pay the cost of preparing a copy for the printer at a rate not exceeding one shilling per brief sheet [now three half-pence per folio],

And likewise the cost of printing such record or appendix,

And that one hundred copies [now seventy-five] of the same be struck off, whereof thirty [now twenty] copies are to be delivered to the agents on each side, and forty [now thirty-five] kept for the use of the Judicial Committee;

And that no other fees for solicitors' copies of the transcript, or for drawing the joint appendix, be henceforth allowed,

The solicitors on both sides being allowed to have access to the original papers at the Council Office,

And to extract or cause to be extracted and copied such parts thereof as are necessary for the preparation of the petition of appeal, at the stationer's charge not exceeding one shilling per brief sheet [now three half-pence per folio].

V. That a certain time be fixed within which it shall be the duty of the Appellant or his agent to make such application for the printing of the transcript, and that such time be within the space of six calendar months from the arrival of the transcript and the registration thereof in all matters brought by appeal from Her Majesty's colonies and plantations east of the Cape of Good Hope, or from the territories of the East India Company,

And within the space of three months in all matters brought by appeal from any other part of Her Majesty's dominions abroad;

And that in default of the Appellant or his agent taking effectual steps for the prosecution of the Appeal within such time or times respectively, the Appeal shall stand dismissed without further order,

And that a report of the same be made to the Judicial Committee by the Registrar of the Privy Council at their Lordships' next sitting.

VI. That whenever it shall be found that the decision of a matter on appeal is likely to turn exclusively on a question of law, the agents of the parties, with the sanction of the Registrar of the Privy Council, may submit such question of law to the Lords of the Judicial Committee in the form of a special case, and print such parts only of the transcript as may be necessary for the discussion of the same; provided that nothing herein contained shall in any way bar or prevent the Lords of the Judicial Committee from ordering the full discussion of the whole case, if they shall so think fit; and that in order to promote such arrangements and simplification of the matter in dispute, the Registrar of the Privy Council may call the agents of the parties before him, and having heard them, and examined the transcript, may report to the Committee as to the nature of the proceedings.

And Her Majesty is further pleased to order, and it is hereby ordered, that the foregoing Rules and Regulations be punctually observed, obeyed, and carried into execution in all Appeals or petitions and complaints in the nature of Appeals brought to Her Majesty, or to Her Heirs and successors, in Council, from Her Majesty's colonies and plantations abroad, and from the Channel Islands or the Isle of Man, and from the territories of the East India Company, whether the same be from courts of justice or from special jurisdictions, other than Appeals from Her Majesty's Courts of Vice-Admiralty, to which the said Rules are not to be applied.

Whereof the Judges and Officers of Her Majesty's Courts of Justice abroad, and the Judges and Officers of the Superior Courts of the East India Company, and all other persons whom it may concern, are to take notice, and govern themselves accordingly.

W. L. BATHURST.

ORDERS
OF
HER MAJESTY IN COUNCIL.

ESTABLISHING CERTAIN RULES AND REGULATIONS IN APPEALS.

AT THE COURT AT WINDSOR,

The 6th day of March, 1896.

PRESENT:

THE QUEEN'S MOST EXCELLENT MAJESTY IN COUNCIL.

WHEREAS there was this day read at the Board a Representation from the Lords of the Judicial Committee of the Privy Council, in the words following, viz.:—

"The Lords of the Judicial Committee of the Privy Council have the honour, with their humble duty to Your Majesty, to represent that it would be advisable that the

Rules, established by Your Majesty's Order in Council of the 31st March, 1870, should be amended; and their Lordships beg leave to recommend that Your Majesty will be graciously pleased to approve the Rules set forth in the Schedule hereunto annexed, and to declare that the said Rules shall be observed by all Proctors, Solicitors, Attorneys, Agents, or other persons employed in the conduct of Appeals, Petitions, or other matters pending before Her Majesty in Council."

Her Majesty, having taken the said Representation and the Schedule of Rules annexed into consideration, was pleased, by and with the advice of Her Privy Council, to approve thereof, and to order, as it is hereby ordered, that the said Rules (copy of which is hereunto annexed) be punctually observed, obeyed, and carried into execution, in lieu of the Rules established by the Order of Her Majesty in Council of the 31st March, 1870.

C. L. PEEL.

SCHEDULE ANNEXED TO FOREGOING ORDER.

RULES.

I. Every Proctor, Solicitor, or Agent admitted to practise before Her Majesty's Most Honourable Privy Council, or any of the Committees thereof, shall subscribe a Declaration to be enrolled in the Privy Council Office, engaging to observe and obey the Rules, Regulations, Orders, and Practice of the Privy Council; and also to pay and discharge, from time to time, when the same shall be demanded, all fees or charges due and payable upon any matter pending before Her Majesty in Council; and no person shall be admitted to practise, or allowed to continue to practise, before the Privy Council, without having subscribed such Declaration in the following terms:—

FORM OF DECLARATION.

WE, the Undersigned, do hereby declare, that we desire and intend to practise as Solicitors or Agents in Appeals and other matters pending before Her Majesty in Council; and we severally and respectively do hereby engage to observe, submit to, perform, and abide by all and every the Orders, Rules, Regulations, and Practice of Her Majesty's Most Honourable Privy Council and the Committees thereof now in force, or hereafter from time to time to be made; and also to pay and discharge, from time to time, when the same shall be demanded, all fees, charges, and sums of money due and payable in respect of any Appeal, Petition, or other matter in and upon which we shall severally and respectively appear as such Solicitors or Agents.

II. Every Proctor or Solicitor practising in London shall be allowed to subscribe the foregoing Declaration, and to practise in the Privy Council, upon the production of his Certificate for the current year; and no fee shall be payable by him on the enrolment of his signature to the foregoing Declaration.

III. Persons not being certificated London Solicitors, but having been duly admitted to practise as Solicitors by the High Courts of Judicature in England and Ireland, or by the Court of Sessions in Scotland, or by the High Courts in any of Her Majesty's Dominions respectively, may apply, by petition to the Lords of the Committee of the Privy Council, for leave to be admitted to practise before such Committee; and such persons may, if the Lords of the Committee please, be admitted to practise by an Order of their Lordships, for such periods and under such conditions as their Lordships are pleased to direct.

IV. Any Proctor, Solicitor, Agent, or other person practising before the Privy Council, who shall wilfully act in violation of the Rules and Practice of the Privy Council, or of any rules prescribed by the authority of Her Majesty, or of the Lords of the Council, or who shall misconduct himself in prosecuting proceedings before the Privy Council, or any Committee thereof, or who shall refuse or omit to pay the Council Office fees or charges payable from him when demanded, shall be liable to an absolute or temporary prohibition to practise before the Privy Council, by the authority of the Lords of the Judicial Committee of the Privy Council, upon cause shown at their Lordships' Bar.

I. All Cases, Records and other Proceedings in Appeals, or other matters pending before Committees of the Privy Council, are henceforth to be printed in the form known as Demy Quarto.

II. The size of the paper used is to be such that the sheet, when folded, will be eleven inches in height and eight inches and a half in width.

III. The type to be used in the text is to be Pica type, but Long Primer is to be used in printing accounts, tabular matter, and notes.

IV. The number of lines in each page of Pica type is to be forty-seven, each line being five inches and three-quarters or 146 millimetres in length.

FORMS

XII.

FORMS.

1. Notice of Appeal.
2. Bond for Security for Costs.
3. Affidavit of Execution.
4. Affidavit of Justification.
5. Order for payment of money into Court as security for costs.
6. Certificate of Settlement of Case.
7. Appointment of Agent.
8. Judgment allowing Appeal.
9. Judgment dismissing Appeal.
10. Order made in Chambers.
11. Appellant's Bill of Costs.
12. Respondent's Bill of Costs.
13. Affidavit of Disbursements.
14. Sheriff's Account.

1. NOTICE OF APPEAL.

IN THE COURT OF APPEAL FOR ONTARIO.

(or as the case may be, giving the style of the Court in which the judgment to be appealed from has been rendered.)

Between
      A. B., Plaintiff (appellant or respondent),
               AND
      C. D., Defendant (respondent or appellant).
         (or as the case may require.)

Take notice, that A. B., the above named plaintiff, hereby appeals from the (judgment, decree, rule, order, or decision) pronounced (or pronounced and entered) in this cause (or matter) by this court (or by Mr. Justice ————) on the day of , 18 , whereby *(as the case may be.)*

The above form, altered to suit the circumstances of each particular case, would be applicable to most cases, but care should be taken to consider the wording of the section or rule requiring notice of appeal to be given and to vary the notice accordingly. For instance, in giving notice of intention to appeal, under section 53 of chapter 16 of 50-51 Victoria, from the decision of the Exchequer Court (see *ante* p. 108), the notice should state "that the Crown is dissatisfied with such decision, and intends to appeal against the same."

And notice of appeal must not be confounded with the notice of hearing required after an appeal is set down for hearing in the Supreme Court (see rules 13, 14 and 15, *ante* pp. 137-8); nor with the notice to be given in Exchequer appeals under section 51 of chapter 16 of 50-51 Victoria, a notice additional to that required by section 53 (see *ante* p. 106); nor with the notice to be given in election appeals, under sub-section 3 of section 51 of the Dominion Controverted Elections Act (see *ante* p. 114). These notices are given after the appeal has been set down for hearing in the Supreme Court of Canada and should be entitled in that court and the style of cause should be the style in that court, and by them the appeal may be limited to any special and defined question or questions.

2. BOND FOR SECURITY OF COSTS.

(To be given under section 46 of the Supreme and Exchequer Courts Act. See *ante* p. 67.)

Know all men by these presents, that we A. B., of the   of   , in the county of   , and Province of   , C. D. of the same place   , and E. F. of the same place   , are jointly and severally held, and jointly bound unto G. H., in the penal sum of $500, for which payment well and truly to be made we bind ourselves and each of us himself, our and each of our heirs, executors and administrators firmly by these presents.

Dated this   day of   , A.D. 18   .

Whereas a certain action was brought in the Queen's Bench Division of the High Court of Justice for Ontario by the said A. B., plaintiff, against the said G. H., defendant. And whereas judgment was given in the said Court against the said A. B., who appealed from the said judgment to the Court of Appeal for Ontario. And whereas judgment was given in the said action in the said last mentioned Court on the   day of   , A.D. 1888. And whereas the said A. B. complains that in giving of the last mentioned judgment in the said action upon the said appeal manifest error hath intervened, wherefore the said A. B. desires to appeal from the said judgment of the Court of Appeal for Ontario to the Supreme Court of Canada.

Now the condition of this obligation is such, that if the said A. B. shall effectually prosecute his said appeal and pay such costs and damages as may be awarded against him by the Supreme Court of Canada, then this obligation shall be void, otherwise to remain in full force and effect.

Signed sealed and ⎫	A. B. (SEAL.)
delivered in presence ⎬	C. D. (SEAL.)
of ⎭	E. F. (SEAL.)

If, during the appeal, an appellant is added or substituted for the original appellant, either a new bond should be filed or an undertaking by the sureties to be bound by the bond, notwithstanding the change of parties.

---

3. AFFIDAVIT OF EXECUTION.

Province of ⎫
County of ⎬
ToWit: ⎭

I, X. Y., of the   of   in the County of   , and Province of   , (*occupation*), make oath and say:

1. That I was personally present and did see the within instrument duly signed, sealed and executed by A. B., C. D. and E. F., three of the parties thereto.

2. That the said instrument was executed at

3. That I know the said parties.

4. That I am a subscribing witness to the said instrument.

Sworn before me at ⎫
the   of   in ⎥
the county of   and ⎬   X. Y.
Province of   this day ⎥
of   A.D. 18 ⎭

(Signed)
        A Commissioner, etc.

222 FORMS.

4. AFFIDAVIT OF JUSTIFICATION BY SURETIES.

I, C. D., of the　　　　of　　　　, in the County of　　　　, and Province of　　　　, make oath and say, That I am a resident inhabitant of the Province of　　　　, and am a freeholder in the　　　　of　　　　aforesaid, and that I am worth the sum of $1,000, over and above what will pay all my debts.

And I, E. F., of the　　　　of　　　　in the County of　　　　, and the Province of　　　　, make oath and say, That I am a resident inhabitant of the said Province of　　　　, and am a freeholder in the　　　　of　　　　aforesaid, and that I am worth the sum of $1,000, over and above what will pay all my debts.

　　　　　　　　　(Signed)　　　　C. D.
　　　　　　　　　　　　　　　　　E. F.

The above named deponents, C. D. and E. F., were severally sworn before me in the　　of　　in the County of　　, and Province of　　, this　　day of　　, A.D. 18　.

(Signed)
　　　　　A Commissioner, etc.

The affidavit should be entitled in the court in which the security is given.

---

5. ORDER FOR PAYMENT OF MONEY INTO COURT FOR SECURITY FOR COSTS.

IN THE SUPREME COURT OF CANADA.

On appeal from the Court of Appeal for Ontario (or as the case may be).

　　　　　　　the　　day of　　, A.D. 18　.

The Registrar in Chambers (or The Honourable Mr. Justice　　in Chambers).

Between

  A. B., (defendant or plaintiff) Appellant ;
    AND
  C. D., (plaintiff or defendant) Respondent.

Upon the application of the above named appellants, and upon hearing what was alleged by counsel for all parties, it is ordered that the sum of five hundred dollars paid into the Bank of Montreal as appears by deposit certificate No. , duly filed as security, that the appellants will effectually prosecute their appeal from the judgment of the Court of (as the case may be), dated the day of , A.D. 18 , and will pay such costs and damages as may be awarded against them by this Court, be and the same is hereby allowed as good and sufficient security.

    (Signed) R. C.
          Registrar.

6. CERTIFICATE OF SETTLEMENT OF CASE.

I, the undersigned Registrar (or Prothonotary, *or* clerk) of the *(name of court)* do hereby certify that the foregoing printed document from page to page , inclusive, is the case stated by the parties (*or* settled by the Honourable Mr. Justice , one of the Judges of the said Court) pursuant to section 44 of the Supreme and Exchequer Courts Act and the rules of the Supreme Court of Canada, in an appeal to the said Supreme Court of Canada, in a certain case pending in the said *(name of court)* between A. B., plaintiff (appellant) and C. D., defendant (respondent).

(If a printed copy of the Bond given as security for costs forms part of the case, the certificate may continue as follows:)

And I do further certify that the said A. B. has given proper security to the satisfaction of the said the Honourable Mr. Justice , as required by the 46th section of the Supreme and Exchequer Courts Act, such security being a bond to the amount of $500, a printed copy of which

224 FORMS.

is to be found on pages   of the said printed document hereto annexed.

In testimony whereof I have hereto subscribed my name and affixed the seal of the said (*name of court*) this (*date*).

See section 44 of the Supreme and Exchequer Courts Act, *ante* p. 64, and rules 1, 2, 3 and 4, *ante* pp. 130, 131. See also section 46, *ante* p. 67, and rule 6, *ante* p. 133.

7. APPOINTMENT OF AGENT.

See Rule 16, *ante* p. 138.

I,   , of the City of   , in the Province of   , practising as an attorney and solicitor in the Superior Courts of the said Province hereby authorize   , of the City of Ottawa, Esquire, to enter his name as my agent, in the agents' book of the Supreme Court of Canada, and to act as such agent in all appeals to that court in which I may be concerned as attorney or solicitor, (*or, if the authority is to be limited*, in the following appeal, viz.,   ) (*date*)

8. JUDGMENT ALLOWING APPEAL.

In the Supreme Court of Canada.
    day the   day of   , A.D. 18 .

Present:

THE RIGHT HONOURABLE SIR HENRY STRONG, KNIGHT, CHIEF JUSTICE.
THE HONOURABLE MR. JUSTICE TASCHEREAU.
  "   "   MR. JUSTICE GWYNNE.
  "   "   MR. JUSTICE SEDGEWICK.
  "   "   MR. JUSTICE KING.
  "   "   MR. JUSTICE GIROUARD.

(*If any Judge has been absent when judgment was rendered* add THE HONOURABLE MR. JUSTICE   being absent, his judgment was announced by THE HONOURABLE THE CHIEF JUSTICE, *or* MR. JUSTICE   , pursuant to the statute in that behalf).

Between A. B. (plaintiff), Appellant;

AND

C. D. (defendant), Respondent.

The appeal of the above named appellant from the judgment of the Court of Queen's Bench for Lower Canada (appeal side) (*or* of the Court of Appeal for Ontario, *or as the case may be*) pronounced in the above cause on the   day of   in the year of our Lord   , reversing the judgment of the Superior Court for Lower Canada sitting in and for the District of   , (*or* of the Queen's Bench Division of the High Court of Justice for Ontario, *or as the case may be*) rendered in the said cause on the   day of   in the year of our Lord   , having come on to be heard before this court on the   day of   in the year of our Lord   , in the presence of counsel as well for the appellant as the respondent, whereupon and upon hearing what was alleged by counsel aforesaid, this court was pleased to direct that the said appeal should stand over for judgment, and the same coming on this day for judgment, this court did order and adjudge* that the said appeal should be and the same was allowed, that the said judgment of the Court of Queen's Bench for Lower Canada (appeal side) (*or* of the said Court of Appeal for Ontario, *or as the case may be*) should be and the same was reversed and set aside, and that the said judgment of the Superior Court for Lower Canada sitting in and for the District of   (*or* of the Queen's Bench Division of the High Court of Justice for Ontario, *or as the case may be*) should be and the same was restored.

And this court did further order and adjudge that the said respondent should and do pay to the said appellant the costs incurred by the said appellant as well in the said Court of Queen's Bench for Lower Canada (appeal side) (*or in* the said Court of Appeal for Ontario, *or as the case may be*) as in this court.

(*In appeals from the Province of Quebec add :* " the said costs *distraits* in favour of Messrs. A. & B., attorneys for the said appellant.")

9. JUDGMENT DISMISSING APPEAL.

(Formal parts as in preceding down to * then proceed as follows :)

that the said judgment of the Court of Queen's Bench for Lower Canada (appeal side) (*or, of the Court of Appeal for Ontario, or as the case may be*) should be and the same was affirmed, and that the said appeal should be and the same was dismissed with costs to be paid by the said appellant to the said respondent.

(*Conclude with distraction of costs as in preceding form.*)

---

10. ORDER MADE IN CHAMBERS.

In the Supreme Court of Canada
the   day of   , 18 .

The Honourable Mr. Justice (*or* The Registrar) in Chambers.

      Between   A. B. (plaintiff), Appellant;
                    AND
                 C. D. (defendant), Respondent.

Upon hearing   , and upon reading the affidavit of   filed the   day of   18 (and   )

It is ordered (*here insert the order made*), and that the costs of this application, which are hereby fixed at the sum of   be paid by the said   to the said

---

11. BILL OF APPELLANT'S COSTS.

In the Supreme Court of Canada,
    Between   Appellant,
                 and
                                    Respondent.

        BILL OF APPELLANT'S COSTS.   FEES. PAYMENTS.

Notice of appeal .... $ 4 00
[In election appeals, when notice limits
    appeal ....   6 00]

Bill of Appellant's Costs.	Fees.	Payments.
Notice of giving security	2 00	
Attendance on giving security and paid..	3 00	
Fee on special case	25 00	
[Not taxable in election appeals.]		
Engrossing and superintending printing of special case, fos. at 15 cents per folio		
[Not taxable in election appeals.]		
Paid printer as per affidavit		
Paid clerk on transmission, etc., of original case, or record in an election appeal		
Paid forwarding copies of case		
Paid filing case with registrar		$10 00
Engrossing and superintending printing of factum, fos. at 15 cents per folio		
Paid printer as per affidavit............		
Fee on factum [in the discretion of registrar to]		50 00
Paid, search and inscribing appeal		$ 35
Allowance to cover fees to counsel and solicitor on hearing [in the discretion of the registrar, to]	$200 00	
Paid postages, telegrams, etc.		
Allowance on account of agent's fees under Rule 82 [in the discretion of registrar, to]		20 00
Paid, search for particulars, to draft minutes		25
Paid entry of judgment................		10 00
Paid taxation and appointment		1 50
Allocatur		1 00
Paid filings [10 cents on each filing]		
Paid certified copy of judgment .... [$1.00, and 10 cents a folio.]		
Registrar's postage		

BILL OF APPELLANT'S COSTS.	FEES.	PAYMENTS
Total fees ....$	$	
Total disbursements		
Taxed off		
Taxed at		

12. BILL OF RESPONDENT'S COSTS.

In the Supreme Court of Canada,

Between   Appellant,

and

Respondent.

BILL OF RESPONDENT'S COSTS.	FEES.	PAYMENTS.
Attendance on giving security	$ 3 00	
[Not taxable in election appeals.]		
Fee on special case	$25 00	
[Not taxable in election appeals.]		
Engrossing and superintending printing of factum, fos. at 15 cents per folio		
Paid printer as per affidavit		
Fee on factum [in the discretion of registrar, to]	50 00	
Allowance to cover fees to counsel and solicitor on hearing [in the discretion of registrar, to]	200 00	
Paid postages, telegrams, etc.		
Allowance on account of agent's fees under Rule 82 [in discretion of registrar to]		$20 00
Paid search for particulars, to draft minutes		25
Paid entry of judgment		10 00
Paid taxation and appointment		1 50
Allocatur		1 00
Paid filings [10 cents on each filing]		
Paid certified copy of judgment		
[$1.00, and 10 cents for each folio.]		
Registrar's postage		

Bill of Respondent's Costs.	Fees.	Payments.
Total fees	$	$
Total disbursements		
Taxed off...................		
Taxed at		

13. AFFIDAVIT OF DISBURSEMENT.

In the Supreme Court of Canada,

Between   Appellant,

                     and

                                               Respondent.

I,   of the   of   in the Province of   (*occupation*)   make oath and say :

1. That I am (*a member of the firm of, etc., or a clerk in the office of, etc.*); the attorneys or solicitors for the above named   and as such have a personal knowledge of the facts hereinafter deposed to.

2. That on behalf of the said (*appellant or respondent*) I have paid   of the   of   in said Province, printers, the sums following for the work mentioned, viz. :

DATE PAID.	PRINTING DONE.	AMOUNT PAID.
	("Case in Appeal." "Appellant's or Respondent's Factum.")	$
	Total, $	

amounting in all to the sum of   dollars.

3. That in addition to the foregoing, I have paid the following sums in this appeal, viz. :

4. That with regard to the foregoing disbursements, I believe that the amount so paid for printing is fair and reasonable, and the usual and lowest price for which that class of work can be done in the said   of

and that the foregoing amounts further paid as aforesaid were reasonable and proper disbursements in this appeal.

Sworn before me at the   (Sgd.)
    of   in the Province of
                 this
       day of   A.D., 18

A Commissioner in the

---

14. SHERIFF'S ACCOUNT.

IN THE SUPREME COURT OF CANADA.

SHERIFF'S ACCOUNT.

Under O. C. 7th June, 1883, and 49 Vic., Chap. 135, Sec. 15.

The Government of Canada,
    To the Sheriff of the County of Carleton.   DR.

Date 189..		$	Cts
Please forward this account to the Registrar Supreme Court of Canada, Ottawa.	To actual attendance in person or by deputy on the Supreme Court at its sittings from the ..... day of .... to the ...... day of		
	............days at $5.00 per day..............		
	........Constables at $1.50 each per day for each day necessarily and actually engaged in attendance during the sittings of the Court, in all.............days...................		
	NAMES OF CONSTABLES TO ATTEND. NO. OF DAYS.		
	....		
	....		
	....		
	....	$	

I CERTIFY that the above account, amounting to........is correct

                               ....
                                              Sheriff.

I CERTIFY that I have examined this account and believe it to be correct.   ....
                                                             Registrar

ADDENDA.

I.

In *Simpson* v. *Palliser*, on Oct. 12th, 1898, the Supreme Court held that an appeal would not lie by the defendant from a judgment of the Court of Review for Lower Canada, which varied the judgment of the Superior Court by increasing the damages thereby allowed, which was not an affirmance of such judgment under sub-sec. 3 of sec. 29 (see p. 47), although it affirmed, in principle, the adjudication against the defendant.

And on Oct. 13th that there is no appeal from an order for a new trial in a criminal case. *Viau* v. *The Queen*.

In the same sitting the Court held that the Act 60-61 Vic. c. 34, limiting appeals from Ontario, did not apply to a case which was pending when it came into force, although the judgment appealed from was not pronounced until several months after. *Hyde* v. *Lindsay*, Nov. 2nd, 1898.

No appeal lies to the Supreme Court from a judgment on proceedings by *quo warranto*: *Walsh* v. *Heffernan*, 14 Can. S. C. R. 738.

II.

Sections of the Railway Act, 51 Vic. cap. 29, respecting cases to be stated for the opinion of the Supreme Court of Canada by the Railway Committee of the Privy Council.

Section 19. The Railway Company may, if it thinks fit, at the instance of any party to the proceedings before it, and upon such security being given as it directs, state a case in writing for the opinion of the Supreme Court of Canada upon any question which in the opinion of the committee is a question of law.

Section 20. The Supreme Court of Canada shall hear and determine the question or questions of law arising thereon and remit the matter to the Railway Committee, with the opinion of the court thereon.

Under these sections, in Dec., 1888, there was stated for the opinion of the court on the application of the Hon. Joseph Martin, Railway Commissioner for Manitoba, a case *in re* the crossing by the Portage extension of the Red River Valley Railway and the Pembina Mountain Branch of the Canadian Pacific Railway.

This is the only case referred under these sections.

INDEX.

ABANDONMENT—
    of appeal by delay, in ordinary appeals, 75, 152.
        in criminal appeals, 102.

ABRIDGING TIME—
    for doing any act or taking any proceeding, 167.

ABSENCE—
    of judge at delivery of judgment, in case of, judgment may be delivered by majority of judges present at hearing, 18.
    examination of any person owing to, may be ordered, 93.

ACT—" the," meaning of, in rules, 170.
    of Parliament of Canada, appeal when question relates to validity of, 39, 90.
    of councils or legislative bodies of territories or districts, appeal when question relates to validity of, 39, 90.

ACTS—
    certain, applied to officers, etc., of Supreme Court, 16.

ADJOURNMENT—
    of sittings of court till quorum present, 19, 169.
    of any session of court from time to time, 19.
        notice of, to be given in *Canada Gazette*, 19.

ADMIRALTY—
    jurisdiction in, given to Exchequer Court, 33, 109.

ADVOCATES—
    of Provinces, may practice in Supreme Court, 17.

AFFIDAVIT—
    in rules, includes affirmation, 170.
    who authorized to administer in, for use in Supreme and Exchequer Courts, 91.
    commissioners for receiving may be appointed, 91.
        how commissioners to be styled, 92.
    before whom to be taken out of Canada, 92.
        no proof of signature or seal of commissioner, etc., required, 92.
    no informality in, to be an objection to, 93.
        nor set up to defeat indictment for perjury, 93.
    that reasons of judges cannot be obtained to be used in case, 65, 130.
    interlocutory applications to be by motion supported by, 150.
    copy of any, to be served with notice of motion, 151.

AFFIRMATION—
See *Affidavit*.

AGENT—
name of, to be entered in "agents' book," 138.
who may be, 138.
must be entitled to practice in Supreme Court, 138.
form of appointment of, 139, 224.
duties of, 139.
notice of motion may be served on, 151.
allowance to be taxed to, 176.

AGENTS' BOOK—
to be kept in office of registrar for names of agents, 138.

AMENDMENTS—
necessary, may be made, 84.
    whether necessity occasioned by party applying or not, 85.
to be made on terms, 85.
case may be remitted for, and when, 85, 131.
    application to remit, should be to a judge, 86, 131.
to judgment, may be ordered, 86.

AMOUNT IN CONTROVERSY—
appeals from Quebec depending on, 39.
and from Ontario, 50.
decisions as to, 40–46, 48.
to be amount demanded, 47, 50.
in Exchequer appeals, 106, 107.
in appeals under Winding-Up Act, 122.

APPEAL—
summary of proceedings on, 4.
what expression includes, 11.
to Supreme Court, in what cases it shall lie, 20.
    from final judgments, 20.
    from judgment upon special case, 20.
        or upon points reserved at the trial, 20.
        or upon motion for new trial, 21.
        decrees, etc., in equity, 22.
        or upon motion to set aside award, 22.
    in cases of *habeas corpus, certiorari*, prohibition, mandamus and municipal by-laws, 22.
    in cases in certain provinces when matter in dispute $250 or upwards, where court of first instance possesses concurrent jurisdiction with a superior court, 24.
from Supreme Court, North-west Territories, 25.
in assessment cases, 26.
in probate cases, 26.
in criminal cases, 33, 101, 153.

APPEAL—*Continued.*
>to Supreme Court in election cases, 33, 112, 155.
>>in exchequer cases, 33, 100, 153.
>>in cases under Winding-up Act, 33, 121.
>
>to be from highest court of last resort, 20, 34.
>>by consent from court of original jurisdiction, 34.
>>*per saltum*, by leave, 34.
>>but not from Province of Quebec, 34.
>>special circumstances to be shown to justify, 35.
>
>none from orders, etc., made in exercise of judicial discretion, 38.
>>exceptions, 38.
>
>from Province of Quebec, in what cases, 39.
>>in cases not originating in Superior Court, 46.
>>to be only from Court of Queen's Bench or Court of Review, 47.
>>amount in dispute to be amount demanded, 47.
>
>right of, limited in Ontario cases, 50.
>in *habeas corpus* cases to be heard at an early day, 53.
>procedure in, to be in conformity with practice of judicial committee, when not otherwise provided for, 59.
>to be brought within 60 days from signing, entry or pronouncing of judgment, 60.
>>exceptions, 60.
>>time may be extended under special circumstances, 62.
>>but not in election appeals, 62.
>
>notice of, in certain cases to be given within 20 days after decision, 21, 61.
>>in criminal appeals within 15 days, 61, 102.
>>in exchequer appeals within 10 days, 61, 106.
>
>security to be given in, 67.
>>approving of, a mode of allowing, 63, 69.
>>obtaining allowance of appeal and giving security sufficient to bring case into Supreme Court, 64.
>
>to be upon a case, 64.
>execution stayed on, if security given, 71.
>discontinuance may be filed in, 74.
>consent to reversal of, may be given by notice, 74.
>>and judgment of reversal given, 74.
>
>dismissal of for want of prosecution, 75, 132.
>>at hearing if appellant fails to appear, 84, 148.
>
>abandoned, if not brought on for hearing within one year after security given, 75, 152.
>parties may be added to by suggestion, 76, 77, 140.
>by or against representative of party dying before judgment appealed from, 79.
>must be heard on case as transmitted, 78.

APPEAL—*Continued.*
    to be set down on list by registrar at least 14 days before hearing, 79, 145.
    hearing of, to be in order in which received for entry, 80.
        and in which set down, 148.
        cannot be set down unless filed 20 clear days before first day of session, 81; 145.
        nor unless appellant's factum deposited, 81.
        may be set down for, *ex parte*, if respondent fails to deposit factum, 143.
        notice of hearing to be given and when, 136.
        form of notice of, 137, 171.
        when notice of, to be served, 137.
        how to be served, 138.
        may be postponed, 148.
        if either party fail to appear at, court may hear other party and give judgment or postpone hearing, 148.
    inscription of, practice generally with reference to, 145.
    quashing, when no jurisdiction, or brought against good faith, 81.
    Supreme Court may dismiss or give judgment court below should have given, 82.
    costs of, may be ordered to be paid, 82.
        execution will not issue out of Supreme Court to enforce payment of general costs of, 84.
        except in election appeal, 84.
        but will for interlocutory costs, 84.
    interest to be allowed when execution delayed by, 86.
    judgment of Supreme Court in, to be certified to court below, 87.
    to Privy Council, practice on, 88, 207.
    from Exchequer Court in certain cases when Act of Legislature of a province passed consenting, 90.
    counsel at hearing of, rules as to, 147.
    orders in, how to be signed and dated, 149.
    interlocutory applications in, to be by motion, 150.
    from Exchequer Court, what rules applicable to, 153.
    in criminal and *habeas corpus* cases, rules governing, 154.
    and in election cases, 155, 156, 186.

APPELLANT—
    to give proper security, 67.
    may discontinue appeal by giving notice, 74.
    may be added by suggestion, 76, 77, 149.
    death of one of several appellants, 76.
        of sole appellant or all appellants, 77.
    insolvency of, 77, 149.
        other causes requiring addition of, 77, 149.

APPELLANT—*Continued*.
    to file case within one month after security allowed, 75, 132.
    to print case, 134.
    to serve notice of hearing, 136.
        when and how, 137, 138.
    appearance by, in person, 141.
    to deposit factum, 142. See *Factum*.
    may inscribe *ex parte* if respondent's factum not deposited, 143.
    to deposit factum in cross-appeal one week after respondent's factum in cross-appeal deposited, 165.
    bill of costs, form, 226.

APPELLATE JURISDICTION—
    of Supreme Court within and throughout Canada, 20.
    See *Jurisdiction*.

APPENDIX—
    contents of, 189.

APPOINTMENT—
    of Judges, 13.
    of Registrar and other officers, 15.
    of Reporters, 16.
    of persons presiding over Assessment Court necessary to give an appeal, 26.
    to tax costs to be obtained from registrar, 160.

ASSESSMENT—
    appeal from judgment of provincial court created to adjudicate on, 26.

ATTACHMENT—
    as for contempt, not to issue for non-payment of money only, 84, 97.
    rules relating to, 178, 181.
    form of writ of, 181.

ATTORNEY—
    who may practice as, in Supreme Court, 17.
    practicing in Supreme Court, to be officers of such court, 17.
    may enter name of agent in agents' book, 138.
    respondent represented by attorney or solicitor in court below may appear in person in appeal on filing suggestion, 139.
    or solicitor representing respondent in court below to be attorney or solicitor in appeal, if no suggestion filed or order made changing, 140.
    respondent who appeared in person in court below may appear by attorney or solicitor in appeal, 140.
    or solicitor may be changed on *ex parte* application, 141.

ATTORNEY-GENERAL—
    of province to be served with notice of appeal in criminal cases, 102.
    what expression includes, 103.

288 INDEX.

AT LEAST—
    meaning of, 168.

AWARD—
    appeal to lie from judgment upon motion to set aside, 22.
        or upon any motion by way of appeal from, 22.

BAIL—
    power to, in *habeas corpus* cases, 52.
    commissioners for administering oaths who reside within Canada may take recognizances of, 96.

BANKRUPTCY—
    See *Insolvency*.

BARRISTERS—
    who may practice as, in Supreme Court, 17.
    practicing in Supreme Court to be officers of such Court, 17.

BILLS—
    private, may be referred to judges by Senate or House of Commons, 59.

BOND—
    copy of, given as security, to accompany case, 134.
    form of, 220.

BOOKS—
    to be kept by registrar to record proceedings, 168.

BRITISH COLUMBIA.
    appeal allowed in cases from, when matter in dispute $250 or upwards, and court of first instance possesses concurrent jurisdiction with a superior court, 24.
    County Court jurisdiction in, 192.
    cases from, to be set down on part three of list of appeals for hearing, 80.
    Act of Legislature of, consenting to exercise of special jurisdiction by Supreme and Exchequer Courts, 91, 207.
    criminal and *habeas corpus* appeals from, when case to be filed, 154.
        and notice of hearing served, 154.

BRITISH NORTH AMERICA ACT, 1867—
    sec. 101, provides for establishment of general court of appeal for Canada, 12, 104.
    sec. 91, No. 27, gives legislative authority to Parliament of Canada over criminal law, excepting constitution of courts of criminal jurisdiction, but including procedure in criminal cases, 104.

BY-LAWS—
    of municipal corporation, appeal from judgment quashing, or refusing to quash, 22.
    decisions on, 24.
    cases of, excepted from effect of certain provisions, 51.

CANADA GAZETTE—
    notice of adjournment of any session of court to be published in, 19.
    notice convening court to be published in, 19.

CAPIAS—
    judgment in proceedings on, appealable, 30.

CARLETON, COUNTY OF—
    sheriff of, to be *ex officio* officer of Supreme Court, 16.

CASE—
    appeal to be upon, 64.
    to be stated by parties, or in event of difference, settled by a judge, 64.
    what it shall contain, 64.
    must be printed, 67, 134.
        exceptions, 67, 154.
    filing of, to be first proceeding in appeal in Supreme Court, 64, 130.
        this subject to right to make applications for certain purposes before case filed, 130.
    must be certified under seal of court appealed from, 130.
    and transmitted by proper officer of court below, 66.
    must contain formal judgment of courts below, 64.
    and reasons of judges of courts below, 65, 130.
        or affidavit that they cannot be obtained, 65, 130.
    also copy of any order enlarging time for appealing, 65, 131.
    may be remitted for addition of further matter, 65, 131.
    matter improperly inserted in, will not be taxed, 65, 131, 135.
    should be filed within one month after security allowed, 66, 132.
        if not, respondent may move to dismiss, 132.
        application for dismissal, to be in chambers, 132.
        but time may be extended, 66, 132, 152.
    must be accompanied by certificate of security having been given and copy of bond, 66, 133.
    and by certified copies of exhibits, unless dispensed with or printed in case, 136.
    must be printed by appellant, 134.
    and twenty-five copies deposited with registrar, 134.
    form and style of, 135.
    application to dispense with printing part of, may be made, and when, 134.
    application to amend should be to a judge, 66.
    in criminal and *habeas corpus* appeals, may be written, 66, 154.
    not to be filed unless rules as to printing complied with, 135.
    fees allowed for printing, 135, 176.
    must be filed twenty clear days before session at which appeal to be heard, 145.
    further time for filing may be given, 152.

CASES CITED—
  table of, xiii.
CERTIFICATE—
  under seal of proper officer of court below that security given to accompany case, 133.
  form of, 223.
  of judgment of Supreme Court to be sent by registrar to court below, 87.
  of costs awarded against Crown to be sent by registrar to Minister of Finance, 186.
CERTIORARI—
  appeal from judgment on proceedings for, 22.
  writ of, may issue, and when, 55.
CHAMBERS—
  registrar appointed to transact business in, 176.
CHIEF JUSTICE—
  word "judge" includes, 11.
  title of, 12.
  salary of, 15.
  oath of office to be administered to, by Governor-General, or person administering government of Canada, in council, 15.
  to administer oath of office to puisné judges, 15.
  may convene court at any time, 19.
CIVIL SERVICE ACT—
  to apply to officers, clerks and servants of Supreme Court, 16.
CIVIL SERVICE SUPERANNUATION ACT—
  to apply to officers, clerks and servants of Supreme Court, 16.
CLEAR DAYS—
  meaning of, 168.
COMMISSIONERS—
  to administer affidavits, etc., for use in Supreme and Exchequer Courts may be appointed by Governor in Council, 91.
  style of, 92.
  of H. M. High Court of Justice in England may take affidavits, etc., to be used in Supreme and Exchequer Courts, 92.
  no proof of signature or seal of commissioner required, 92.
  residing within Canada, may take acknowledgments of recognizances of bail in Supreme Court, 96.
COMMITTAL—
  judgment or order requiring the doing or abstaining from any Act, other than payment of money, may be enforced by, 178.
COMMON LAW—
  the Supreme Court, a court of common law and equity, 12.
COMPUTATION OF TIME—
  rules as to, 168.

CONSENT—
    hearing before four Judges by, 19.
    appeals from court of original jurisdiction by, 34.
CONSOLIDATED REVENUE FUND—
    salaries and retiring allowance of judges to be paid out of, 13, 14.
    costs awarded against Crown to be paid out of, 98.
    proceeds of sale of stamps to be paid into, 98.
CONSUL—
    affidavit, etc., may be administered before, 92.
CONTEMPT—
    no attachment as for, to issue for non-payment of money, 97.
    for non-compliance with order, how punished, 161, 178.
    form of writ of attachment for, 181.
CONTROVERTED ELECTIONS—
    See *Election Appeals.*
CONVENING COURT—
    by notice, 19.
CONVICTION—
    See *Criminal Appeals.*
CORONERS—
    process to be directed to, when sheriff disqualified, 96.
    to be paid same fees as sheriffs, 185.
COSTS—
    no appeal lies for deciding mere question of, 31.
    of appeal may be taxed when discontinuance filed, 74.
        and judgment signed for, or order for their payment obtained, 74.
    may be ordered to be paid when appeal quashed for want of jurisdiction, 81.
        but not when objection taken by court at hearing, 81.
        when objection taken at earliest moment, general costs of appeal, and fee on motion to quash given, 81.
    general power in Supreme Court to order payment of, in ordinary appeals, 82.
    and in election appeals, 84, 115, 120.
    judges of Supreme Court, or any five, may make rules regulating, 82, 97.
    to be taxed pursuant to tariff, 83, 157.
    tariff of, 173.
    provisions as to, generally, 82, 157.
    practice on taxation of, 160.
    between solicitor and client, not taxed by registrar, 160.
    as a general rule allowed to successful party, 83.
    but no costs given when appeal allowed on point first taken at hearing, 83.
    nor when court equally divided, 83.
        C.S.E.C.—16.

COSTS—*Continued.*
>   not given in *habeas corpus* appeals, 83.
>   nor in criminal appeals, 83.
>   in interlocutory applications may be fixed, 83, 160.
>   payment of, may be enforced by such writs as court prescribes, 84, 96.
>   of appeal will not be enforced by execution from Supreme Court, 84.
>   but otherwise with interlocutory costs, 84.
>   and costs in election appeals, 84.
>   in election appeals, provisions as to, 115, 120.
>   distraction of, when granted, 84.
>   awarded to or against Crown, how to be paid, 98, 186.
>   appeals under Winding-up Act not proceeded with may be dismissed with or without, 122.
>   security for, when and how to be given. See *Security*.
>   hearing of appeal may be postponed upon terms as to, and when, 148.
>   court or judge may order payment of fixed sum for, 160.
>   how payment of, may be enforced, 160, 178.
>   allowance to be taxed to entered agent in discretion of registrar to $20; 176.
>   forms of bills of, 226-229.

COUNSEL—
>   who may practice as, in Supreme Court, 17.
>   practicing in Supreme Court to be officers of such court, 17.
>   on reference by Governor-General in Council may be assigned, 56.
>   no more than two to be heard on any appeal and one in reply, 147.
>   cases in which this rule has been relaxed, 147.
>   order in which heard, 147.
>   on motion, only one heard, 148.
>   fee to, on motion to quash, 82
>   fees to, generally, 157.

COUNTIES—
>   sheriffs of respective, to be *ex officio* officers of Supreme Court, 96.

COUNTY OF CARLETON—
>   sheriff of, to be *ex officio* officer of Supreme Court, 16.

COUNTY COURTS—
>   jurisdiction given to Supreme Court in cases originating in, and when, 24.
>   statutes regulating jurisdiction of, in Nova Scotia, 25, 190.
>   in New Brunswick, 25, 191.
>   in British Columbia, 25, 192.
>   in Prince Edward Island, 25, 196.
>   no appeal in cases originating in, of Ontario, 134.

INDEX.

COURT—
    appealed from, the, what expression means, 11.
    of appeal for Ontario, rule of, as to printing additional copies of case for Supreme Court, 134.

COURT OF PROBATE—
    appeal from judgment in case originating in, 26.

COURT OF REVIEW—
    in Quebec, appeals from, 47.

CRIMINAL APPEALS—
    Act relating to, 101.
        meaning of expressions in, 103.
    notice of appeal to be given in, 61, 102.
    may be on written case, 66, 154.
    no security required in, 67.
    no costs given in, 83.
    who may bring, 102-
    how Supreme Court may deal with, 102.
    no appeal allowed if court affirming conviction unanimous, 101, 102.
    notice in writing to be served on Attorney-General for province within 15 days after affirmance, 102.
    judgment of Supreme Court in, to be final and conclusive, 102.
    when new trial may be granted in, 102.
    no appeal to Privy Council in, 102.
    rules relating to, 105, 153-4.
    no printed case or factum required, no fees to be paid registrar and no security to be given in, 105, 145, 154.
    practice as to setting down for hearing, 147.
    certain rules not to apply to, 153.
    case in, from British Columbia to be filed two months before first day of session, 154.
    from other provinces to be filed one month before, 154.
    notice of hearing in, when to be given, 154.

CRIMINAL CASES—
    an Act respecting procedure in, 50-51 Vic. c. 50: 2.
        See *Criminal Appeals*.

CRIMINAL JURISDICTION—
    of Supreme Court, appellate within and throughout Canada, 20.
        See *Criminal Appeals*.

CRIMINAL PROCEDURE ACT, THE—
    sections of, relating to appeals to Supreme Court repealed and others substituted, 101.

CROSS-APPEALS—
    not necessary for respondent to give notice of motion by way of, 162.

CROSS-APPEALS—*Continued.*
>but he should give notice of intention to contend that decision of court below should be varied, 162, 163.
>>effect of omission to give such notice, 162, 163.
>>fifteen days' notice to be given, 165.
>
>factums in, when to be deposited, 165.
>practice of Judicial Committee of Privy Council as to, 163.

CROWN—
>appeal in matter relating to money payable to, 39, 46.
>judges may make rules as to payment of costs in favor of and against, 97.
>costs awarded against, how to be paid, 186.

DEATH—
>of one of several appellants, 76.
>of sole appellant, or all appellants, 77.
>of one of several respondents, 77.
>of sole respondent, or of all respondents, 77.
>of party before judgment appealed from, 79.
>of any party, additional party or parties may be added by suggestion, 149.
>>such suggestion may be set aside on motion, 150.
>
>in event of, between hearing and judgment, judgment may be entered *nunc pro tunc*, 78, 149.

DECLARATION—
>See *Affidavit.*

DECREE—
>or decretal order, appeal to be from any, in any action, suit, cause, matter, or other judicial proceeding instituted in any Superior Court of Equity, 22.
>>or in the nature of a suit of proceeding in equity, 22.
>>except in Province of Quebec, 22.

DELAY—
>dismissal of appeal for, 75, 132.
>>See *Dismissal of Appeal.*
>
>for certain proceedings.
>>See *Time.*

DEMURRER—
>appeal lies from judgment on, which finally puts an end to part of an action, 30.

DEPOSIT—
>as security, in exchequer appeals, 106.
>in election appeals, 113.

DEPOSITIONS—
>taken under S. & E. C. A. may be used in evidence, and when, 95.

DISCONTINUANCE—
>notice of, may be given by appellant, 74.
>>proceedings thereon, 74.

DISCRETION—
>   no appeal from orders made in exercise of, 38.
>   exceptions, 38.
>   of Supreme Court to order payment of costs of appeal or of court below, 82.
>   and to order new trial, 82.

DISMISSAL OF APPEAL—
>   for want of prosecution under section 53 of Act, 75.
>   motion for, should be made to a judge, 75.
>   and now in election appeal, 75.
>   appeal held abandoned without motion for, if not brought on for hearing within one year after security allowed, 75, 152.
>   the practice of Judicial Committee as to, 76.
>   Supreme Court may dismiss, or give judgment court below should have given, 82.
>   at hearing, in default of appearance by appellant, 84, 148.
>   for not filing case within one month after appeal allowed, 132.
>   for not filing factum, 142.

DISTRACTION OF COSTS—
>   when granted, 84.

DISTRICTS OF CANADA—
>   appeal when question relates to any Act or ordinance of, 30.

DOCUMENTS—
>   certified copies of, used in evidence to be deposited with registrar, 136.
>   but order may be obtained for transmission of originals, 136.

DOMICIL—
>   may be elected by practitioners and entered in agents' book, 138.
>   election of, by respondent appearing in person in appeal, 140.

DOMINION OF CANADA—
>   Exchequer Court to have jurisdiction in controversies between Dominion and any province passing an Act agreeing thereto, 89.
>   or between provinces passing such an Act, 90.
>   an appeal to Supreme Court in such cases, 90.
>   when Act of Parliament of, in question, Supreme Court to have jurisdiction, when Legislature passes enactment, 90.
>   procedure in such cases, 90.

DUTY—
>   payable to H. M. appeal lies when question relates to, 39, 46.
>   in Exchequer appeals, 107.

ELECTION APPEALS—
>   special provisions relating to, 112.
>   appeal to lie from judgment, etc. 1. On preliminary objection, and when. 2. On question of law or of fact of judge who has tried petition, 112.

ELECTION APPEALS—*Continued.*

    rule laid down as to reversing on matters of fact in, 112.

    what a preliminary objection from judgment on which appeal will lie, 113.

    appellant to make a deposit within eight days of $100 as security for costs and $10 for transmitting record, 113.

    clerk of court below to transmit record in, 114.

    registrar of Supreme Court to set appeal down for hearing at nearest convenient time, 114.

    take precedence on list for hearing. 81.

    provision as to extending time for appealing does not apply to election petition. 62,. 114.

    rules specially applicable to. 66. 114, 155, 186.

    appellant to give notice within three days of setting down, 62, 114.

        time may be extended, 114.

        may limit appeal by such notice, 115.

    Supreme Court to give decision, court below should have given, 115.

    and may make such order as to deposit and costs as it thinks just. 115.

    execution for costs may issue in. 84.

    when evidence has been improperly rejected may cause witness to be examined, 115.

    judgment in, to be certified by registrar to Speaker of House of Commons, 116.

    judgment in final, and no appeal to Privy Council, 116.

    what judge of court below to report in election case, 119.

    Supreme Court may adjudge as to costs of court below, 120.

        how costs of court below to be recovered, 120.

    motion for dismissal of election appeal, 75.

    factum in, to be printed and interchanged as in ordinary appeals, 146, 156.

        and to be deposited three days before session, 146, 156.

    factum in, may be dispensed with, 156.

    practice as to inscription of, for hearing, 114, 146.

    certain rules not applicable to, 155.

    appellant to obtain from registrar certified copy of record and have same printed, 155, 186.

    forty-five copies of record to be printed, 155, 186.

    appellant to deliver thirty copies of record to registrar, 156, 186.

    respondent to receive five copies from registrar, 156, 186.

    fees for printing record, 156, 186.

    printing of record may be dispensed with on application, 156.

ELECTION PETITION—

    See *Election Appeals.*

EQUITY—

appeal to lie from judgment, decree, decretal order, or order, in proceedings in, or in nature of proceedings in, 22, 38.

    except in Province of Quebec, 22.

appeal *per saltum* from judgment, etc., in, 34.

the Supreme Court a court of common law and, 11.

ERROR IN LAW—

when alleged, proceedings in Supreme Court to be in form of appeal, 64.

EVIDENCE—

provisions respecting, 91.

although verdict against weight of, new trial may be ordered by Supreme Court, 82.

when new trial ordered by court below, because verdict against weight of, Supreme Court will not entertain appeal, 82.

when improperly rejected at trial of election petition, the Supreme Court may cause witness to be examined, 115.

    See *Examination.*

EXAMINATION—

of any person may be ordered to be taken on interrogatories or otherwise, 93.

before whom, 93.

order may contain directions respecting, 93.

party examined called a "witness," 94.

duty of person taking, 94.

further, may be ordered, 94.

penalty for non-compliance with order for, 94.

notice of, to be given to adverse party, 94.

refusal to attend, a contempt of court, 94.

as to production of papers at, 95.

consent of parties to, to take place of order, 95.

to be returned to court, 95.

depositions taken on, may be used in evidence, and when, 95.

taken out of Canada, how proved and returned, 95.

notice of return of, may be given by any party examined, 96.

reading of, must be objected to within time and manner prescribed by general order, 96.

EXCHEQUER APPEALS—

excepted from effect of certain provisions, 51.

special provisions relating to, 106.

$50 to be deposited with registrar of Supreme Court as security in, within thirty days after final judgment, 106.

    time may be extended by judge of Exchequer Court, 106.

notice of appeal in lieu of deposit to be given by Crown, 62, 108.

EXCHEQUER APPEALS—*Continued.*
    to be entered on list for Province where case tried, 80.
    to be set down for hearing on first day of next session by registrar when deposit made or notice given, 106, 146.
    notice of setting down, to be given within ten days, 61, 106.
        may limit appeal to any defined questions, 106.
    matter in controversy must exceed $500, 106.
        exceptions, 107.
            in excepted cases appeal to be allowed by a judge of the Supreme Court, 107.
    procedure in, governed by ordinary rules of Supreme Court, 108.
    certain rules specially applicable to, 153.
    how procedure in, differs from that in ordinary appeals, 153.

EXCHEQUER COURT—
    continued by 50-51 Vic., c. 16: 1.
    jurisdiction, taken away from Supreme Court judges, 2.
    meaning of expression, 11.
    special jurisdiction may be given to, by Act of Legislature of any province: 1. In controversies between Dominion and such province. 2. In controversies between any two provinces, 89, 90.
        appeal lies in such cases to Supreme Court, 90.
    to have jurisdiction in admiralty, 33, 109.

EXECUTION—
    stayed upon certain conditions when appeal brought, 71.
    cases relating to stay of, 74.
    such writs of, to be issued as court prescribes, 84, 96, 178.
    writs of, prescribed by rule, 84, 178.
    not issued from Supreme Court to enforce payment of general costs of appeal, 84.
        except in election appeals, 84.
    will issue for interlocutory costs, 84.
    when delayed by appeal, interest to be allowed, 86.
    process of, to enforce payment of money, 96.
    general order regulating writs of, and practice relating to, 97, 178.

EXHIBITS—
    material parts of, to be printed in case, 66, 136.
    certified copies of, to be deposited with registrar, with case, 136.
    but order may be obtained for transmission of originals, 66, 136.

EXTENDING TIME—
    for bringing an appeal, 62.
    for giving notice in criminal appeals, 102.
    for appealing in Exchequer cases, 106.
    for filing case or factum, or for inscribing, 152.
    generally, for doing any act, or taking any proceeding, 167.
    grounds on which application for, may be granted, 168.

EXTRADITION—
    no appeal in case of proceedings for or upon writ of *habeas corpus* arising out of any claim for, 52.

FACTUM—
    each party to deposit twenty-five copies of, with registrar fifteen days before first day of session at which appeal to be heard, 142.
    what to contain, 142.
    to be printed in same manner and form as case, 142.
    if not deposited by appellant in proper time, respondent may move to dismiss appeal, 142.
    if not deposited by respondent in proper time, appellant may inscribe cause for hearing *ex parte*, 143.
        such inscription may be set aside on application, 143.
    first deposited to be kept under seal, 143.
    parties to interchange three copies of, 143.
    may be supplemented by list of additional authorities, 143.
    further reasonable time for depositing may be given by court or judge, 152.
    none required in criminal or *habeas corpus* appeals, 105, 145, 154.
    in election appeals, to be printed as provided for ordinary appeals, 146, 156.
        to be deposited three days before session, 146, 156.
        may be dispensed with, 156.
    in cross-appeal, of respondent to be deposited within two days after notice given him under Rule 61: 165.
        of appellant, to be deposited within one week after service of notice, 165.
        such factums to be interchanged, 165.
    translation of, may be required by any judge, 165.
        party depositing shall cause translation to be printed, 166.

FEE OF OFFICE—
    appeal when action, etc., relates to, 39, 46.
        and in Exchequer cases, 107.

FEES—
    to registrar to be paid in stamps, 98, 157.
        tariff of, 157, 172, 178.
    between party and party to be taxed pursuant to tariff, 157.

FIAT—
    to sheriff, to stay execution when security perfected, 73.
    for increased counsel fee, 160.

FIERI FACIAS—
    See *Execution, Writs*.

FINAL JUDGMENTS—
    appeal to be from, 20, 29, 30.
        exceptions, 29, 30.
    cases in which judgment held final, 29.
    judgment on demurrer, not finally putting an end to any part of an action, not final, 29, 30.
    of Exchequer Court, appeal to be from, 106.

FINANCE MINISTER—
    moneys or costs awarded to Crown to be paid to, 98.
        and against Crown to be paid by, 98.
    judgment or order awarding payment of costs by Crown to be certified to, 186.

FORMA PAUPERIS—
    no power to admit an appeal in, 68, 157.

FORMAL OBJECTION—
    no proceeding to be defeated by, 167.

FORMS—
    affidavit of disbursements, 229.
    affidavit of execution of bond, 221.
    affidavit of justification, 222.
    appointment of agent, 224.
    bill of costs, appellant's, 226.
        respondent's, 228.
    bond for security for costs, 220.
    certificate of settlement of case, 223.
    judgment, allowing appeal, 224.
        dismissing appeal, 226.
    notice of appeal, 219.
    notice of hearing appeal, 171.
    notice calling special session, 171.
    order made in chambers, 226.
    order for payment of money into court as security for costs, 222.
    writs of *fi. fa.*, 179.
        of *ven. ex.*, 180.
        attachment, 181.
    præcipe for writ, 182.
    - sheriff's account for attending court, 230.

FORTHWITH—
    meaning of, 168.

FUTURE RIGHTS—
    appeal when question relates to, 39, 46, 50.
    the same in Exchequer appeals, 107.
    and in appeals to Provincial Courts under Winding-Up Act, 121.

GOVERNOR IN COUNCIL—
    oath to be administered to Chief Justice before, 15.
    may appoint such clerks and servants of Supreme Court as necessary, 15.
    may appoint reporter and assistant reporters, 16.
    may refer certain matters to court for consideration, 55.
    may appoint commissioners for taking affidavits, etc., to be used in Supreme and Exchequer Courts, 91.

HABEAS CORPUS—
    judges of Supreme Court to have concurrent jurisdiction with courts or judges of several provinces to issue, 52.
    power to bail, discharge or commit prisoner, 52.
    writ of, will not be issued where matter disposed of by appellate court of province, 54.
    nor where conviction regular, 54.
    court will set aside writ of, if improvidently issued by Judge under sec. 32; 54.
    after conviction for felony by court having general jurisdiction over offence charged, writ of, an inappropriate remedy, 54.
    cannot be issued in case of murder, or other cases at common law, 54.

HABEAS CORPUS APPEALS—
    to lie from any judgment for or upon writ of *habeas corpus*, not arising out of criminal charge, 22.
    excepted from effect of certain provisions, 51.
    no appeal in matters arising out of claim for extradition, 52.
    appeal to lie to court if judge of Supreme Court refuses writ or remands prisoner, 52.
        prisoner need not be present in court, 53.
    to be heard at an early day, 53.
    costs not given in, 53.
    appeal will not lie if prisoner at large, 53.
    security for costs in, not required, 53, 67.
    certain rules not applicable to, 153.
    rules applicable to, 53, 154.
    may be on written case, certified under seal of court appealed from, 66, 154.
    no factum to be deposited in, 145, 154.
    practice as to setting down for hearing, 147.
    case to be filed, two months before first day of session when from British Columbia, 154.
        one month, from other provinces, 154.
    notice of hearing, when to be given, 154.

HEARING—
    of *habeas corpus* appeals at early day, 53.

252 INDEX.

HEARING—*Continued.*
    on reference by Governor in Council, Lieutenant-Governor of Province may be notified of, 56.
        or person or class interested, 56.
        counsel may be assigned for, 56.
    of appeals, order of, 79.
    when objection to jurisdiction first taken at, no costs given, 81.
    inscription for, by appellant may be *ex parte*, if respondent fails
        such inscription may be set aside, 143.
        or further time given, 152.
    counsel who may be heard, and order in which heard, 147.
        on motions, 148.
    may be postponed by the court, 148.
        or when parties consent, 148.
    when either party fails to attend, court may give judgment or postpone hearing, 148.

HOLIDAY—
    what expression includes, 169.

HOUSE OF COMMONS, THE—
    may refer private bills to court, 59.

INDEX—
    must be added to printed case, 135.

INFERENCES OF FACT—
    shall be drawn by Supreme Court from facts stated in special case, 20.

INJUNCTION—
    interim, order dissolving, not a final judgment from which an appeal will lie, 31.

INSCRIPTION—
    of appeals, order of, 79.
        when to be made, 145.
    practice as to, generally, 145.
    ex parte by appellant, if respondent fails to deposit factum, 143.
        may be set aside on application, 143.
    appeals to be heard in order of, 148.
    further time may be given for, 152.

INSOLVENCY—
    in case of, of original party, additional party or parties may be added by suggestion, 149.
        suggestion may be set aside on motion, 150.
        how questions of fact arising on, to be determined, 150.

INTEREST—
    may be allowed for time execution delayed by appeal, 86.

INTERLOCUTORY APPLICATIONS—
    costs may be fixed in, 83.
    in Supreme Court to be by motion, 150.

INTERLOCUTORY COSTS—
    may be fixed by order, 83.
    execution may issue to enforce payment of, 84.

INTERPRETATION—
    in Supreme and Exchequer Courts Act, 11.
        meaning of expressions "the Supreme Court," "the Court," "the Exchequer Court," 11.
    "judge," includes chief justice, 11.
        meaning of expressions "judgment," "final judgment," "appeal," "the court appealed from," 11.
    in Act respecting Criminal Appeals, 103.
    in rules, of word "judge," 170.
    words importing singular number to include plural, and *vice versa*, 170.
    words importing masculine gender to include females, 170.
    of word "party" or "parties," 170.
    of "affidavit," to include affirmation, 170.
    of words "the Act," 170.

INTERROGATORIES—
    examination of any person on, may be ordered, 93.
        party examined called a "witness," 94.
    duty of person taking examination on, 94.
    further examination on, may be ordered, 94.
        penalty for non-compliance, 94.
    notice prescribed in order to be given adverse party, 94.
    neglect or refusal to attend for examination on, a contempt of court, 94.
    as to production of papers, 94.
    consent of parties to examination may take place of order, 95.

JUDGE—
    includes chief justice, 11.
    meaning of, in rules, 170.
    may pronounce judgment of reversal on consent, 74.
    may dismiss appeal for want of prosecution, 75.

JUDGES—
    of court below, reasons of, should form part of case, 65, 130.

JUDGES OF SUPREME COURT—
    who may be appointed, 13.
    two to be from Province of Quebec, 13.
    to hold no other office of profit, 13.
    residence of, to be at Ottawa, or within five miles thereof, 13.
    tenure of office, 13.
    salaries, 13.
    retiring allowances of, and how payable, 14.
    oaths to be taken by, and how to be administered, 14, 15.
    not necessary for all who have heard argument to be present at delivery of judgment, 17.

JUDGES OF SUPREME COURT—*Continued.*
    majority of, present at hearing, may deliver judgment, 18.
    may hand opinion in writing to be read or announced in open court, 18.
    when disqualified from hearing appeal, 18.
    opinions of, on case referred by Governor-General in Council, 56.

JUDGMENT—
    meaning of word, 11.
    final, meaning of, 11.
        appeal to lie from, 20, 29.
        what are final judgments, 29.
    may be delivered by majority of judges present at hearing, 18.
    upon special case, appeal from, 20.
    upon motion to enter verdict, or non-suit, upon point reserved at trial, 20.
    upon motion for new trial, 21.
    in proceedings in equity, or in nature of proceedings in equity, 22.
    upon motion to set aside award, or upon motion by way of appeal from award, 22.
    in *habeas corpus* proceedings, not arising out of a criminal charge, 22.
    in proceedings on *certiorari* and prohibition, 22, 23.
    in proceedings on mandamus, 22, 23.
    or on municipal by-law, 22, 24.
    distinction between final and interlocutory, 33.
    appeal to be brought within 60 days from signing or entry or pronouncing of, 60.
        exceptions, 60.
    upon motion to enter verdict or non-suit upon point reserved, or upon motion for new trial on ground that Judge has not ruled according to law, notice of appeal from, to be given within twenty days, 61.
    may be signed for costs when discontinuance filed, 74.
    of reversal, to be pronounced on consent, 74.
    nunc pro tunc may be entered in event of death of party between hearing and judgment, 78, 149.
    may be given, which court below should have given, 82.
    when varied, reversed or affirmed, Supreme Court may order payment of costs, 82.
    may be amended in certain cases, 86.
    of court below, when affirmed, interest to be allowed, 86.
    of Supreme Court, to be certified to court below, 87.
        and to be final and conclusive, 88.
    as to finality of, in criminal appeals, 104.
        and in election appeals, 116.
    of Privy Council, may be made an order of Supreme Court, 89.

INDEX. 255

JUDICIAL COMMITTEE OF H. M. PRIVY COUNCIL—
    practice of, to be followed in appeals to the Supreme Court, when no other provision, 50.
    practice of, as to dismissal of appeals for want of prosecution, 76.
        on cross-appeals, 163.
    order of, may be made an order of Supreme Court, 89.
    no appeal lies to, in criminal cases, 102, 104.
    statutes and orders in council regulating practice in appeals to, 207.

JUDICIAL PROCEEDING—
    what a, within meaning of Act, 40.

JURISDICTION OF SUPREME COURT—
    to be general within and throughout Canada, 20.
    provisions relating to, 20.
    essentials to exercise of, 27.
    in appeals from final judgments of highest court of last resort, 20, 29.
    court of original jurisdiction must be a superior court, 20.
        except in certain cases from New Brunswick, Nova Scotia, British Columbia and North-west Territories, 24.
        and in assessment and probate cases, 26.
    in appeals, from judgment upon special case, 20.
        or upon motion to enter verdict, or non-suit, upon point reserved at trial, 20.
        or upon motion for new trial, 21.
    or from decrees, etc., in equity, 22.
    or from judgment, etc., to set aside award, 22.
    or from judgment in any case of proceedings in *habeas corpus*, *certiorari* and prohibition, mandamus, and municipal by-laws, 22.
    in certain cases from New Brunswick, Nova Scotia, and British Columbia, wherein matter in dispute $250 or upwards in which court of first instance possesses concurrent jurisdiction with a superior court, 24.
    in appeals from Supreme Court of North-west Territories, when case has not originated in a superior court, 25.
    in criminal cases, 33, 101.
    in exchequer cases, 33, 106.
    in election cases, 33, 112.
    in cases under The Winding-up Act, 33, 121.
    in *habeas corpus* cases, 22, 32.
    in special cases referred by Governor in Council, 55.

JURISDICTION OF SUPREME COURT.—*Continued.*
>   special, when legislature of any province passes an Act agreeing thereto—
> >   1. In controversies between Canada and province, and between provinces, by appeal from Exchequer Court, 89, 90.
> >   2. When validity of Act of parliament or of legislature in question, 90.
> >   procedure in such cases, 90.
> >   such jurisdiction only in civil cases, 91.
>   quashing proceedings for want of jurisdiction, 81.
> >   costs may be given, 81.
> >   but not when objection taken by court, 81.

KEEWATIN—
>   in district of, any person dissatisfied with order or decision of the court or a single judge in any proceeding under Winding-up Act, may, by leave of a judge of the Supreme Court of Canada, appeal to that court, 121.
>   practice on such appeal, 121.
>   [in the Winding-up Act the word "court" means in the District of Keewatin such court or magistrate, or other judicial authority, as is designated from time to time by proclamation of the Governor in Council, published in the *Canadian Gazette.* See Winding-up Act, sec. 2, par. (*d*); see also R. S. C. c. 53.]

LACHES—
>   in prosecuting appeal. See *Dismissal.*

LAND—
>   appeal lies when question relates to title to, or where future rights may be bound, 39, 46, 50.
> >   in Exchequer appeals, 107.
>   practice as to seizure and sale of. See *Writs.*

LEAVE—
>   to appeal in Ontario cases, 50.
>   to appeal, under special circumstances, to be given, 62.
>   to appeal from Exchequer Court to be obtained from Judge of Supreme Court in certain cases, 107.
>   to appeal in cases under Winding-up Act to be obtained from Judge of Supreme Court, 122.

LEGISLATURE—
>   of province may pass an Act agreeing to exercise of special jurisdiction—
> >   1. By Exchequer Court in controversies between Dominion and any province, or between provinces, 89, 90.
> >   appeal in such cases to Supreme Court, 90.
> >   2. By Supreme Court, when validity of Act of Parliament of Canada, or a legislature of any province in question, 90.

INDEX. 257

LIBRARY OF SUPREME COURT—
    under control of registrar of Supreme Court, 16, 198.
LIMITATION—
    on right to appeal in assessment cases, 26.
        in probate cases, 26.
        in cases from Province of Quebec, 39.
        from Province of Ontario, 50.
        in Exchequer cases, 107.
        in cases under Winding-up Act, 122.
LIST—
    cases for hearing to be set down on, 79.
    how divided, 79.
MANDAMUS—
    appeal to lie from judgment in proceedings for or upon writ of, 22.
    decisions on, 23.
    cases of, excepted from effect of certain provisions, 51.
MANITOBA—
    cases from, to be set down on part three of list of appeals for hearing, 80.
    criminal and *habeas corpus* appeals from, to be filed at least one month before first day of session, 154.
        notice of hearing to be served one month before, 154.
MARITIME PROVINCES—
    cases from, where to be entered on list of appeals, 79.
        in October session, order of hearing, 80.
MATTER IN CONTROVERSY—
    meaning of, 40.
MAYOR—
    affidavits, etc., may be taken out of Canada before, 92.
MINISTER OF FINANCE AND RECEIVER GENERAL—
    costs awarded to Crown to be paid to, 98.
    costs awarded against Crown to be paid by, out of consolidated revenue fund, 98.
    certificate of costs awarded to or against Crown, to be sent to, 186.
MONEY—
    order for payment of, may be enforced by writs prescribed, 84, 96.
        writs prescribed by general order, 178.
    no attachment to issue for non-payment of, 84, 97.
    awarded to or against Crown, how to be paid, 98, 186.
    payment of, into court, how made, 166.
    out of court, must be on order upon notice, 166.
        and by cheque of registrar, countersigned by a judge, 167.
C.S.R.C.—17

MONTH—
    meaning of word, 168.

MOTION—
    to enter verdict, or non-suit upon point reserved, or for new trial, appeal from judgment on, 20.
        notice of appeal to be given in such cases, 61.
    by respondent to dismiss appeal, if appellant's factum not filed, 142.
    to set aside suggestion adding parties, 150.
        course which may be taken on such, 150.
    all interlocutory applications to be made by, 150.
    notice of, when to be served, 151.
        how to be served, 151.
        service of, to be accompanied by copies of affidavits filed, 151.
    to be made before court to be set down on list and called on each morning of session before hearing of appeals, 151, 152.

MUNICIPAL BY-LAWS—
    appeal from judgment quashing, or refusing to quash, 22.
        decisions on, 24.
    cases relating to, excepted from effect of certain provisions, 51.

NAME—
    Supreme Court of Canada, continued under such name, 12.

NEW BRUNSWICK—
    appeal in cases from, when amount in dispute $250 or upwards, and court of first instance possesses concurrent jurisdiction with a superior court, 24.
    jurisdiction of County Courts of, 25, 191.
    Act of legislature of, consenting to exercise of special jurisdiction by Supreme and Exchequer Courts, 91, 207.
    cases from to be set down on part of list of appeals for hearing, 79.
    criminal and *habeas corpus* appeals from, to be filed at least one month before first day of session, 154.
        and notice of hearing to be served three weeks before, 154.

NEW TRIAL—
    appeal to lie from judgment upon any motion for, 21.
        when moved for on ground of improper ruling notice of appeal to be given, 21, 61.
    cases of new trials excepted from effect of certain provisions, 51.
    may be ordered by Supreme Court, on ground verdict against weight of evidence, 82.
    but court will not entertain appeal when court below has ordered new trial, on ground verdict against weight of evidence, 82.
    may be granted in criminal cases, 102.

INDEX. 259

NON-SUIT—
    appeal to lie from judgment upon motion to enter, upon point reserved at trial, 20.
        notice of appeal to be given, 61.

NORTH-WEST TERRITORIES—
    appeal lies from decision of Supreme Court of, 25.
        although matter may not have originated in a superior court, 25.
    expression "province" includes, 25.
    expression "Superior Court" means Supreme Court of, 25.
    Acts of Parliament of Canada to apply to, 25.
    appeals from, to be entered on list of appeals, 25. 80.
        on part three of list, 80.
    leave to appeal in cases from, by whom to be granted, 25.

NOTICE—
    of adjournment, 19.
    of appeal, from judgment on special case, or upon motion to enter verdict or non-suit upon point reserved, or upon motion for new trial upon ground judge has not ruled according to law, to be given within twenty days, 21, 61.
        in criminal cases, 61, 102.
        in exchequer appeals, 61, 106, 108.
        giving such notice a condition precedent 62.
        to be published in *Canadian Gazette*, 137.
        to be published in *Canadian Gazette*, 137.
        form of, 171.
    of cross appeal to be given, 162.
        to be fifteen days notice, 165.
    by Crown, in lieu of deposit in exchequer appeal, 108.
    of discontinuance, may be given, 74.
    of examination upon interrogatories to adverse party, 94.
    of return of examination, 96.
    of hearing, to be given and when, 136.
        form of, 137, 171.
        when to be served, 137.
        how to be served, 138.
    of motion, when to be served, 151.
        and how, 151.
    of reversal of judgment, may be given, 74.
    of setting down exchequer appear, 106.
        such notice may limit appeal to defined questions, 106.
    of setting down election appeal, 115.
        such notice may limit appeal to defined questions, 115.

NOVA SCOTIA—
    appeal in cases from, where amount in dispute $250 or upwards, and court of first instance possesses concurrent jurisdiction with a superior court, 24.
    jurisdiction of county courts of, 25, 190.
    Act of Legislature of, consenting to exercise of special jurisdiction by Supreme and Exchequer Courts, 91, 207.
    cases from, to be on part one of list of appeals for hearing, 79.
    criminal and *habeas corpus* appeals from, to be filed one month before first day of session, 154.
        and notice of hearing to be served three weeks before, 154.

NUNC PRO TUNC—
    judgment or order may be entered, in event of death of party between hearing and judgment, 78, 149.

OATH—
    to be taken by judges of Supreme Court, and how to be administered, 14, 15.
    of allegiance, 15.
    who may administer for use in Supreme and Exchequer Courts, 91.
    commissioner to administer oaths may be appointed, 91.
        style of such commissioner, 92.
    made out of Canada, before whom to be taken, 92.
        no proof of seal or signature of commissioner, etc., required, 92.

OBJECTION—
    See *Formal Objection*.

OFFICERS—
    of Supreme Court to be appointed by Governor in Council, 15.
        certain Acts to apply to, 16.

ONTARIO—
    cases in which appeals from, will lie, 50.
    cases from, to be on part three of list of appeals for hearing, 80.
    Act of Legislature of, consenting to exercise of special jurisdiction by Supreme and Exchequer Courts, 91, 205.
    Court of Appeal for, rule of, as to printing additional appeal books for use in Supreme Court, 134.
    criminal appeal from, to be filed at least one month before first day of session, 154.
    and notice of hearing to be given two weeks before, 154.

ORDERS—
    enlarging time for appealing, a copy of, to be in case, 131.
    in appeal, how to be signed and dated, 149.
        may be dated *nunc pro tunc* in certain cases, 78, 149.

INDEX.   261

PAPERS—
 service of, on respondent, who elects to appear by attorney, 140.
  on respondent, who elects domicil, 140.
  on respondent appearing in person without electing domisil, 141.
  on new attorney or solicitor, 141.
 certiorari may issue to bring up, 55.

PARLIAMENT—
 general rules and orders to be laid before Houses of, 98.

PARTIES—
 may be added in appeal by suggestion, 76, 77, 149.
  in case of death of one of several appellants, 76.
  or death of sole appellant or all appellants, 77.
  or of one of several respondents, 77.
  or of sole respondent, or of all respondents, 77.
  when necessary from any other cause, 149.
   dying before judgment appealed from, appeal by and against representatives, 79.
 in event of death of party between hearing and judgment, judgment may be entered *nunc pro tunc*, 78, 149.
 where improperly joined, will be struck out, 78.
 may be allowed to prosecute an appeal in name of plaintiff, though not on record, 78.

PAUPER APPEALS—
 Supreme Court has no power to admit, 68, 157.

PAYMENT—
 of money into court, how made, 166.
  out of court, order must be obtained for on notice, 166.
  and paid on cheque of registrar, countersigned by judge, 167.

PENSIONS—
 of judges. See *Judges*.

PERISHABLE PROPERTY—
 may be ordered to be sold, 73.

PERJURY—
 no informality in affidavit to defeat indictment for, 93.

PER SALTUM—
 by leave, appeal may be allowed, 34.
 but not from Province of Quebec, 34.
 special circumstances to be shown to justify such appeal, 35.

PETITION—
 for private bill, may be referred to court, 59.

POINTS RESERVED AT TRIAL—
 appeal to lie from judgment upon any motion to enter verdict or non-suit upon, 20.

POSTAGE—
    on transmission of original documents to be paid by appellant, 136.
    reasonable allowances for, in taxing costs, 174.

POUNDAGE—
    party entitled to execution may cause to be levied, 182.

PREROGATIVE OF CROWN—
    to allow appeals, 88.
    not to be exercised in criminal cases, 102.

PRINCE EDWARD ISLAND—
    appeal in cases from, when matter in dispute $250 or upwards, and court of first instance possesses concurrent jurisdiction with a superior court, 24.
    County Court jurisdiction in, under appealable amount, 25, 196.
    cases from, to be set down on part one of list of appeals for hearing, 79.
    criminal and *habeas corpus* appeals from, to be filed at least one month before first day of session, 154.
        and notice of hearing to be served three weeks before, 154.

PRINTING—
    of immaterial documents will not be allowed on taxation, 65, 131.
    of case, rules as to, 66, 134, 135.
        See *Case*.
    of factum, 142.
        See *Factum*.
    in election appeals, of record, 155, 186.
        of factum, 156.
    of record or factum in election appeals, may be dispensed with, 156.
    in criminal appeals, of case or factum not required, 154.
    certain rules as to, amended, 176.
    in appeal to Privy Council, requirements as to, 210, 216.

PRISONER—
    court or judge has power to bail, discharge or commit, 52.
    need not be present in court, 53.

PRIVATE BILLS—
    may be referred to court, 59.

PRIVY COUNCIL—
    See *Judicial Committee of H. M. Privy Council*.

PROBATE COURT—
    appeal from judgment of, 26.
    except in Province of Quebec, 26.

INDEX. 263

PROCEDURE—
>in appeals, to be in conformity with practice of judicial commitee, when not otherwise provided for, 59.
>under special jurisdiction, to decide questions relating to validity of an Act of Parliament of Canada or of the legislature of any province, 90.
>judges may make general rules of, 97.

PROCESS—
>of Supreme Court, runs throughout Canada, 96.
>>how tested and directed, 96.
>>>See *Writs.*

PROCTORS—
>who may practice as, in Supreme Court, 17.
>practising in Supreme Court, to be officers of such court, 17.

PROHIBITION—
>appeal from judgment on proceedings for, 22.
>juridiction of court as to, 23.

PROSECUTION—
>of appeal.
>>See *Appeal, Dismissal of Appeal.*

PROVINCE—
>expression includes North-west Territories, 25.
>legislature of any, may pass an Act agreeing to exercise of special jurisdiction by Supreme and Exchequer Courts, 80.

QUASHING PROCEEDINGS—
>by Supreme Court, when taken against good faith, or appeal does not lie, 81.
>when appeal quashed, court may order payment of costs, 81.
>when objection taken by court at the hearing, no costs will be given, 81.
>motion to quash should be to the court, at earliest convenient moment, 81.
>general costs of appeal given, and counsel fee on motion, 81.
>>fee of $25 may be allowed, subject to increase, 82, 173.

QUEBEC, PROVINCE OF—
>cases in which appeals from, will lie, 39.
>>cases not originating in superior court, 46.
>>to be only from Court of Queen's Bench, or Court of Review, 47.
>amount in controversy to be amount demanded, 47.
>cases from, to be on part two of list of appeals for hearing, 80.
>criminal appeals from, to be filed at least one month before first day of session, 154.
>>and notice of hearing to be served two weeks before, 154.

QUORUM—
    any five judges shall constitute, 17.
    four judges may constitute in certain cases, 18.
    majority of judges present at hearing may deliver judgment, 18.
    judge or judges present may adjourn sittings till quorum present, 19, 169.

QUO WARRANTO—
    no appeal in case of proceedings by, 231.

RAILWAY ACT, 1888—
    references to Supreme Court under, 231.

REASONS—
    of judges of courts below to form part of case, 130.
        or affidavit filed that they cannot be procured, 130.
        translation of, may be ordered, 166.

RECEIVER-GENERAL—
    moneys awarded to Crown to be paid to, 98.
    and to pay moneys awarded against Crown, 98.
    certificate of costs awarded to or against Crown to be sent to, 186.

RECOGNIZANCES—
    in Supreme Court, may be taken by commissioners, 96.

RECORD—
    Supreme Court of Canada continued as a court of, 12.

REGISTRAR OF SUPREME COURT—
    provision respecting appointment of, 15.
    has authority of a judge of the court sitting in chambers, 16, 97, 176.
        except in matters of *habeas corpus* and *certiorari*, 177.
        may refer any matter to a judge, 177.
        orders made by, to be as binding as if made by a judge, 177.
        orders to be signed by, 177.
        appeals from order of, and mode of procedure, 177.
        when to sit for transaction of business, 178.
    publisher of reports, 16, 98.
      has management and control of Supreme Court library, 16, 198.
    to set down appeals for hearing on list, 79.
    to certify judgment of Supreme Court to court below, 87.
    to certify judgment in election cases to Speaker of House of Commons, 116.
    to keep necessary books, 168.
    fees to be paid to, in stamps, 98, 157.
        tariff of, 172.

RENT—
    payable to H. M., appeal lies when question relates to in Quebec cases, 39, 46.
        and in Exchequer Court cases, 107.
        annual or other, appeal in Ontario cases as to, 50.

REPORTS OF SUPREME COURT—
    reporter and assistant reporter to prepare, 16.
    to be published by registrar, 16, 98.

REPORTERS—
    provision respecting appointment of, 16.
    to report decisions of Supreme Court, 16.

RESIDENCE—
    of Supreme Court Judges, to be at Ottawa, or within five miles thereof, 13.
    of registrar to be at City of Ottawa, 15.

RESPONDENT—
    entitled to costs when appellant discontinues, 74.
    may consent to reversal of judgment, 74.
    may move to dismiss appeal for want of prosecution, 75, 132.
    suggestion of death of, may be filed, 77.
    may be added by suggestion, 77, 149.
    notice of hearing to be served on agent of, 138.
    represented by attorney in court below may file suggestion of appearance in person in appeal, 139.
    who has appeared in person in court below, may file suggestion of appearance by attorney in appeal, 140.
        if no suggestion filed, attorney in court below deemed attorney in appeal, 140.
    appearing in person may elect domicil for service, 140.
    how papers served on, if no domicil elected, 141.
    may move to dismiss if appellant fails to deposit factum, 142.
    may give notice by way of cross appeal, 162.
        such notice to be fifteen days notice, 165.
    to file factum in cross appeal two days after notice, 165.

RETIRING ALLOWANCE.
    to judges of Supreme Court, 14.

REVENUE—
    appeal when question relates to in Quebec cases, 39, 46.
        and in Exchequer cases, 107.

REVERSAL—
    of judgment, to be pronounced on consent, 74.

REVISED STATUTES OF CANADA—
    proclamation bringing into force, 1.
    not to operate as new laws, 1.

RULES AND ORDERS—
    court may make, respecting matters to be referred by Governor-General in Council, 57.
    judge may make, 97.
    to what they may extend, 97.
    copies of, to be laid before Houses of Parliament at session next after making, 98.
    table of, 127.
    made under repealed Act to continue valid, if not inconsistent with substituted Act, until annulled, or others made in their stead, 130.

SALARIES—
    of judges of Supreme Court, 13.
    of Registrar, 15.

SEAL—
    of city, court, notary public, consul, etc., on affidavits, etc., to be used in Supreme and Exchequer Courts, proof of, not required, 92.

SCHEDULES TO RULES—
    A. notice convening special session, 171.
    B. notice of hearing of appeals, 171.
    C. tariff of fees to be paid registrar, 172.
    D. tariff of costs, 173.
    tariff of fees to sheriffs, 184.

SECURITY—
    terms as to, may be imposed when appeal allowed under special circumstanies, 62.
    approving of, a mode of allowing appeal, 63, 69.
    after allowanse of, court below *functus officio*, 63, 69.
        and proceedings governed by Supreme Court rules, 63.
    in appeals from district of Keewatin under Winding-up Act, to be given according to practice of court below, 68, 121.
    in other appeals under that Act to be given under section 46 Supreme and Exchequer Courts Act, 68, 122.
    on appeal, to be $500 under section 46, 67.
        this section not to apply to election, criminal, exchequer or *habeas corpus* appeals, or appeals by or on behalf of the Crown, 67.
    application to allow, should be made within sixty days, 63, 69.
        court below may extend the time under special circumstances, 63, 69.
    case to be filed within one month after allowance of, 66, 132.
        but time may be extended on application, 66, 152, 167.
    certified copy of bond given as, to accompany case, 66, 133.
    no power to dispense with, 68.

SECURITY—*Continued.*
    bond for, should provide for costs of appeal only, 69.
    objection to form of bond how urged, 69.
    amount of, cannot be increased, 70.
    no appeal from judge refusing to allow, 70.
    personal, sufficient, 70.
    interpretation, 71.
    examination of sureties, 71.
    deposit of money in court as, 71.
    execution stayed upon giving, 71.
    when perfected, fiat may issue to sheriff to stay execution, 73.
    in exchequer appeals, $50 by deposit, 106.
        when appeal on behalf of Crown, notice to take the place of, 108.
    in election appeals, by deposit of $100, 113.
    in appeals under Winding-up Act, 121, 122.

SERVICE—
    of notice of hearing, when to be made, 137.
        and how, 138.
    of papers on attorney or solicitor of respondent who has appeared in person in court below, 140.
    of papers at elected domicil of respondent who appears in person on appeal, 140.
    by affixing papers in registrar's office when respondent appears in person without electing domicil, 141.
    of notice of motion, how made, 151.
    of notice of hearing of criminal or *habeas corpus* appeal, 154.

SENATE, THE—
    may refer private bills to court, 59.

SESSIONS OF SUPREME COURT—
    three yearly: 3rd Tuesday in February, 1st Tuesday in May, 1st Tuesday in October, 19.
    to be continued till business disposed of, 19.
    court may adjourn any session from time to time, 19.
    notice of adjournment of, to be given in *Canada Gazette*, 19.

SHERIFFS—
    sheriff of County of Carleton, to be *ex officio* officer of Supreme Court, 16.
    remuneration of, for attendance regulated by order in council, 16.
        form of account for, 230.
    of respective counties, or divisions of any province, *ex officio* officers of Supreme Court, 96.
    when sheriff disqualified, process to be directed to any of the coroners of the district, 96.

SHERIFFS—*Continued.*
    Fiat may issue to, to stay execution when security perfected, 73.
        proviso as to poundage, 73.
        money levied by and not paid over before fiat, to be repaid, 73.
    practice on issuing process of execution to, 96.
    tariff of fees to be paid, 184.

SITTINGS—
    of Supreme Court. See *Sessions.*

SOLICITORS—
    who may practise as, in Supreme Court, 17.
    practising in Supreme Court to be officers of such court, 17.
        See *Attorneys.*

SPECIAL CASE—
    appeal to lie from judgment upon, 20.
    Supreme Court to draw inferences of fact from facts stated in, 20.
    notice of appeal to be given within twenty days after decision upon, 61.
    may be referred to court by Governor in Council, 55.

SPECIAL CIRCUMSTANCES—
    to be shewn to justify appeal *per saltum*, 35.
    appeal may be allowed after time limited, by court below under, 62.
    what are, for this purpose, 63.

SPECIAL JURISDICTION—
    given Supreme Court in certain cases when legislature of any province passes an Act agreeing thereto, 89.
    procedure in such cases, 90.

SPECIAL SESSIONS—
    of Supreme Court, may be convened, 19.
    form of notice convening, 171.

STAMPS—
    fees to registrar, to be paid by means of, 98, 157.
    to be issued and sold by Minister of Inland Revenue for the purpose, 98.
    proceeds of, to be paid into Consolidated Revenue Fund, 98.
    tariff of fees to be paid by, 172.

STATUTES—
    outline of, 1.
    Imperial:
        British North America Act, 1867, ss. 91 and 101, 12, 104.
    of Canada:
        38 Vic. c. 11: 1.
        39 Vic. c. 26: 1.
        40 Vic. c. 22: 1.
        42 Vic. c. 39: 1.

INDEX.   269

STATUTES—*Continued.*
   of Canada:
      43 Vic. c. 34: 1.
      49 Vic. c. 4, s. 8: 1.
      49 Vic. c. 25, s. 2: 25.
      50-51 Vic. c. 16: 1, 196.
      50-51 Vic. c. 50: 2, 101.
      51 Vic. c. 37: 2, 197.
      51 Vic. c. 43: 2.
      52 Vic. c. 37: 2, 198.
      53 Vic. c. 35: 2, 200.
      54-55 Vic. c. 25, 2, 200.
      54-55 Vic. c. 26, 3, 203.
      54-55 Vic. c. 29: 3, 109.
      55-56 Vic. c. 29: 3, 101.
      56 Vic. c. 29: 3, 204.
      59 Vic. c. 14: 3, 205.
      60-61 Vic. c. 34: 3, 50.
      Dominion Controverted Elections Act (R. S. C. c. 9): 112.
      Supreme and Exchequer Courts Act, 1875: 1.
      Supreme Court Amendment Act, 1876: 1.
      Supreme Court Amendment Act, 1877: 1.
      Supreme Court Amendment Act, 1879: 1.
      Supreme and Exchequer Court Amendment Act, 1880: 1.
      Supreme and Exchequer Courts Act, 1886 (R. S. C. c. 135): 11.
      Supreme and Exchequer Courts Amendment Act, 1887: 196.
      Supreme and Exchequer Courts Amendment Act, 1888: 197.
      Supreme and Exchequer Courts Amendment Act, 1889: 198.
      Supreme and Exchequer Courts Amendment Act, 1890: 196, 200.
      Supreme and Exchequer Courts Amendment Act, 1891: 200.
      Supreme and Exchequer Courts Amendment Act, 1893: 204.
      Supreme and Exchequer Courts Amendment Act, 1896, 205.
      Winding-up Act (R. S. C. c. 129): 121.
   of New Brunswick:
      45 Vic. c. 9, ss. 2 and 3: 25, 191.
      Consolidated Statutes, c. 51, s. 51: 25 192.
      51 Vic. c. 9: 91, 207.
   of Nova Scotia:
      Revised Statutes, 5th series, c. 105, ss. 16, 17 and 27: 25, 190.
      Revised Statutes, 5th series, c. 91: 191.
      Revised Statutes, 5th series, c. 111: 91, 207.

STATUTES—*Continued.*
    of Ontario:
        Judicature Act, s. 43: 50.
        Revised Statutes, 1897, c. 49: 91, 205.
    of Prince Edward Island:
        41 Vic. c. 12: 25, 196.

SUGGESTION—
    may be filed in case of death of one of several appellants, 76.
    or of sole appellant, or all appellants, 77.
    or of one of several respondents, 77.
    or of sole respondent, or all respondents, 77.
    additional party may be made by, 77, 149.
        mode of setting aside such suggestion, 77, 150.
        or of trying question of fact arising out of it, 150.
    to be filed by respondent who desires to appear in person, 139.
    form of, 139.
    if none filed, the solicitor or attorney of respondent in court below shall be deemed to be his solicitor or attorney in appeal, 140.
    to be filed by attorney or solicitor of respondent who has appeared in person in court below, 140.
    to be filed by respondent appearing in person, to elect domicil, 140.
    how service of notice of hearing to be made on respondent appearing in person, or who has filed suggestion of appearance in person, 141.

SUPERANNUATION—
    of judges of Supreme Court, 14.
    Act respecting, to apply to officers, clerks and servants of Supreme Court, 16.

SUPERIOR COURT—
    meaning of expression as regards North-west Territories, 25.
    case must have originated in, to give jurisdiction to Supreme Court, 20, 27, 39.
        except in certain cases where court of original jurisdiction possesses concurrent jurisdiction with, 24, 25.
    and in cases from North-west Territories, 25.
        in assessment and probate cases, 26.
        in certain cases from Quebec; 46.

SUPREME COURT OF CANADA—
    outline of statutes relating to, 1.
    continued as a court of record, 11.
    provision for establishing, sec. 101 B. N. A. Act, 12.
    established and organized in 1875, 12.
    constitution of, 12.
    who may be appointed judge of, 13.
    two judges of, to be from Quebec, 13.

SUPREME COURT OF CANADA—*Continued.*

appointment of registrar and other officers of, 15.
who may practice in, as barristers, advocates, counsel, attorneys, solicitors and proctors, 17.
practitioners in, may enter name of agent in agent's book, 138.
    or elect domicil, 138.
to hold three sessions yearly, 19.
may adjourn any session from time to time, 19.
may be convened at any time, 19.
    notice convening, to be published in *Canada Gazette*, 19.
to have, hold and exercise appellate, civil and criminal jurisdiction within and throughout Canada, 20.
in what cases appeal shall lie to, 20, 33.
special jurisdiction of, in criminal appeals, 101.
    in exchequer appeals, 106.
    in election appeals, 112.
    in appeals under Winding-up Act, 121.
appeal to, to lie from court of last resort, 20, 34.
but from court of original jurisdiction, by consent of parties, 34.
and by special leave in certain cases, 34.
no appeal to, from orders made in exercise of judicial discretion, 38.
    with certain exceptions, 38, 51.
appeals to, to be from final judgments, except as otherwise provided, 20, 39.
appeals to, from Province of Quebec, limited, 39, 46.
    and from Province of Ontario, 50.
no appeal to, in cases of extradition, 52.
jurisdiction of judges of, in *habeas corpus* cases, 52.
certiorari may issue out of, in certain cases, 55.
Governor in Council may refer matters to, for hearing and consideration, 55.
proceedings on reference, 56.
    Court may make rules, 57.
the Senate or House of Commons may refer private bills to, 59.
no writ required to bring appeal to, 64.
when error in law alleged, proceedings to be in form of an appeal, 64.
appeal to, to be in form of a case, 64.
case to be transmitted by proper officer of court below to, 66.
security to be given on appeal to, 67.
    execution stayed on appeal to, on what conditions, 71.
may pronounce judgment of reversal on consent, 74.
may dismiss appeal for want of prosecution, 75.
or quash, where appeal does not lie, or brought against good faith, 81.

SUPREME COURT OF CANADA—*Continued*.

    may dismiss appeal, or give judgment which court below should have given, 82.

    may order payment of costs of court appealed from, 82.
        or of the appeal, 82.

    when equally divided does not give costs, 83.

    powers of amendment of, 84.

    to allow interest for time execution delayed by appeal, 86.

    judgment of, to be certified to court below, 87.
        to be final and conclusive, 88.
            special provision as to finality of, in election cases, 116.
        and in criminal cases, 102, 104.

    to have special jurisdiction when Act of legislature of province passed agreeing thereto, 1. On appeal from Exchequer Court in controversies between Dominion and province, and between two provinces. 2. When validity of Act of legislature in question, 89, 90.

    procedure in such cases, 90.

    such jurisdiction to be exercised only in civil cases, 91.

    process of, to run throughout Canada, 96.
        how to be tested and directed, 96.

    sheriffs of respective counties or divisions to be *ex officio* officers of the court, 96.

    order in, for payment of money, how enforced, 96.

    judges of, may make rules of procedure, 97.

    reports of, to be published by registrar, 98.

    may order transfer of proceedings under Winding-up Act from one court to another, 122.

    references to, under railway Act, 231.

TARIFF—
    of fees to registrar, 172.
    of costs, 173.
    of fees to sheriffs, 184.

TAXATION—
    of costs, generally, 157.
        See *Costs*.

TERRITORIES—
    of Canada, appeal from Quebec when question relates to ordinance or act of councils or legislative bodies of, 39.

TIME—
    computation of, 168.
        meaning of expressions "clear days," "at least," "forthwith," "month," "holiday," 168, 169.

TIME—*Continued.*
    for bringing appeal, 60 days, 60.
        exceptions:
            criminal appeals which must be brought at session of Supreme Court during which affirmance of conviction takes place, or next session if Supreme Court not then in session, 102.
            exchequer appeals, to be brought within 30 days, 106.
            election appeals, to be brought within 8 days, 113.
            appeals from District of Keewatin under Winding-up Act, to be brought within 14 days, 121.
    rule as to, when 60 days begin to run, 60.
    may be extended under special circumstances in ordinary appeals, 62.
        and in criminal appeals, 102.
        exchequer appeals, 106.
        and appeals from District of Keewatin under Winding-up Act, 121.
        copy of order extending time to be in case, 131.
    allowance of security, 66, 132.
    case to be filed, in ordinary appeals within one month after allowance of security, 66.
        and 20 clear days before first day of session at which to be heard, 145.
        in criminal and *habeas corpus* appeals from British Columbia, two months before first day of session, 154.
        from other provinces, one month, 154.
    for filing case, may be extended, 66, 132, 152.
    factums, to be deposited 15 days before session, 142.
        further reasonable time may be given, 152.
        in election appeals to be deposited three days before session, 156.
        in cross appeal by respondent within two days after notice under rule 61, 165.
        by appellant in cross appeal, within one week after notice, 165.
    inscription of appeal, to be 14 days before session, 145.
        time may be extended, 152.
        election appeal, to be set down when record received and fee on entering appeal paid, 114.
        in such appeals notice of setting down to be given within three days, 114.
        or within extended time, 115.

TIME—*Continued.*

notice of appeal, from judgment on special case, or upon motion to enter verdict or nonsuit upon point reserved at trial, or for new trial, upon ground judge has not ruled according to law, to be given within 20 days. 21, 61.

    in criminal appeals, to be served on Attorney-General of province within 15 days after affirmance of conviction, 102.

    in cross appeal, 15 days' notice to be given, 165.

notice of hearing, to be given fifteen days before session, 137, 138.

    except in criminal and *habeas corpus* appeals, in which, from Ontario and Quebec, two weeks; from Nova Scotia, New Brunswick and Prince Edward Island, three weeks; from Manitoba, one month; and from British Columbia, six weeks, 154.

notice of motion, to be served four clear days before time of hearing, 151.

security to be given within 60 days, 63.

    in exchequer appeals, 30 days, 106.

    in election appeals, 8 days, 113.

    in appeals from District of Keewatin, 14 days, 121.

    when given in court below, time may be extended under special circumstances, 62.

unless appeal brought on for hearing within one year after security allowed, held abandoned, 152.

enlarged or abridged for doing any act or taking any proceeding upon terms, 167.

    grounds on which application to eslarge or abridge time may be granted, 167.

TRANSCRIPT—

of reasons for judgment of judges of courts below to be in case, 130.

of record to be sent to Privy Council, 208, 210.

    fee on certifying, 172.

TRANSLATION—

of factum may be ordered by any judge, 165.

    to be printed by party depositing, 166.

of opinions of judges in courts below, 166.

TRIAL—

appeal from judgment upon motion to enter verdict or non-suit upon point reserved at, 20.

or upon motion for new trial, 21.

    notice of appeal to be given in such cases, 21, 61.

in criminal appeal, Supreme Court may grant new trial, 102.

INDEX. 275

TRIAL.—*Continued.*
    when verdict against weight of evidence new trial may be ordered, 82.
        but if new trial ordered by court below on this ground, the appeal will not be heard, 82.

VACATIONS—
    at Christmas, 169.
    long vacation, 169.
    chambers not held during, 170.
    computed in time for filing case under rules, 170.

VENDITIONI EXPONAS—
        See *Writs.*

VERDICT—
    appeal to lie from judgment upon any motion to enter, upon point reserved at trial, 20.
    notice of appeal to be given, 61.
    when against weight of evidence, new trial may be ordered, 82.
        but if new trial ordered on this ground by court below, Supreme Court will sot hear appeal, 82.

WINDING-UP ACT, THE—
    special provisions as to appeals under, 121.
    who may appeal from decisions under, 121.
    and from what courts, 121.
        in Keewatin appeals to be to Supreme Court of Canada, 121.
        practice in such appeals, the practice of court appealed to, 121.
        steps to be taken within fourteen days to perfect appeal and to give security, 121.
        appeal may be dismissed for want of prosecution with or without costs, 122.
        appeal to Supreme Court if amount over $2,000, 122.
    proceedings under Act may be transferred from one court to another by order of two courts, or of Supreme Court of Canada, 122.
    procedure in Supreme Court to apply to appeals under, 123.

WITNESS—
        See *Evidence, Examination.*

WRITS—
    order for payment of money may be enforced by such writs as court prescribes, 96.
    general order prescribing and regulating practice, 178.
        judgment or order for payment of money may be esforced by *fi. fa.* goods or lands, 178.
        judgment or order requiring any person to do or abstain from doing any act, other than payment of money, may be enforced by attachment or committal, 178.

WRITS—*Continued.*
    general form of writ of *fi. fa.*, 179.
        writ of *ven. ex.* may issue to compel sale of property seized, 180.
        form of writ of *ven. ex.*, 180.
        in mode of selling and advertising, laws of province to be followed, 181.
        no writ of attachment to be issued without an order, 181.
        form of writ of attachment, 181.
        " writ of execution," what expression includes, 181.
            writs, how issued and indorsed, 181.
        form of præcipe for, 182.
        judgment or order to be produced to officer issuing writ, 182.
        interest, poundage fees and expenses may be levied, 182.
        direction to sheriff to be indorsed, 182.
        how long a writ shall remain in force and how renewed, 183.
        execution may issue within six years after judgment or order, 183.
        after that, by order, 183.
        stay of execution or other relief may be asked for, 183.
        writ may be amended, 184.
        schedule of fees to sheriffs and coroners, 184.
        corners to be entitled to same fees as sheries, 185.
        order of a judge may be enforced in same manner as order of the court to same effect, 185.
        no execution to issue against Crown, 186.
        order directing Crown to pay money to be certified to Minister of Finance, 186.

4-5 EDWARD VII.

CHAP. 47.

An Act to amend the Supreme and Exchequer Courts Act.

[Assented to 20th July, 1905.]

HIS Majesty, by and with the advice and consent of the Senate and House of Commons of Canada, enacts as follows:—

1. Section 7 of *The Supreme and Exchequer Courts Act*, being chapter 135 of the Revised Statutes, as amended by section 57 and schedule A of chapter 16 of the statutes of 1887, is repealed, and the following is substituted therefor:— {R.S.C., c. 135, new s. 7.}

"**7.** There shall be paid and payable out of the Consolidated Revenue Fund of Canada, the yearly sums following, as and for the salaries of the said judges, that is to say: to the chief justice, the sum of ten thousand dollars, and to each of the puisné judges the sum of nine thousand dollars, which sums shall be paid, free and clear of all deductions whatsoever, by monthly instalments; the first payment shall be made *pro ratâ* on the first day of the month which occurs next after the appointment of the judge entitled to receive it; and if any judge resigns his office or dies, he or his executor or administrator shall be entitled to receive such proportionate part of the salary aforesaid as has accrued during the time that he has executed such office since the last payment." {Salaries of judges of Supreme Court.}

2. Section 5 of chapter 16 of the statutes of 1887, is repealed, and the following is substituted therefor:— {1887, c. 16, new s. 5.}

"**5.** There shall be paid and payable out of the Consolidated Revenue Fund of Canada, the yearly sum of eight thousand dollars as and for the salary of the said judge, which sum shall be paid, free and clear of all deductions whatsoever, by monthly instalments; the first payment shall be made *pro ratâ* on the first day of the month which occurs next after the appointment of the judge; and if the judge resigns his office or dies, he or his executor or administrator shall be entitled to receive such proportionate part of the salary aforesaid as has accrued during the time that he has executed such office since the last payment." {Salary of judge of Exchequer Court.}

"2. There shall be paid to the said judge for travelling allowances his moving expenses and the sum of six dollars for each day during which he is attending as such judge any court at any place other than the city of Ottawa."

3. No judge mentioned in this Act shall, either directly, or indirectly as director or manager of any corporation, company, or firm, or in any other manner whatever, for himself or others, engage in any occupation or business other than his judicial duties; but every such judge shall devote himself exclusively to such judicial duties.

www.ingramcontent.com/pod-product-compliance
Lightning Source LLC
Chambersburg PA
CBHW030020240426
43672CB00007B/1024